A YEAR AT THE
CHÂTEAU

Dick and Angel Strawbridge

SEVEN DIALS

First published in Great Britain in 2020 by Seven Dials
an imprint of The Orion Publishing Group Ltd
Carmelite House, 50 Victoria Embankment
London EC4Y 0DZ

An Hachette UK Company

1 3 5 7 9 10 8 6 4 2

A CIP catalogue record for this book is
available from the British Library.

ISBN (Hardback) 9781841884615
ISBN (Export Trade Paperback) 9781841884622
ISBN (eBook) 9781841884646

Typeset by Born Group
Printed and bound in Great Britain by Clays Ltd, Elcograf S.p.A.

MIX
Paper from
responsible sources
FSC® C104740

www.orionbooks.co.uk

A YEAR AT THE
CHÂTEAU

To Arthur and Dorothy, you are the reason we do what we do!

Contents

Foreword   ix

Introduction   1

JANUARY   23

FEBRUARY   51

MARCH   85

APRIL   119

MAY   141

JUNE   161

JULY   173

AUGUST   193

SEPTEMBER   219

OCTOBER   233

NOVEMBER   253

DECEMBER   279

Afterword   287

Acknowledgements   289

About Us   293

Foreword

Firstly, thank you for buying this book and giving us the opportunity to relive our first year together at the château. This year, 2020, has been a year like no other and at times incredibly hard for many of us. We embarked on our first-ever speaking tour in February and arrived back mid-March. We travelled overnight to get home and hug the children. The next day, 12 March, the French president announced that schools and universities were going to close. By 17 March there was mandatory home confinement across the country ... For us, this pause gave us the chance to reflect on the remarkable journey we have been on, as well as the opportunity to put pen to paper and capture our story of the first year in our new home, Château-de-la-Motte Husson. We have loved writing this book and it has brought back so many happy memories for both of us: we have laughed, cried and honestly felt every emotion again. It's been beyond a pleasure.

We will not lie to you, this is a love story – not just between us, but also with the château. This book celebrates what we have done to get our château habitable and turn it into a true family home. Our aim is to share both what we have learnt and what we have loved, as well as some of the details of our journey, from the food to the flies! There has never been a dull moment, and that first year was the most ridiculous of them all. It has truly been a rollercoaster, so buckle up.

It's impossible to tell the story of our first year – the adventures, the challenges, the highs and the lows, the whirlwind romance, the tears and the laughter – without first telling you a bit about how and why we ended up buying our château.

This is our family story, our shared adventures, but at times we have slightly different memories of exactly what occurred, or exactly how it unfolded – you'll find all that in here as well.

Before we go any further, we should explain one thing: when you see words in bold that's me, Angel, telling the story.

And when you see them like this, that's me, Dick.

So, let's get started, back to when we first set eyes on our dream home: October 2014. We hope you enjoy sharing our journey with us!

Introduction

I will never forget the moment we first saw Château-de-la-Motte Husson. We had been in France searching for our forever home when the details were emailed over to us. I had butterflies in my belly – the good ones that make you feel a little sick with nerves. I knew this was the one and I spent the next four-and-a-half-hour drive fretting that someone would put an offer in before we got to see it. The drive was painfully slow and with all the excitement we nearly missed the turning. As we rounded the corner for the very first time, we gasped. It was majestic, so much more than we could ever have imagined and most certainly the one. In fact, I would liken it to the very first time I met Dick.

The château itself was beautifully balanced with the twin towers I'd been dreaming about; even the trees were symmetrical. Coming round the corner, we immediately focused on the château, but it took only seconds before we also became aware of the island and the moat surrounding it, then the abundance of huge old trees, then the outbuildings, each of which was a substantial stone building. And as we got closer the scale of the moat became apparent – it was a huge lake! Everything on our wish list was right there in front of us.

That first impression, that feeling of finally being home, is imprinted in my mind's eye for ever. As I write this, I have tears in my eyes just remembering the beauty of the surroundings. I have never tired of turning that corner – and I know with all my heart that I never will.

I've never wanted to do the maths to work out exactly how many hours we spent looking on the internet, driving through France and visiting estate agents in search of our dream home, but four years on from when we had made the decision to move it must have amounted to weeks, if not months. It had been a long, arduous and at times incredibly frustrating process.

The drive to view this very special château was beautiful. Driving in France is like a Sunday drive in the country used to be in the UK. In rural areas it feels like there is so little traffic. It's a big country and the countryside is not densely populated. Unless we had a lot of miles to cover, we stayed off the autoroutes, three-quarters of which are toll roads. If you are near a large city they can be crowded, but in the country they tend to be quiet, so you don't miss the sense of being somewhere different. Unlike motorways and many A roads in the UK, the *Routes Nationales* often take you through villages or around towns, so you get to see where and how people live.

There are lots and lots of trees in France and no shortage of old deciduous woodlands. It feels peaceful and a little bit exotic as the houses and villages are so very different from anything back home.

The idea of moving to France first came to us in 2012 while we were on holiday in the small fortified village of Caunes-Minervois near Carcassonne in the south of France. Dick had been living in Cornwall when we met in 2010 and I was based in east London.

Relationships are tricky at the best of times, especially with over 300 miles between you. The old adage 'absence makes the heart grow fonder' is all well and good at the beginning but it wasn't sustainable for us. We were on a mission to find somewhere we both wanted to call our home, in the geographical sense!

At first I moved up to London but I am definitely a country boy at heart – London isn't my scene. Angela had been on *Dragon's Den* and was very busy growing her elegant events company, the Vintage Patisserie. She had found run-down premises in Hackney, overlooking the St-John-at-Hackney church, and I was helping decorate and install kitchens so all her tea parties finally had a home. But even with all this activity going on we knew we had our life and family to build and the really big question was, where should we live?

We could go anywhere as long as we had a plan. I must admit I had an aversion to being inside the M25 and even found all the home counties too busy and frantic. As I'd lived in Dorset and Cornwall before, the West Country would never have been 'ours', so we started to look further afield. I was brought up in Northern Ireland and know full well there is a very good reason for Ireland being 'green' – it rains a lot! Wales, Cumbria and Scotland have the same 'soft' climates, which meant we crossed them off our lists. There are some truly beautiful, vibrant places in the UK but none of them had grabbed us and made us think we must move there, so we were a bit stuck on where we would make our home.

A solution to our dilemma as to where, and how, we would live came out of the blue when we took a holiday to the south of France. Neither of us had really had a proper holiday for many years and so we headed off for a romantic break to start 2012, all loved up. We stayed in a lovely little gîte in the old part of Caunes-Minervois and, having stocked up on wine, *foie gras,* cheese and other delicacies we settled down to chill and cuddled up on the sofa in front of the blazing log fire, watching *A Good Year*, a romantic comedy with Russell Crowe. If you don't know the film, it's about a successful city worker who inherits a run-down château and, after many ups and downs, ends up living happily ever after, forsaking life in the city for an idyllic existence making wonderful wine. It's fair to say it got us thinking.

Who hasn't been on holiday, relaxed and pondered living without the stresses, pressure or work of everyday life? The difference with us was that we took it a step further. Passing a local *notaire's** office, we discovered a small townhouse like the one we were staying in would cost about €30,000, which, at the time, was equivalent to about £20,000. Our gîte was not huge but it was in a beautiful setting. It was a terraced building with a cobbled street out in front of it. There was nowhere to park within about 100 metres but that was easily overlooked. On the ground floor there was a spacious sitting room, dining room and kitchen with a set of French windows (we did wonder, do they just call them windows in France?) that led to a small walled courtyard. Spiral stone stairs led to two more floors, each of which had a large bedroom and a stunning en suite bathroom. It was all beautifully French, with exposed stone walls and it raised some huge questions – did we really want to have a massive mortgage that needed to be serviced? What did we want from life? Did we want to live to work or work to live?

We are lucky enough to have some incomes that are not tied to our current jobs or where we live: Dick's small army pension and some royalties from books we have written. It isn't a lot, but we knew it could help us to simplify our lives. We definitely wouldn't stop working, but when work came in we could travel to do jobs,

---

* The notary.

so we concluded that it would be relatively easy to change our life-styles. Living in France would mean that we could buy somewhere outright *and* put some money in the bank, and, in addition, any future children we had would be bilingual. The simple life was calling us . . .

However, the internet didn't take long to disrupt our plans. For a while, searching for small elegant townhouses with a glass of wine in hand kept us amused, and we found lots of properties that were too perfect to believe. Though our understanding of French geography was such that we didn't even look in a specific area; we did a search of the whole of France (did you know France is big? Four times the size of England, in fact!). This is when the internet changed our plans.

We were looking at sweet little buildings, both in villages and in the country, when the first '*manoir*' made an appearance on our screen. It may have been old, run-down and needed a lot of work, but it was only about £50,000 – for a manor house! Our search parameters changed and – guess what? Next thing you know we were 'oohing' and 'aahing' over amazing *manoirs* when the first little château appeared on our screen. It was for sale at about £100,000 and needed lots of work, but it was a castle! At that exact moment our lives changed irrevocably.

Within ten minutes the screen was full of 'château porn' and we were gazing adoringly at multi-million-pound, truly amazing properties. Obviously those fantasies didn't last long but the seeds had been sown and the simple life in a small, cosy French cottage never got a look in again. We needed a château. And we knew that if we found the right one – with Angel's events experience – there would be the potential to build a business there as well.

The rest of the holiday just reinforced our decision. We took trips to explore the country that was to be our future home. We went to a natural spa in Ax-les-Thermes, driving through stunning countryside up into the foothills of the Pyrenees. We ate out, usually at lunchtime. There is something so special about a couple of hours of unhurried dining and it must have been normal as everyone else seemed to be doing it too – even on a work day! We loved the diversity of the restaurants we found. One day we'd be in the Pyrenees in a small family-run café eating *pommes aligot** served with duck breast and gizzards, from a very limited-choice '*menu du jour*', then the next we'd pop down to a touristy restaurant by the Mediterranean and feast on a platter of fresh seafood.

We discovered that eating out at lunchtime was a very reasonably priced way to experience great food. One of our forays led us to a little hilltop village called Aragon and, in the middle of nowhere, we found a very posh, totally adorable restaurant. We were there just a little after midday and we spent hours enjoying a menu of regional specialities. We loved the way little extras kept turning up in addition to the three courses we had ordered. The plate of little bites of fungi and truffle to tempt us with flavours from the local forest while we had our aperitif was amazing, then our *amuse-bouche* was a trio of dishes made from local *sanglier*†. After starters of tasty morsels of fish and barely cooked vegetables there was a palate-cleansing sorbet of cucumber and mint before our main courses of guinea fowl stuffed with chorizo, which made us realise just how close to Spain we were. Everything was cooked to perfection and when the dessert arrived it looked like we'd each been give a small chocolate football. When we smashed our way into the cold, crisp, wafer-thin chocolate, we found a velvety-smooth chocolate-orange mousse. After we had savoured every mouthful, and were

---

* Aveyron cheese and potato puree – what's not to love about that?
† Wild boar.

too full for comfort, they placed a selection of irresistible petit fours in front of us alongside our espressos. It was no wonder that we rolled down the hill afterwards. Just to put this into context, this particular menu was less than £20 per head with a bit extra for the aperitif and glass of wine, but definitely not bad for an amazing experience that we still talk about. It's fair to say we were falling in love with the French way of life.

This was our first holiday together. And not only that but, while we had grabbed a few weekends away when work allowed, this was the first real holiday either of us had taken for years. That alone made it incredibly special. Though neither of us could have predicted how this holiday would change the direction of our lives. However, while we knew what we wanted, we also knew it would take time to work everything out and we needed to be patient. It was not a matter of just stopping our lives and changing everything. We are both planners as well as doers, so we were in total agreement that the transformation of our life had to be orderly.

Once we got back to London, our search for the perfect home took some time every day, but life carried on and we kept working, trying to grow our pot and our family. Marriage was also on the cards, but when, where and how was never top of our urgent to-do list.

With a thriving events company and other people's celebrations taking up lots of our lives, Angela stated categorically – and on several occasions, m'lud – that she did not want a big wedding, just something intimate with our parents followed by a glorious honeymoon. To coin a phrase from my youth: 'you little fibber!' Above marriage, and right at the very top of our list was kids: on 29 January 2013 the wonderful Arthur Donald Strawbridge entered the world and, just over a year later, 8 April 2014 marked the arrival of the beautiful Dorothy Francis Strawbridge. We knew our family was complete (reinforced by Angela booking me into a clinic near Southend!) and we were in the process of organising the how and when of getting married, as well as searching frantically for somewhere to start the next phase of our adventure, when we found our château and everything changed, but that is jumping ahead . . .

As yet, we had not narrowed down our search for a specific type of property or even location. It felt like we were looking at every doer-upper in every part of France. Every day I would send Dick a list of ten possible properties, but in my heart I knew that I hadn't yet found one that ticked all the boxes – and most importantly one we could afford!

We knew that location was key. It's textbook, but it's really hard to stay focused when there are so many temptations in France with stunning properties in the middle of nowhere! That was a major hurdle and it is very humbling to confront your ignorance, but we really had little idea about what sort of country France was. Neither of us were accomplished French speakers and, though Dick had a good grasp of the geography, we were completely unaware of the regional characteristics.

Being British we 'know' the difference between, say, Yorkshire and Cornwall, for example, and we all tend to have our own views on the people and how friendly they are, the landscape and how desirable it is to live there. We know the people of Northern Ireland will talk to everyone, and in a doctor's waiting room you can expect everyone to join in the conversation and give you a diagnosis and reassurance long before you see the doctor. We know in London everyone is busy and there is a lack of eye contact, so saying hello to a stranger or thank you to a bus driver identifies you as a bit odd. We have a feel for what Lincolnshire is like compared to Cumbria, and what Herefordshire house prices are compared to Hampshire. Bournemouth and Birmingham are about the same distance from London but they are very different places, and we feel we 'know' the difference between Torquay and Scarborough even if we have not visited either. This is something we've absorbed over years but when we were thinking about where to live in France we didn't have any of this. Our solution was quite simple, if a bit of a gamble: see what we find and then see what the area is like.

For some reason we were more drawn to the western half of France – the properties seemed a touch more elegant, the countryside was rolling, and there were lots of châteaus.

After months of intense searching and viewings of several châteaus, we found a property that was definitely worthy of a visit: a very special château near Saint-Jean-Pied-de-Port, the start of the famous pilgrimage route, the Camino Francés, that goes over the Pyrenees and across the north of Spain to Santiago de Compostela and the tomb of St James.

The main house was beautiful and looked over the foothills of the Pyrenees. There were magnificent glass doors that opened onto a terrace where you could just imagine drinking your evening aperitif. In addition to the main house there was a perfectly habitable gatehouse and some outbuildings, all set in lovely wooded parkland. The château had once belonged to one of Napoleon's marshals and that was probably the reason it was a 'heritage' building. It was beautiful but needed a lot of love, having been attacked by termites and suffering neglect. Over the last two winters, a large hole in the roof had got bigger and all the running water had caused significant damage, removing the majority of the plaster on the inside walls. Some lovely murals on the walls had survived, but even they would need lots of attention. We knew it would need a lot of work, but there is financial support for such buildings to help protect them, so we definitely felt it was worth exploring.

I went to visit this château on my own initially. The plan was I would go to see exactly how bad a state it was in before the whole family committed to a trip. Even though the damage was extensive, it was beautiful, in a lovely hilltop setting. There was no doubt that we could have done something special there.

It all sounds very rock and roll: a quick return trip to Biarritz to check out a château, but it didn't turn out quite like that. As I was returning the hire car to Biarritz airport, there was a snap air traffic controller strike called across France. The only airport that Angela could find open for me to get back home was in Perpignan, a four-and-a-half-hour journey away, all the way along the Pyrenees from the Atlantic coast to the Mediterranean. And I had just over four hours to get there or I'd need to drive for nearly eleven hours to Calais in the hire car. I did just manage to get there, with one minor speeding infringement, but it made us think again about where exactly we were looking for in properties. Top of the new list of criteria: we needed it to be located in a part of France that allowed us to return to London in less than a day, no matter what.

Over the course of a couple of years we got into a fairly slick routine when it came to viewing properties. I would scour the internet to find beautiful 'maybes' in the correct price bracket (we were looking at properties listed for between £100,000 to £300,000), then we would contact the estate agent to see where exactly the properties were so we could get a feel for the surroundings. This was notoriously difficult as the estate agents are very secretive as there is sometimes more than one selling agent and they don't want to lose possible commission.

On one occasion we made a rather long trip to visit a château only to discover it shared the forecourt with a garage. On another we visited a truly beautiful château that had an industrial chicken farm less than thirty metres from the back door. The agents just did not want to give exact addresses in case you find this stuff out, but we are fast learners and Dick started to use Google Maps to have a good look around first. He would even look for shadows to determine the orientation of the building. We also started to ask for the *cadastral**. They were invaluable and meant we could get a real feel for what we were going to see. I love a surprise as much as anyone, but not after a day's travel with two young kids to find it was not worth it! When we had lined up enough properties of interest, we would organise a trip, sometimes as a family and sometimes for Dick to go and view a few in one day.

We were serious about buying our new home and consequently my day trips were gruelling, and frequent. I'd leave home at 4am and get the 6am Eurotunnel, drive down to the area where the properties were, view a couple and then get back for the late-evening train, which meant I got home between midnight and 2am. We tried to do as much research as possible in advance but sometimes I just had to see for myself. One château I visited was absolutely massive and on the edge of a national forest. The décor had been trashed as it had been used for raves, but it came with many acres, lovely outbuildings and a habitable cottage. From the photos it looked too good to be true … until you saw it. Never mind the decoration, walls had been removed, mass toilet complexes had been (badly) installed and every bit of wiring and plumbing had been ripped from the walls and floors. Squatters had turned it into what looked like an horrific modern installation. Needless to say, it was not for us.

There were many frustrations and disappointments before we found the 'one'. And, as time went on, our list of wishes (and

---

* The plan of the plot with each building and subplot numbered and detailed as to whether or not it is included in the sale.

wish-nots) grew. I never knew what an orangery was until I started looking, but once I saw one it went on the 'must-have' list. In a practical sense an orangery is a building, or conservatory, to protect your citrus trees from frosts during the depths of winter. But they tend to be beautiful, elegant winter gardens and are truly magical to look at. Dick's dream was to have workshops, a walled garden and a moat. And we both knew that we needed to find a property with a roof in goodish order as our budget would never stretch to a new one straight away.

In early 2014, we found the 'nearly one': a beautiful property on the outskirts of Châteauponsac, near Limoges. It was nearly right. It lacked the fairy-tale symmetry we had been searching for, but it was affordable and in a lovely location – it even had a gorgeous *boulangerie* at the end of the road where we could see my mum and dad taking the kids to get their fresh baguettes in the morning.

Some months later, we returned to see the château near Châteauponsac to confirm if the outbuildings had as much potential as we remembered. Angel's parents, Jenny and Steve, had come with us on this trip and we were having breakfast in the hotel when an email arrived that gave all of us goosepimples. An estate agent with whom we had seen a previous property had sent us the details of a château that was about to go on the market. When we opened the email the pictures alone made us catch our breaths. It was classified as a 'small château' but it looked exactly like what we had dreamt of. If not better. It had a moat, an orangery, a walled garden, tons of outbuildings and it looked like the interiors had been untouched – and, best of all, the price was also within our budget. On 9 October 2014 we met Château-de-la-Motte Husson, and it was love at first sight.

There had to be a catch, but our excitement was such that we were packing up and organising an immediate viewing within minutes.

With apologies to the agent who was supposed to be showing us around that day, we headed north. I can't remember anyone even mentioning the idea of stopping for a pee break. We were on a mission. A mission that took four and a half hours. Angela must have said 'We should call and put an offer in' every ten minutes. I did try explaining that we had an appointment at 2pm and that the agent wouldn't be showing anyone else around in the interim but still Angela fretted. I have to be honest, if something had happened in that period, I'm not quite sure what Angela's response would have been, but I know it would have been bloody. But as my mum always says, 'If it's meant for you, it'll not go by you.'

Being sent what I believed we had been looking for, for four years, was a big deal. I just knew it was going to be our happy ending – or, I should probably say, our happy beginning. Not only was this place like a fairy tale, it had everything on our list and had only ever been owned by one family: the Bagliones. I guess there is no point in picking old scabs, especially as all worked out OK in the end, but writing this and reliving my aggravation, Dick not allowing us to put in an offer still makes no sense to me nearly six years later!

When we arrived at Martigné-sur-Mayenne, we were very pleasantly surprised. To be honest we had not heard anything about the *département** of the Mayenne, which is just south of Normandy and to the very north of the Pays de la Loire. There are so many stunning villages in France: the flowers, the artisan bakers, the butchers. Many are simply idyllic and you quickly get a sense of how large or small the community is. Most have a pharmacy and a hairdresser, some also have a *boulangerie* and a few have a couple

---

* *Départements* are the administrative divisions within France. There are ninety-four in total.

more shops beyond. As we drove across France that morning, we decided it was essential to have at least a *boulangerie*. It was important for how we saw our life.

The village definitely fell into the idyllic category. It was small and felt very friendly. Tick. There was a charming *mairie*[*] with an abundance of flowers outside. Tick. A *boulangerie*, a convenience store, two hairdressers, two banks, a restaurant, a *tabac*, a primary school and rather grand church, a florist and a beauty salon. Tick, tick and tick.

I cannot explain the desire for this to be our forever home and for everyone to love it. I knew I already did but Dick was playing with a poker face, I think to calm me. And I also wanted my parents to love it. I could not imagine my mum and dad not moving to France with us, and being part of our adventure.

So that brings us back to the start, the beginning and the unforgettable moment when we all gasped in astonishment as we saw the Château-de-la-Motte Husson for the very first time.

As we turned the corner, the elegance of the château took hold of every sense. But the 200 metres stretching ahead of us up the driveway before we arrived at the front door allowed my mind not to panic and take everything in. Dick drove slowly, or it seemed slow. The forest of trees on the left and the right were gorgeous but I had no idea how exciting it really was or how much fun exploring them would bring to our family. The standalone 1920s orangery was as glorious as it was in the picture. I remember thinking nothing is ever as good in real life, but this was better. Even the outbuildings, which we'd found are often ugly, had their own elegance. I must have had hundreds of thoughts within seconds: what part of the château would we live in? Which areas would we

---

[*] The *mairie* is the administrative centre of a town or village. Similar to a town hall or mayor's office.

use for the business? Which rooms would be good for Mum and Dad? And endless other possibilities and questions that nearly stopped me talking. Then we were there: the front door. And what a front door it was!

I'm sure Angela and I both had the same mix of excitement and relief at this point because we had done it; we'd found our château. Though I think I proved that I am at least a little bit sensible by insisting that we look inside before the offer was made. Which is exactly what we did. Climbing the fourteen majestic, very solid granite steps up to the 'ground' floor just increased our anticipation. The key to get in the imposing front door was huge and in keeping with a château, which pleased us. Turning it made a meaty clunk as the lock mechanism rotated and, after a bit of jiggling with the handles, we got our first view of the insides.

We had to pause and breathe so we could take in the high ceilings, the sculptured stonework, the enormous doors into the rooms and the amazing double staircase that led away and swept up to the left and right . . . It was spectacular. It was dark and smelt musty and the peeling wallpaper was very busy but wonderfully original. Looking around the ground floor, the salon, the small snug, the dining room, the service kitchen and the bureau showed every room to be tired but thankfully untouched. We galloped around the rest of the château to confirm there were no walls missing or major disaster areas. We commented on every view and marvelled at every room but we did it in a blur, as we knew this was right and we had to get down to business. Within twenty minutes we had made an offer and it had been accepted. Well, sort of.

The truth is, it actually took longer than expected to have our offer accepted, mainly because there was an anomaly on the *cadastral*. While the walled garden was included on the map, one quarter of it was not coloured in. The agent told us, 'Oh, that bit is being sold separately as a plot with the large barn that has permission to be a three-bedroom house.' Well, there was no way we could have someone living in our walled garden. It was a deal-breaker for us. We made our position very clear and, as the buyer was still a couple of days away from committing and signing, the sellers decided they would sell us everything. The price went up by €50,000 to €395,000 but it was still within our budget and the sale was agreed.

We knew from experience how easy it was to forget the details when you were back in the UK, so as we set off to explore our château in full, we took copious notes, photos and videos. In my videos you will see the location of old electric cables, sewage and plumbing issues, the condition of windows and general areas to be addressed. For me, if you are looking around a property seriously you have to pause in every doorway, orientate yourself and methodically sweep around the room. There were just so many rooms. Apart from the ground floor and the first floor, where the rooms were traditionally for 'high-status' guests, and the only rooms guests could expect to see, every other floor had lots of functional rooms for children, or the staff, for storing, for ironing or for working in.

In the basement, the cellarage took up half the floorspace with cider *caves*, good and less good wine *caves*, and then there were the preserves rooms, with shelf upon shelf of empty glass preserve jars and containers. The utility room was all but empty but in the cold room there were the remains of the cupboards with fine-mesh windows, which is where cheese and meat and other perishables would have been kept in the days before refrigeration. There was an amazing sink for cleaning vegetables in the base of the western tower, adjacent to the main kitchen and pantry. It was nearly six feet across but only four inches deep, complete with hand pump, though sadly not connected. Every window on this level had sturdy bars securing it.

I knew just by what Dick and I were filming that we had different agendas. It's who and what we are. In my footage, you see the wonderful wallpaper, the incredible floors, the views of dappled light, the woodwork, the steel works – not plumbing and electrics. The contrast is clear to see. We are a team and, without even discussing it, we had divided up the tasks and captured it all.

First impressions are everything and, when I walked through the front door across the hexagonal flooring and pictured our guests walking in and having the same experience, excitement filled my heart. The grand wooden symmetrical doors that lead off the breathtaking entrance into the salon and the *salle-à-manger* were exactly the right height. The staircase – the double-revolution staircase – was too much to take in and I could hardly speak for excitement. It's hard to articulate this, but there is the finest line in having a grand house. We wanted somewhere that was impressive enough to hold weddings but would also feel like a home. What I was seeing was perfection. The château was a happy place and you could feel it. Every room I entered showed signs of elegance and that the previous custodians had cared for every detail. Faded glory came to mind. Every room told a different story and even though there was no furniture, the curtains, wallpapers, windows and flooring were more than enough to bring the picture to life.

It felt like a couple of hours passed in seconds as we moved through all forty-five rooms in turn. Then we started to investigate the outbuildings and the grounds. As we did, a tractor turned up, driven by Jacques De Baglion, a very French gentleman with open arms and a big smile. He was being followed on foot by his wife, Isabelle De Baglion, who we watched walk round from the far side of the moat with their dog Inox to come and welcome us.

We all said our *bonjour*s and Dick and Jacques made me giggle: they are both such alpha males, but within an instant a firm handshake turned into a hug. It felt to me like the Bagliones needed to meet us (and to like us); as if they needed to see who the next custodians of their family home would be. We were to become only the second family ever to have owned this château after all. They seemed delighted that it was going to a family and could not have been more helpful and lovely. Within no time at all, Jacques had Arthur up on the tractor driving around. They were buddies.

Then we all walked across to the orangery together, where we spotted an ancient quince tree laden with fruit. It smelt incredible and a bit of pidgin French later we quickly discovered that they harvested the '*coing*' every year and made quince cheese or jelly. We love quince and were really excited as we had never had the ability to make our own jelly. It felt pretty presumptuous to just take the quince, but Isabelle and Jacques must have realised this and instructed us to help ourselves. We did and promised to bring them back some of our preserves. They said we'd do a swap for some of theirs and an *entente cordiale* was well and truly established. We ended up with a huge bag of the pear-like fruit to take back to the UK. The sweet, perfumed smell in the car all the way home was a brilliant reminder of what was to come.

We spent hours walking and talking, first on our own, then with Jacques and Isabelle, planning and looking at what was soon to be ours. Along the southern side of the walled garden, away from the château, we discovered that, in addition to the barn we had stopped being sold to someone else, we had also bought a second barn with planning permission for a three-bedroom residence. It was all getting better and better. No doubt this would have been the next bit of the estate to have been sold off, but, no matter, it was to be ours now.

We fought our way into the walled garden, where we discovered the *potager**; it had been neglected for decades but the potential was immense. Walking in the walled garden was not easy. Nature had reclaimed its 2,800 square metres and underfoot was a tangle of brambles, grasses and weeds, but were some ancient fruit trees that alluded to its former glory. Against the walls were some deformed old pear trees that would once have been pruned to perfection, and a plum and a cherry tree that now appeared randomly placed, but must have been positioned with some thought in the garden's heyday. A true indication of the neglect were the numerous forty-foot-high sycamore trees that had started as self-seeded weeds and were now a major feature of the garden. They'd have to go. We knew the garden would have to wait, as our priority had to be the château, but nonetheless the potential was incredible and my smile was making my face ache.

By the time we had to leave or else camp out for the night, we were deeply happy and excited for what lay ahead. Our minds were racing. It was purely by chance that we had a cameraman with us the very first time we saw the château. We always thought it was an interesting idea to make a television series about the adventure we had planned and were filming a bit of a 'taster' video. There was so much we could do, and so much we would do. Now we had to arrange all these thoughts into a sensible order so a plan could form.

---

*   The vegetable garden.

An original architectural illustration of Château-de-la-Motte Husson.

CHAPTER ONE

JANUARY

·2015·

The short days and cold, damp conditions of January always have you looking to the future. It's fair to say that in the UK we usually have to endure this dreary sort of weather a lot more than the crisp, clear days that are the optimum version of winter. It is in these gloomy conditions that we make and try to keep our New Year's resolutions as well as dreaming about what the next year will bring. Looking ahead in January 2015, we knew it was going to be an interesting year. Instead of snuggling down with warming hotpots and log fires, we were just about to launch into the adventure of a lifetime.

The first tranche of paperwork had been signed in November and the last legal opportunity to change our minds had passed, but that never occurred to us. This year we would be starting our new lives in a castle! There was a lot to do to organise ourselves to start afresh in France.

Conducting a legal transaction in a foreign country with a rudimentary grasp of the language is both stressful and seriously difficult. The purchase of the château was conducted in two phases and, after our initial commitment, we were given a very weighty tome to digest. We were handed a large envelope and within this was a report on the château with literally hundreds of pages about all the things that were wrong with it. It was enough to scare any sane person. We immediately punched holes in every page and created a very scary file. Obviously, it was all in French; however, we hadn't really thought about the difficulty of translating hard copies of paper documentation. We could not copy and paste it into Google Translate. Each report had been done by a specialist who must have charged by weight or word count.

With a failed French O level dating back to 1976, I would have thought I would have been the last person to be given the task of working out what the reports said. However, as a student I had sold doughnuts on the beaches of the south of France and in my youth had also earned my French 'wings' by training and jumping out of aeroplanes with the French army, so that was enough justification for Angela to say 'catch' and the coup de grâce was the throwaway, 'They're technical and that's your department.'

There were a couple of things I learnt very quickly: firstly, every report contained a significant amount of generic filling and fluff that I soon realised I could skate over; and, secondly, it pays to read the last page first before launching into the complete document. This latter point became apparent when I decided to read the report on asbestos first to see just how big a problem we had. There were more than forty pages and I ploughed my way through translating description after description of how terrible *amiante friable* was, be it white, brown or blue. Over the course of several hours I began to feel a tightening in my stomach and a rising panic. It was only when I reached the conclusion that I realised that the 'report' was mainly an education document and that the totality of the risk at the château was centred around a handful of new tiles on the sides of a dormer window in the hay loft of an outbuilding. It simply means that disposal of these 'slates', in fifty years' time, will probably involve double bagging them first. Lesson learnt.

The 'file of doom' was never going to be my job. I struggle reading English, let alone French. Oh no, my job was to make Dick tea, rub his shoulders and make all the right sounds when asked a question. My heart melted watching Dick in his office night after night with his phone trying to capture the text into a PDF translator, but it would have cost thousands to get it all translated professionally – and that thousands could buy us a new bathroom suite.

The château had not been lived in for some time and the list of jobs that needed to be done was extensive: there was a significant amount of lead paint that had to be stripped; masses of windows that were lacking glass, or at the very least were cracked and broken; the entirety of the electrics had to be replaced, as did all the plumbing; the sewage needed sorting as a matter of urgency and there was no central heating. It was a long list and they were all mammoth jobs. Not for the first time, we reminded ourselves it was all about the planning – and that you eat an elephant a bite at a time. Looking on the bright side, there was one working tap – admittedly it was in the cellar, nowhere near a sink, but at least it worked.

Having ploughed our way through the paperwork and made a plan, of sorts, we were assailed with another raft of documents: the legal paperwork to actually buy the property. France is known to be bureaucratic, so it came as no surprise when we got a very thick envelope that required a straight back and bent knees to pick up. This time we had to bite the bullet and paid for a translator to ensure we did not miss anything important – after all, to coin a poker phrase, we were going all in. Despite chasing, we only received the translations a couple of days before our meeting with the *notaire*, Monsieur Blot, and every minute thereafter was spent excitedly pawing over them.

The signing was probably one of the biggest commitments either of us had ever made. It was not just the buying of a house, which is a very grown-up thing to do; it was the sinking of all our money and hopes into a building that no one else seemed to want to buy. Added to that, on a scale of hugeness, it was enormous, and also a very long way from being habitable. We knew these stark facts but, quite frankly, it didn't matter. We just knew it was right for us and right for our family. It might sound a bit odd, but we didn't doubt we were doing the right thing, though we were a little curious as to how we were going to do all that had to be done. Angela and I are positive people and we knew we'd overcome anything thrown at us, but at this point we didn't really know what those things would be.

We travelled in style to the signing in France. We hired a van in Southend-on-Sea and filled it with items we knew we would need the moment we got the keys – and then we headed off to take the final steps to owning our very own château. Arthur stayed with Grandma and Grandad but Dorothy, who was still very attached to Mummy's boobs, came with us. The journey south was very special; we chatted all the way, with Dorothy, sat in her car seat between us, watching us as avidly as any fan at the centre court of Wimbledon.

It was a fairly unimpressive January day and we arrived at the *notaire's* office in good time. We had agreed to allow Monsieur Blot to act for us, even though he was also acting for the Bagliones because he was based in the village and spoke English – two very good reasons. On our arrival, we discovered that the office was indeed in the village and that Monsieur Blot's claim to fluency in

English was based on his ability to communicate on several fishing trips to Scotland. We would have loved to have been a fly on the wall when he and his gillie were chatting in a pub after a day on the water. Fortuitously, we had decided before Christmas that we'd invest in an interpreter to be in attendance and to translate the documentation we were to sign. We felt that if there had been any misunderstandings, our limited ability to understand French would not have been a defence for us . . .

We convened at 3pm on 12 January 2015. In the office there was the *notaire*, the estate agent, our interpreter, Jacques, and the three of us. It was a marathon session: each page had to be read, explained and then initialled. There is so much arse-covering going on you have to know that it is definitely a case of '*Caveat emptor*' – let the buyer beware – though it was actually very exciting when each parcel of land was discussed and confirmed to be in the sale. We had visited the property a couple of times, but we still hadn't actually walked the boundaries. That was all to come . . .

Dorothy was so well behaved we hardly knew she was there (she was probably doing her bit to ensure it all went smoothly). There was only one small sticking point and that was to do with a tax that has to be paid for the year. Legally this was due to be paid by the person owning the property on 1 January. Obviously that wasn't us, and we'd done our research so we knew what bills we would expect and when. Initially it was stated that it was for us to pay, then it was acknowledged that it was not actually our debt, however, ultimately we had to pay it anyway, because that was what was done. Apparently custom and practice is as important as the law in rural France.

After five hours, on a dark, chilly January evening, we finally had the keys to our own château in our hands. After the warm handshakes and thanks we headed off to our new home. Château-de-la-Motte Husson was officially ours and our smiles could have lit up

all the Mayenne. Jacques invited us to his house for a celebratory drink but first we had to pop 'home' and drop off the contents of our van. In some ways it was good that our first visit as owners had to be quite short as otherwise we would have probably spent most of the evening and night starting our list of things to do.

Five minutes later we reversed up to the steps leading to our front door. Our front door key is truly a thing of beauty: it's huge and when you open the door it makes a significant clunk. Opening our massive front door for the first time that evening and going into our château was very special. We both had tears in our eyes – we had done it. We now owned the château of our dreams. We were realistic and knew full well that now the work would really begin, but our family had actually bought a fairy-tale castle to live in. We had talked about putting down roots for generations ahead and this was where we were going to do it. Our goosebumps were nothing to do with the temperature: we owned a f***ing château!

We savoured our achievement for a few moments but then it was time to focus and we went back outside, opened the back of the van and proceeded to empty it. First out of the van came our battery-operated work lights: we illuminated our way and, after a quick sweep, the first room we occupied was the *salle-à-manger*, the dining room. Some glass was missing from the windows but the shutters were sound. And, most importantly, it was on the ground floor, even though there were fourteen stone steps to be negotiated to get up there. Time was against us, so we shot up and down like people possessed.

First up was a large rug and play pen. Dorothy was wrapped up like a Michelin man and plonked, happily, in her cage. Next up came masses of cleaning equipment, a leather chesterfield sofa bed – which was a bugger to get up there – bedding, towels, assorted tools, clothing and a basic camping kit (gas stove, pans, loo rolls, bowls). Every time we went up and through the front door we smiled. This beautiful place was ours. We 'moved in' in record time but couldn't dwell long as we had to pop next door to Jacques and Isabelle's for drinks before heading off to find our hotel.

So, reluctantly, we locked up and the three of us drove to see our new neighbours: Jacques and Isabelle. They only live five minutes' walk away, and four of those minutes are the walk from the château and round the moat, then it is just a skip and hop to their home, which is two huge old farmhouses from the original estate. But with Dorothy only being nine months old, we drove – it was just easier because of the amount of stuff a nine-month-old needs.

Their house was stylish, rustic, homely and inviting. With six children it did not have room to be anything else. They had two entrance ways: the main one was seldom used and opened into a hallway in the oldest part of the building; the other was the doorway into the kitchen, which was clearly the heart of their home. The kitchen was filled with shelves upon shelves of herbs, seasonings, preserves; there was a gigantic cooker, a huge table and a smaller breakfast table. You could clearly see how they lived life just from their kitchen.

Around the corner was what looked like an old hunting room with stone walls, exposed dark beams and a huge fire and mantel-piece that was the focus of this room. This was their salon (back home in Northern Ireland this would have been called the front room: somewhere to bring guests that was usually tidy and, with a fire in the grate, would be welcoming). In Jacques and Isabelle's room, comfy green and burgundy chairs had been carefully arranged round the fire. It was a cosy room, but it did feel like it was saved for special occasions.

Jacques and Isabelle were prepared for us. There was a bottle of champagne in the fridge and homemade nibbles on the table:

bread, olives and charcuterie. They warmly welcomed us into their lives and Jacques stood up and said a few words before everyone cheered '*Santé!*' It was a very special moment between families. And although we had TV cameras with us that day, Isabelle made it very clear that her family would never be on TV. We loved her for this – she was the boss and that was that.

The Baglion family had been masters of this land for over four centuries. They had acquired the rights to the original twelfth-century castle and the lands and had built the 'new' château 150 years earlier. Our château had been built for Countess Dorothée, who had wanted a grand château on the site of what would have been a fort when she married into the family. Her main residence was to be at their château in Nantes, a hundred miles to the south -west of here, where they spent winters in the milder maritime climate. Château-de-la-Motte Husson was the family's summer home. We did not pry into how the fortunes of the family had faired in recent years, but it was clear that they had not used the château as a primary residence for a long time and, upon the death of the late count, it had been sold so the proceeds could be divided amongst the children.

With only the one château, we prepared ourselves to spend our winter and our summer there, and we were truly excited to do so.

After the epic session at the *notaire's* office, followed by drinks at Jacques and Isabelle's house, we should have been on our chin straps but the excitement had us buzzing. We were staying at the Marjolain, a hotel only seven minutes from the château. The rooms were simple but clean and the grounds were stunning, with a beautiful water feature to welcome you. Driving into the hotel, I thought to myself: *Do we need a water feature at the château?*

It took me less than fifteen minutes to get changed, feed Dorothy, pop her into her papoose and get my red lippy on.

With my hair already done I was eager to get downstairs to their highly-recommended restaurant.

I would love to say that the service was welcoming but, alas, I think no one could get over the fact that I had a baby attached to my hip. But I was all dressed up, having just bought our first château, and a sleeping Dorothy was not going to stop us celebrating. In fact, she was part of it. We sat down and giggled like naughty told-off children. 'Does no one go out with babies?' I remember Dick saying, but we soon got distracted by a plate of deliciousness and a menu.

We tried their local aperitif to start with, which was a variation on kir royale, made with champagne and an apricot liquor. It was very nice and a great way to kick off. I watched as Dick scanned the thirteen-page wine menu and eventually said, 'Let's go for a *Chinon*. It's a local wine and I've never tried it.' Sometimes we like to pair our wines with our food and other times we just like to get stuck into one good bottle that both of us fancy. Today was definitely a case of the latter. When the 2012 *Chinon Les Perruches Pascal Lambert* arrived, it was delicious, rich and smooth.

By this point we were both smiling from ear to ear. Aside from having just completed on our new home, it was not very often that we got to go out any more. It was a date – and we were definitely going to enjoy it! There was a *formula*, or set menu, available for €24, but we decided to take the tasting menu. I think it's fair to say moments like these are few and far between. It was a very special meal.

On the day we became château owners we ate the following:

Snails with pork ears
Lobster with fresh thyme
Veal sweetbreads with langoustines
Philippe Delaunay young pigeon with blackberry sauce
A trio of chocolate desserts

The courses were small but bursting with flavours. There were a few combinations that we discussed quietly between ourselves. 'They nearly worked' was the general theme, but that only gave us more lovely conversations on what we thought went well together.

Breakfast at the Marjolain was a little more relaxed: fresh juice, jams, warm croissants and crunchy baguettes with butter that you wanted to put your bread onto (Dick's saying!). We ate early and then, with our one and only key safely clasped in our hands, we headed to the château (I must have checked that I had that key a dozen times. I blame my baby brain for checking that I had the key, forgetting I had the key, checking, forgetting).

When we arrived, Dorothy had fallen asleep, so we took the opportunity to take a few selfies with our gigantic key outside our massive, and very much in need of love, front door. Another special moment from this trip.

It was the first full day of officially owning our new home. I remember thinking it was a dream. It had not sunk in yet. How on earth have we ended up owning a château? Our plan today was to look around and work out in what order we would do things in, but in reality that was Dick's area. I did cosmetics. As we walked around the rooms again, in my mind's eye I saw how each room might look: where the lights would be, where the Christmas tree might go. I even saw the rooms filled with people, drinking and laughing. I saw the potential. As I entered the salon, with the old duck-egg blue and gold wallpaper hanging off the walls, the silk curtains in need of attention, and an electric fire blocking the mantelpiece, I pictured what it would have been like in its heyday with the bustle of noise and life.

Then suddenly with a bang I had to step back to reality. Dick was talking about flue liners, the electrics, the heating and how we would need to 'chase' everything into the walls*, the woodworm, the damp and the flies. Yes, it's fair to say, my feet were firmly back down on solid ground. Room by room, Dick and I went around the château discussing phase one of our (his) plans and what each room might be used for in the future.

One of the first things we came to terms with was realising that we are custodians of the château and that we were there to bring it back to life. Every lock in the château – the doors, the wine cellars and all the cupboards – had keys in them or hanging on a nail beside them. Jacques had mentioned this to us briefly as we were leaving their house the evening before. It was clear that our château had been cared for.

Looking objectively at what we got for our money, it was lots. It was no longer one of the grand estates owned by the aristocracy, but it was still very special. Our plot is about twelve acres altogether; within that we have mixed pasture, woods, a moat and a very neglected walled garden. In addition to the château, which was huge, lovely and in need of attention, we had a collection of other buildings: an orangery and seven outbuildings, including two barns, each with planning permission to become three-bedroom houses, a coach house and stables that we subsequently got permission to convert into a seven-bedroom home, four other agricultural buildings, plus several ruins – a piggery, a building down below the moat and a tower in the walled garden. And, last but not least, we had all the contents the family left behind.

We had a close shave with that and nearly missed out on lots of the treasure the château had to offer, as the Baglion family had

---

* I now know that 'chasing' involves digging out the wall to sink in ducting, but at the time I didn't really understand what he was talking about.

started to clear out all the old 'rubbish' in the château before we took possession. Fortunately, we had arranged for a visit to take some measurements and found them throwing out lots of early twentieth-century clothes, magazines and papers. They were all being taken outside for burning! Being good buyers, we insisted that they just leave it and we'd sort it out when we moved in. That one bit of fortunate timing meant we had a treasure trove of goodies for crafts and decorating the château.

We were very fortunate to also be given the original architectural plans for the building and all the bills associated with the rebuild that took place between 1868 and 1874. There have been a number of changes over the last 150 years but none that were significant. The old plans were incredibly useful when it came to planning routes for the utilities. The truth is that we had a blank canvas: there was just one 'functioning' toilet (we had to fill the cistern with a jug, but when you flushed it the contents went round the bend – although it was to be nearly a year before we found out what happened to the poop).

Our first big decisions all centred around what was to go where in the château. Our plans had always revolved around finding a dream home that worked as a wedding venue. With my twenty years' events experience and Dick's love of cooking we are a great team. I love, *love, love* (I know it sounds cheesy, but it is true!) hosting weddings. I know I'm good at it, but who would not want to host an event that is full of joy and will be remembered for ever?

One evening in Southend we had opened a bottle of wine and talked though dozens of different business ideas, from high-end foodie weekends to Dick hosting residential courses to build rocking horses. We tried to think of ideas that gave good revenue streams but we also wanted variety. French law says you can have

up to five letting rooms and operate as a *chambre d'hôte*[*] without having to meet lots of official rules. If you have more accommodation you have to comply with hotel regulations, which are much more complicated. Ultimately we knew we wanted quality rather than a big operation, so this sealed our fate and we decided that we would not have more than five suites.

We decided that our family suite (for us to live in) would be on the first floor, then there would be the honeymoon suite and three other suites on our floor and the one above. We roughly knew the role of each room and exactly where we wanted each of the bathrooms and toilets to go. That was the most important part for Dick so he could plan the utilities.

There were a few changes along the way but not many, which is always the sign of a good plan, and we were sensible enough not to try to do everything at once. We knew we wanted a home and a lifestyle that was as sustainable and self-sufficient as possible, but I've enough experience to know how much effort that requires, so we parked it and prioritised the urgent important tasks first. It was going to be hard work but we couldn't wait to get started.

I grew up knowing and watching hard work. My parents, Jenny and Steve, were both grafters. When my dad was sixteen he did an apprenticeship in Hatton Gardens to become a jeweller and he remained a jeweller until the day he moved to the château. First, he rented a tiny space within another shop, then a few years later he moved next door to a small shop of his own, then five years later he moved to a bigger shop, and on it went. I knew from a very early age what you can achieve with hard work. Now we were going to be pouring all of that into our very own château.

---

[*]   Basically a bed and breakfast.

It was really interesting working with Angela on the plans for the château. She'd had several businesses before. The first was a vintage experience business, then she started a company that printed personalised T-shirts and most recently she had been running Vintage Patisserie, an events company that specialised in vintage-style parties. But these were her businesses, so right from the very first time I helped her prepare for an event back in London I did things her way – she set the standard for everything. To put that into context, I still have the notebooks in which I wrote down her instructions on how to make a ham and mustard sandwich and how to boil an egg the way Angela wanted. That may sound ridiculous since I'm a competent chef (I've run kitchens and restaurants) but, as the saying goes, democracy can lead to mediocrity, and that is not something you can accuse my girl of!*

The château was our project and our skills are definitely complementary. To start with it was going to be a lot of physical, repetitive tasks and getting the basics done. Then Angela's creativity could be let free. That said, the decisions about what each room would be used for and where the facilities would go had to be made right at the beginning and to do that I had to educate her on the limitations of the laws of physics and the fact that sewage has to flow downstream! To her credit, Angela now fully understands that dealing with the waste from sinks, showers, baths and toilets is far more problematic than putting in electricity and hot and cold water. Having just read the last sentence, I know it to be completely true, but if I was to be asked if it makes a difference as

---

*   As a side note, Angela's boiled eggs are 'egg'cellent (sorry!). You place the eggs into cold water just covered, bring them to the boil, turn off and cover. After thirteen minutes, empty out the water and run cold water over them until they are cold. When peeled they will be cooked to perfection and look great – give it a go, and don't spare the salt.

to where Angela would decide to position things to be aesthetically pleasing, the answer would still definitely be no. But at least she now understands why I get grumpy!

It is nonsensical to start a major refurbishment project in January. Winter is the time of least productivity, especially if you have no power available and are reliant on daylight. But we had no choice in the matter, so before we moved out to France, we had already started sourcing materials and working out what had to be done first and why. We had worked out the routes for all our electricity, hot and cold water and waste, and exactly what each room would be used for. There were some challenges; however, we kept it as simple as possible with the flexibility to expand in the future. With a project as large as the château, one principle we set in stone was that we would only do things that we would not have to undo later – this was to save both money and effort. It was a good principle, though it did mean we had to wait a while for some things. For example, the service kitchen on the ground floor was very limited in functionality and storage but it didn't get any love until we were ready to address it properly, after eight months of making do. Suffice to say, when it was finally done we really, really appreciated it.

During all the planning, I'd had my lesson in the physics involved in sewage systems and I learnt about heating: 'square metres', 'volumes', 'outside walls' and 'cubic heat things'. We had already decided to source all our radiators in advance so they would be ready to install when we arrived in France. I knew what I was looking for in terms of size and output, but finding radiators that delivered in style as well as performance was another matter altogether.

Radiators are useful, ugly bits of metal. They are essential to keep you warm and to dry your wool socks on but not in any way aesthetically pleasing. I did the classic 'look on Pinterest'

for inspiration but anything I liked was either not available or far beyond our price range. I soon realised that I wanted a classic look: a cast-iron Victorian radiator. Dick and I are huge fans of buying second-hand – firstly, because you can often grab a bargain, and secondly because it allows you to reuse an item. But on this occasion, it was not to be. I was shocked at the second-hand market for radiators. Most of them are used until they are ready for the graveyard, and it takes a lot of money and love to bring them back from the dead. We just did not have enough of either in the early days. Luckily, this style of radiator was in vogue and often used in renovations of old buildings, so I decided finding new cast-iron radiators was the way forward. I got the look I wanted as well as the peace of mind that they would be reliable.

The next lesson I learnt was that radiators don't come with a thermostat. And it came as a shock to me that these cost half the price of the cast-iron radiator and were also ugly. Instead of anything thermostatically controlled, I settled for a manual screw twist, as they were cheaper and a bit less ugly. Five years on, Dick still chunters at my decision and the fact he has to run around our big house turning radiators on and off. I have to say, on this occasion he was right, but he'll have to read this book to find that out, as I will not say it out loud to him!

* * *

I'll never forget the date we made the 'Oh, there is no turning back' move to France: 30 January 2015. Not just because it was a big deal. Obviously it was, but there are lots of significant dates I can't remember: for example, I can't remember the date that Arthur or Dorothy said their first word or took their first step. The feeling is imprinted in my memory but the date is totally gone. However, our big move came the day after Arthur's second birthday, so I will never forget it. And, because as a mum I didn't want it to affect his birthday (don't get Dick started on whether or not a two-year-old would remember), all our friends and family gathered in Southend to celebrate. We dressed up as pirates, walked along the pier and ate Chinese food. Then the next day we had to work out how to fit all the pressies in the car! If I'm honest, that detail still makes me laugh. What was I thinking?!

It was pitch black when we left Southend with all our possessions squeezed into the car and very cold. Emotions were all over the place. We were mostly excited but also nervous, even a little anxious. Similar to any move, I guess. Mum and Dad came to wave us off and then we were driving the familiar route out of Southend. Leaving at 4am on a Friday morning had its advantages: the roads were quiet and peaceful, and it allowed us both a moment to reflect. We were driving to a new life! Although it sort of felt like we were off on holiday, to be honest.

Angela is a great, caring mum, but sometimes she worries about things that aren't a problem. I'd say having a two-year-old's birthday party a couple of days early isn't a crime but maybe I'm wrong. Honestly Angela, Arthur would never have known – he was only two! If it wasn't for the fact we wanted the family to be involved we could even have waited until we reached our new, temporary home in France, which was to be a gîte not far from the château, where we would stay until the château was habitable.

For the children, leaving England was a non-event. After the normal bit of chatting and fidgeting they slept all the way to Folkestone. The tunnel crossing gave us the opportunity to get them out of their car seats and we played in the terminal, changed nappies and grabbed a bite to eat. As the train arrived into France it was a matter of drinks, a dummy for Arthur and securing them in for the first leg of our journey to the Mayenne. With 450 kilometres to go we were keen to get some miles under our belts before Arthur and Dorothy protested too much and we had to stop to allow them to burn off some energy.

It couldn't have gone smoother: we found our way out of Calais and headed south and very soon joined the *péage** south of Boulogne-sur-Mer. With all our travelling to and fro to try to find a château, we had reached the stage where we accepted that taking the fastest route was going to cost us money. Having said that, we wouldn't have road tax to pay so it was swings and roundabouts. With much less traffic than the English motorways and a speed limit of 130 kilometres per hour, which is reduced to 110 kilometres per hour in the rain, the *péage* is a great way of getting from A to B as efficiently as possible. Such positive thoughts seemed to tempt fate though.

We'd been driving for about an hour. Angela, Arthur and Dorothy were all asleep and the temperature outside was around 3 or 4 degrees, so I was keeping the speed down to about 110 kilometres per hour. Then suddenly there appeared to be a line across the road and the temperature dropped instantly by six degrees. Freezing rain – a phenomenon that is not very common but quite brutal – had left the surface of the motorway like glass. Before I knew it, the car lost all traction and went into a skid. There were a couple of cars just ahead of us and three or four visible in the rear-view mirror. Time seemed to slow down. I managed to keep the car on the road and skidded and slipped for what felt like the best part of a kilometre, before a gentle left-hand curve meant we ran out of road, and hard shoulder, and the right wheel ended up in the drainage ditch. It was only then that I hit the brakes and put my left arm across Angela's chest to keep her back in her seat. I think I shouted, 'Oh f***!' as the drainage ditch came to an abrupt end and the front wheel hit the concrete. At this point things moved very quickly and I had little control. Airbags went off. The car jumped into the air and ground

---

* Toll road.

to a standstill in the middle lane some fifty metres further on.

Now, there were several things I was unaware of when it comes to airbags. Firstly, the powder that the airbags are packed in makes the inside of the car look likes it's full of smoke, which makes your bum twitch after an accident. Secondly, and I should have thought of this, they inflate so quickly they shoot out with some force. It didn't help that I was leaning across to try to hold Angela back as I was braking.

I very quickly confirmed that Angela was OK and that Arthur and Dorothy were not injured (and I will always be thankful that we invested in the best child's seats we could find and that they were rearward facing) before jumping out to start evacuating. Taking in the scene made me thank my lucky stars – and the training I had on skid pans while serving in Germany in the early 1980s. I could see about a dozen cars that had also skidded on the ice, some had collided and others had come off the road. The nearest vehicle behind us was well over half a kilometre away amongst a scene of carnage. Some vehicles were up the bank and others turned over.

I phoned emergency services who were aware of the accident and, rather than having the family leave the vehicle in the sub-zero temperatures, I threw on a jacket, grabbed the obligatory fluorescent jacket and triangle and set it up a 200 metres behind the car to slow down anyone who tried to pass. It was bloody freezing and I have to say the response of the emergency services was impressive, though it was some time after they attended the scene before they found us way down the road.

I had been in quite a deep sleep holding the kids' hands – I tended to travel with my arm back through the gap between front seats stroking or touching the children if they fretted. Dorothy was only nine months old and still fed every few hours, so with the build-up of the move and all the packing, the white noise of the

car had allowed me to have some rest. I woke up seconds before we hit what must have been a low wall. I must have sensed something but I was oblivious to what was really happening. I glanced at Dick and saw a look in his eye that I'd never seen before, or since, and then the airbag hit him very hard in the face. But it was the smoke that terrified me as I thought the car was alight. Dick's nose was broken instantly but thankfully other than that he was fine. He got out of the car, calmly put on his bright yellow jacket and started ensuring the safety of his family. I know I have a good man but moments like this remind you and also make you realise how precious life is.

As we were all unharmed (other than Dick's broken nose and black eyes), we were taken to the garage to have the vehicle assessed. Unsurprisingly the car was going nowhere, so the insurance company organised for us to be transported to a vehicle rental place in a nearby town so we could grab a vehicle and then come back for all our belongings. All of this took time and our intention of arriving at our new home with lots of daylight to settle the children was obviously not going to happen.

It was five minutes to twelve when we arrived at the car rental office and we had our first experience of the importance of lunch in France . . .

The scene is simple to picture: Dick looked like a grumpy, unsuccessful boxer; I was worrying about Arthur and Dorothy, and trying to make sure they didn't pick up on any of the vibes; and Arthur and Dorothy were wondering why we were in an industrial estate that didn't look like much fun. We launched into our best French to try to explain what we were after but we were talked over by the lady behind the desk who told us to come back at two o'clock. We were struck dumb for a couple of seconds, then launched into a tirade of French, English (and Dick may have even used some Gaelic), all to no avail. It was now midday and there was no one available to process the vehicle to allow us to take it away until after lunch.

The impotence of not being able to ascertain who was in charge, not being able to demand the name and contact details of everyone superior in the organisation and not being able to make her give a shit was disheartening. We had no choice but to accept the particular kind of Gallic shrug that emanates from someone that knows they don't have to be helpful and who has lunch waiting for them. What could we do? The answer was to breathe slowly for a few moments, find our centres and go for lunch ourselves.

Of all the meals to eat out in France, lunch is probably the most French experience. We searched on our phones for a local restaurant within walking distance and headed off to fill the next two hours dining. We were not spoilt for choice but that didn't matter as all we wanted to do was find somewhere comfortable that had something the children would eat. Like all small family-run restaurants, the offerings were limited, but that is often what makes it such a lovely experience. As always, when presented with two choices for starters, mains and desserts, we ordered one of each, and would decide who got what when it arrived.

Drinks were included, but as we were only at the start of our journey, we opted for soft drinks rather than the wine and cider the other diners were enjoying. Arthur's child's meal was fish and rice and, as it turned up with a tasty sauce that was very like a *'beurre blanc'*, it boded well for our meal. Our starters of terrine and cornichons, and a salad of lardons and goat's cheese hit the spot, though we were still coming to terms with the fact that butter seems to be rationed in little restaurants and the French don't seem to have the same appetite we do for mopping up sauces with the wonderful fresh baguettes. Arthur loved the fish and it was obvious he appreciated the flavour, and Dorothy played with enough food to keep her happy as we fed her with what we had brought with us. Our main courses didn't disappoint either: we had an adult portion of Arthur's fish and an unidentifiable cut of beef, cooked well, and served with chips and a sauce that was a Béarnaise but not quite – lovely! To finish we had the ubiquitous *iles flottante** and a chocolate mousse, to which both Arthur and Dorothy gave their seal of approval. The irony of having *crème anglaise* (that's custard to us) the first day away from England was not lost on us.

At €12 for adults and €8 for Arthur the total bill came to €33 (with an extra euro for an espresso), which was just over £20. It was a bargain and the slow pace had us feeling a lot less stressed.

As soon as the rental office reopened we were there. Following telephone conversations with the insurance company and a bit of toing and froing, we had the biggest hire car we could get, which sadly was nothing like the size of the seven-seater MPV we had been driving. Our five-seater SUV looked woefully small as we drove back to the garage to collect our belongings.

The transfer of our belongings from one car to the other was like a high-stakes game of *Tetris*. If you consider that we were moving and starting a new life, our MPV was properly full, so things had to be prioritised. Arthur and Dorothy's seats were put in first. Then it was all about increasing the density of the packing. All air gaps had to be eradicated, which meant cases and boxes had to be emptied and repacked with a lot of the contents stuffed in between them and some of the containers left at the garage. It took well over an hour and every area of the car had something in it (apart from the driver's footwell). It would have been comical if it had not been so serious. Obviously there was no visibility out of the rear-view window – in fact, it was a bit of a challenge to see the children, as they nestled in

---

*   Floating islands – a dessert of French origin, consisting of meringues floating on *crème anglaise*.

amongst the masses of clothing that had been packed around them.

It was late afternoon and getting dark when we started on the road again. With stops, we knew we had at least another five or six hours to go. I absolutely love the drive from Calais to the château – as well as the slowly changing countryside and the regional food and drink to be explored, it's like a live history lesson, cued by all the place names. When the children are older, I'll bore them with stories about the centuries when Calais was part of England, then as we pass Crécy they need to understand the power of a British archer, the three million who fought in the Somme offensive and the sadness and waste of the million casualties. Then there are all the cemeteries and as you cross the Seine at Rouen you can clearly see its cathedral towers that are testament to the Second World War . . . Who needs a car stereo?

Thankfully, the remainder of the journey was uneventful and, with just a single pit stop to wear out the children, feed, water and clean bums, we finally made it to our gîte about 10.30pm. We had been in touch with the lady who owned the gîte, Madame Olga Louvel, and given her progress reports so she knew we were going to be late. But it is fair to say we didn't exactly get a warm welcome. Our petite hostess was all rules and business as we were processed. Readings were taken of gas, electric and water, details of when we could use the laundry facility, where to put rubbish and a plethora of other rules were given thick and fast. We then wrote a sizeable cheque, to be held, uncashed, as security, just in case we started holding wild parties with the taps running. Despite our very, very long day we did try to keep smiling but it was fair to say our responses were probably equally terse.

After the best part of an hour, we were in our very spacious temporary home, with the doors locked, the heating on and our essentials brought in from the car. That didn't include any food, as our cunning plan to pop into a local supermarket to stock up after we'd moved in didn't happen. We had a miscellaneous collection of snacks and drinks scavenged from the car but very little that responsible parents would give their children, or themselves. But it didn't matter – we ended up having a picnic and it was at this point Arthur and Dorothy got their second wind and proceeded to settle in by exploring, running, crawling, gurgling, laughing and generally being so happy it was contagious. We didn't give a shit about how we had got there – we were just happy to have arrived and to be able to breathe.

Our journey may have been out of a book of nightmares, but in hindsight we were so very lucky that we had planned to be in France as soon as we could. We were obviously lucky to survive our accident largely unscathed but it was also fortuitous that we moved that day, as it meant we had been living in France for exactly five years and one day on the official Brexit date: 31 January 2020. Being here more than five years put us into the category of those who pre-dated Brexit and had different rights, but of course we didn't know that at the time as 'Brexit' had not even entered our vocabulary back then . . .

* * *

Our first home in France, La Picherie, was one of two large converted barns. It had spacious dormitory-sized rooms, a couple of bathrooms and a massive sitting/dining area. There were a lot of tiles and very little carpet, which was a bit of a problem with very young children but the main rug in the sitting area became the centre of all play and Arthur didn't seem to mind the cartoon characters on the telly talking a high-speed Gallic gibberish. Bedding was all provided but somehow we had missed that there were no cots for children. But it was a minor problem and our first romantic night was spent on a massive bed made up of four singles pushed together with pillows (Square pillows? What is that about?) stuffed down in the gaps and Mummy and Daddy bookending our precious little ones. When sleep came it was deep and wonderful.

Our time in the gîte was comfortable and happy, especially after we popped out and picked up a couple of cots. We had a rolling rental as we did not know when we could move into our château and, despite first impressions, we soon discovered Olga's brusque demeanour was absolutely not the whole story. She and her son lived in the farmhouse and, since her French husband had died, they had been making plans to move back to Russia. That was to be after her son finished his formal education, so they earned their living from the gîtes that had been made from converting the barns, and she worked part-time in the village school. Olga proved to be a font of knowledge and always had a warm smile for the children.

It was the last day of January when we took the children to see their new home. As we left our gîte, I checked I had the key maybe five times (something that would become a bit of a habit of mine) and we drove the seven minutes to the château. As we turned the corner, my breath was taken away all over again. I wondered then if I would ever tire of turning that corner. It was the depths of winter: the trees were bare, the skies were white and the château looked stunning. We marvelled at the idea that this was to be the only home Arthur and Dorothy would remember as they grew up. It was the first time all four of us had been here together since we made the offer. It felt different and I had to stop myself from running inside to 'get on'. Arthur was toddling around the front of the château, my heart was melting and we needed to savour the moment. Of course, the kids were too young to understand what was happening. They were just happy being with us and our joy was probably infectious. Dick and I had been brought up in more conventional houses but they were filled with love and we knew that we were ready to turn this massive, beautiful building into a home.

Today was 'drop-off day' and we were very sensible. Instead of lingering, it was a case of a quick unload and off to the supermarket to stock up. We have always loved going food shopping in France. It all feels so foreign and exciting. With two trolleys and the children ensconced we prepared to dash around. The baguettes were warm so we broke the end off one and gave a bit to each of the children and then we didn't hear another word from them, so off we went. Everything was interesting: even the loo rolls were different. When we arrived at the delicatessen and butchery departments it was gloves off, as we bought all sorts, justified by the fact that we'd need 'picnics' when we were at the château. The salmon and spinach quiche was a particular favourite, as was the smoked chicken. For some reason, France seems to be the place to have smoked chicken. Passing the abundant seafood counters reminded us just how close we were to the coast of Brittany and that this was the season to enjoy mussels, oysters, whelks, clams, cockles, crabs and lobsters (when we had more time).

We noticed the lack of 'out of season' fruits straight away. We bought lots of fresh fruit and vegetables, but there were no strawberries or raspberries, or indeed any soft fruits apart from some very expensive Moroccan blueberries. It is easy to think of strawberries in the middle of the winter as being normal but they don't taste as good if they are force-reared in the middle of winter, so we had to assume that the consumers in France were fussier and didn't buy them, and that was why the supermarkets didn't have them on the shelves. It is not a hardship waiting until the right time of year to buy seasonal fruit – if anything, the anticipation makes their arrival all the more special. First shop in France complete, we were off 'home' to enjoy some of our local delicacies.

In the overall scale of things it has to be said that January 2015 was a big month for us. We'd packed up our lives in the UK, bought our château, said our goodbyes and moved the family out to France. Arthur had turned two and we had all come through what could have been an horrific car accident. It was cold in the Mayenne – not the damp cold of home but it was still not the weather to be working in without creature comforts and our château was definitely lacking in those. It's true we had not yet sampled the lifestyle we had aimed for, but we knew the ports of Brittany had stocked the local markets with masses of fresh seafood. So even if we hadn't yet had the chance to appreciate the shellfish, we were here and the world was our oyster, whelk, clam, cockle, crab, lobster and mussel . . .

CHAPTER TWO

FEBRUARY

In the short, dark days of February, without lighting in the château, productivity was limited by daylight. It just doesn't yet feel like the promise of spring is round the corner, however the hardy snowdrops do make an appearance and we were delighted to have clumps of them round the moat and in the woods over by the orangery. But you always have to be wary of feeling too confident about the changes happening through the months. The old saying goes, 'As the day lengthens so the cold strengthens'. It may have been the lack of glass and sources of heat in the château, but that winter was cold in a way that went into your bones. We even saw the moat freeze for the first time in that first February. Although the freeze wasn't deep, definitely not deep enough to allow us to walk on it, it was sufficient to foil the herons and king-fishers. But we were a little preoccupied sorting out the alligators nearest to our canoe to notice the wildlife during our first winter at the château.

We were very aware that the French enjoy the seasonality of food but the food that is available to be eaten and harvested at this time of year is traditionally very limited. Some things have been stored, such as apples and potatoes, but other vegetables are still available to harvest. Root vegetables, *choux** and brassicas of every type were on sale. We also noticed sacks of leeks and boxes of carrots that were all sandy coming on sale the very first time. Surprisingly, *topinambour*† are widely available and even though we affectionately refer to them as 'fartichokes' because of their ability to cause 'gas', they do make an extremely tasty soup.

With a lot of worthwhile tasks, it is often the case that things get a lot worse before they get better. That was certainly the case with the château. We decided to start by cleaning the areas of the château that the children would be in and that was not trivial. First the entrance hall got a quick lick, then we moved onto the dining room, which needed a lot more attention as that was where we were going to base ourselves. The tower off the dining room had a toilet and a bath. We never understood how the Bagliones could have a high-status *salle-à-manger* and then a toilet so close but it worked out conveniently and we brought the toilet (not the bath) back to life fairly quickly, initially with jugs filled from the tap in the cellar.

On our first inspection, the toilet had driven Angela from the room gagging, so that made the decision about who was going to clean it. I'd brought up a couple of huge metal jugs of water, then proceeded to fill and flush the cistern until there were no lumps! After that it was all about brushing and then scrubbing with sprays

---

* Cabbages.
† Jerusalem artichokes.

and cloths. Now, cleaning rooms on our ground floor really has to be explained to be understood, as the ceilings are fifteen feet high and they needed to be brushed too, so it was a physical but I have to say satisfying task. After a couple of hours, I felt it was safe for Angela and the children to go in. All germs had been dealt with, the cistern charged, some spare jugs filled and even the sink and ancient bath looked acceptable, if not desirable. As the waste was going into the moat and there was definitely no septic tank or holding tank, we made the decision that paper and anything that didn't come out of your body had to go into a little waste bin we put in there. It reminded me of holidays to hot Mediterranean countries decades before, and the feeling that this was all a bit uncivilised. However, the thought of used loo roll floating around the moat was horrible, so we resigned ourselves, and our guests, to the indignity of the bin until our new sewage system was up and running. I also made the decision to feed the children more sweetcorn (it was bound to pay dividends when I started fishing). Within a couple of weeks we had connected the cistern to the mains water. It had its own pipe that went from the tower on one side of the cellar across to the tower on the other. It passed through open doors and was attached to nails in the ceiling so no one would trip over it. It was ugly, but it was only temporary, and it worked.

There were a couple of other tasks that had to be done immediately and it was safer for Angela and the children not to be around, so I dropped them back at the gîte and set about sorting them. Problem number one was the threshold into the entrance hall – it was seriously dodgy. When I walked on it, it flexed a matter of inches and it was obviously about to give way. It's not particularly welcoming if your first words to anyone who turns up are 'Be careful!' or 'Don't step there!' I made the decision to do a temporary fix as long as it was safe – our rule about only doing things that we would not have to undo later did not apply where our immediate safety was at stake. I only understood the extent of the issue when I removed the plaster and lath ceiling in the *sous sol** below – a dusty, messy and generally unpleasant job.

The tiled entrance above was basically levitating and it needed to be braced ASAP. I had set up my workshop in the cellar cider store so I went and grabbed every sort of bracket I could find. Within a couple of hours, I had put together a seriously Frankenstein arrangement that could have easily supported the Irish rugby team jumping on it. It reminded me of my *Scrapheap Challenge* days, when I always subscribed to functionality first – looks were irrelevant. I don't think Angela ever saw the monstrosity but it lasted the couple of years I needed it to until it was time to replace all the joists and redo the ceiling in what was to become our boot room. Cleaning up took as long as the job but it was great to be able to forget about the danger of walking through the door.

The next job was equally pressing but not as obvious. The buyer's report highlighted the front door as having lead paint on it and as it was in constant use it had to be stripped. I was reminded every time I walked through the door. We had had time to plan our priorities and do our research so we were not going to go down the route of using a heat gun and sanding, instead we had sourced an eco-chemical that held the lead compound in suspension that was then was easily disposed of. *Carpe diem.* It was just a matter of getting on with it. But the temperatures were low and it was cold outside, so it ended up requiring longer to 'cure' than anticipated.

Once applied, I put cling film onto the chemicals, then, after an hour of chemical action, I scraped off the paint and the chemical goop and collected it into a large drum. Then it was time to wash it all down, rinsing the cloths regularly to capture the lead in solution. The only water I had was cold and so, despite my Marigold gloves,

---

* The basement.

Château-de-la-Motte Husson, 2015.

'Untouched'. The day we first saw
the château, October 2014.

'Untouched' interior pictures on the same day in October 2014. Including the wallpaper in the entrance hall and the snug.

Signing day! Getting the keys. January 2015.

Arthur's first tractor outing with Jacques De Baglione. Our *cave* with handmade glass bottles.

my hands were a little chilly and, after a while, a little numb. It's a big door so it was a long job and I ended up working on it until late into the night. With no lights to turn on, I illuminated our front door with work lamps and, when those batteries failed, I ran the car with the headlights on so I could get it finished.

The front door was undoubtedly the hardest thing we had to strip as it was intricate and very big, so to reach the top required large stepladders. It was with great relief that I finished it and tidied away all my equipment eight hours later. The next day in the daylight it didn't look that bad, which was a great relief as it took us several months before we got around to repainting it.

Thereafter all our work was geared towards getting the plumbing and electrics in. That meant clearing routes to be ready for drilling holes, putting in pipes and cables and getting the infrastructure ready.

I love getting my hands dirty and with so much to be done and Dick on his own, I desperately wanted to help, but I fully understood that on this occasion the château was just not safe enough for the children. It was also frightfully cold, so the decision for me to stay at gîte was sensible but annoying.

With all the expenses of moving to France, we knew categorically that we didn't have anything like enough money to do all we wanted to in our first year. We had some money coming in from the television series, but to be honest that was never going to be enough, so we had to plan what we spent our money on very carefully.

I was still working as a television presenter as well. It meant I would have to travel and spend time away but it would bring in enough to tide us over until our business was built up and could sustain us. Before moving to France, we had worked out a business strategy that would enable the château to start paying for itself. We had gone through a list of possible revenue streams, the investment required to realise them, how much they could earn and then, most importantly, how much we wanted to do it. The result was interesting and our eventual plan was based around offering high-end experience weekends and some events. But for all of these we needed to have the château functioning.

I had been across to America during the autumn of 2014 to audition for a survival series for National Geographic. It was called a 'chemistry test' and lots of different applicants played at survival and showed off their skills. The idea was that there would be three chaps heading off on their adventures: a survival guru, a fabricator (someone who builds things) and an 'alternative' engineer (this was my group). The audition was great fun and I had a couple of days in New Jersey with some really interesting people. I was the only Brit and the oldest person there, but I did have some advantages: firstly, I was a country boy who loved the outdoors and knew how to enjoy myself; secondly, I had twenty years' military experience; and, thirdly, I used to teach survival.

Before we left the UK, the formal offer had come in and I was due to start filming in early March, so we had to get organised for me to be able to leave Angela and the children for two and a half weeks at a time. As if that wasn't enough, I had to try to get up to Paris to the American embassy to get a visa as an 'extraordinary alien' so I could work there. That would have been relatively easy but I had a broken nose and black eyes, which were not exactly photogenic. It was a matter of waiting as long as I could so my face could heal, but not too long as I needed my passport, complete with a visa, on 1 March.

Our gîte was advertised as sleeping sixteen people, but the reality was it had four very large rooms with dorm-style beds, all with plastic sheets on them. But we soon made it feel like home. Our trip to the supermarket and a scattering of kids' toys was all that

was needed. The floor tiles were very shiny and a little slippy, but we realised the benefit of them when we bought ten-month-old Dorothy a seat on wheels. Dick called it her 'trundle buggy'. It was orange, sturdy and had a little tray to hold, well, grubby stuff. In between feeding, pooping and sleeping it gave the non-walking Dorothy freedom and she whizzed around the entire gîte on it! At first it nearly gave me a heart attack but I relaxed after a few days when I realised it wouldn't topple.

The living space may have lacked a little 'something' but its redeeming feature was a huge oak table that seated sixteen comfortably. This table really came into its own when people started to come and stay. First to visit were my dad and Lee and Kyle, our father-and-son plumbers. I had known Lee and Kyle for many years. Lee was my plumber when I lived in east London. He lived in Hackney and I was in Mile End. As I lived in an old schoolhouse, with old pipes everywhere, he did tons of work for me over the years. He was kind and never let anyone down but was always late. His son Kyle had just started to train as a plumber. Lee joked that he was taking over the business when he retired, but we knew that would probably never happen. Lee loved his work.

Trustworthy friends and family that were handy were the order of the day and they were a much-welcomed addition to the team, which was currently just Dick, Arthur, Dorothy and myself. True to form, Lee and Kyle arrived late and blamed the laden van – which contained the huge shopping list of bits we had requested, including the cast-iron radiators – and the terrible weather. I was looking forward to seeing my dad for many reasons, not least the fact he could spend some time with the kids so I could finally get my hands dirty.

The next morning, everyone was up bright and early and I was taking orders in the kitchen: warm chocolate-milk served in a bowl for Kyle; fresh baguettes, jam, cereals, toast, cheese and eggs for everyone else. **Arthur was in his high chair throwing his food around and Dorothy was in her trundle buggy dashing around the room. Work had begun and the gîte had a whole new energy; it was pleasantly exciting.**

We had not yet mastered how to shop for technical supplies in France so when Lee and Kyle arrived their van packed was to the gunwales with every sort of fitting and pipe we might need. They were even collecting items the night before they travelled. They are total stars! It was so lovely to see a father and son working together and I recognised lots of the same pluses and minuses I had experienced when working with my big boy, James. Two things shone through: how much they cared for each other and how much they cared about getting the best job possible done. It was an absolute pleasure working with them, but the work wasn't easy, and it didn't go to plan.

After a walk around to talk through the details of the routes the plumbing and electrics would follow and to confirm that we were all singing from the same song sheet, it was about unloading and getting started. The first job was to sort the heating and to do that we had to get the customised thermal store we had bought into the *grenier**. As the name suggests, a thermal store is a place where you store heat. If you want any hot water or heat for your radiators, that's where you get it from. We were going to be generating heat from back boilers on wood-burning stoves, the gas boiler on our Rayburn, an immersion heater and, in the future, a solar thermal system. The thermal store would enable us to prioritise where the heat came from, so if our wood burners or a solar thermal system were operating heat would come from there, rather than burning gas in a boiler. It's all very clever and logical. At nearly £3,000 it

---

* The attic.

was quite a commitment, but it did everything I wanted it to for the heating and hot water in the château. But it is also bloody heavy. And from the bottom of the château to the *grenier* we have ninety-two stairs.

Lee and Kyle are both fit and strong and I am not exactly feeble, so we decided to just go for it. There followed a significant amount of grunting, swearing, sweating and general abuse of an inanimate object. It was the last two staircases through the floors where the staff and the children would have lived that caused the most difficulty. They are tight and steep, so the store had to be moved vertically one stair at a time, with each move being greeted with the sound of men doing themselves mischief. Eventually we got there and placed it directly above a main load-bearing wall, as we knew that, though it may have felt heavy now, once installed and filled with water it would be well over 500kg heavier.

The very first pipe we installed went from the one and only tap in the cellar to the thermal store in the attic, five floors up, and then down the far side of the château to the main kitchen fifteen metres away. It was our mains water feed and – to give you a feel for our pain – the water arrived at ground level in the eastern tower. It then went up to the ceiling of the basement in the tower, across the tower, across the main cider cellar at ceiling level (and through wall: hole #1), then across the secondary cider cellar (and through wall: hole #2), into and out of the expensive wine cellar (through the floor: hole #3), up through the playroom, through a series of floor joists (holes #4, #5, #6, #7), up the rear stairwell and through the ceiling (hole #8), then up the attic stairwell and through the ceiling (hole #9) before coming across the attic in ducting to save drilling through two more significant walls to the thermal store. So that was nine holes and masses of piping (all 32mm, for the techies). And to reach the kitchen down the other side was equally involved – on that pipe alone we put nine 'Ts' and full-bore isolators to allow us to break out. With hundreds of metres of pipe to lay it was daunting but, bless them, Lee and Kyle just got on and did it.

Lee is a great thinker and problem-solver, so we had discussed the project in some detail and, even though he and Kyle had no experience with it, we went for multicore piping that was made up of multiple layers of aluminium and plastic – it was strong yet a bit flexible and could be jointed and terminated in a robust way using a powerful compression tool. The main 'highways' for our hot and cold water were all through 32mm pipes to ensure the flow and the elements used in the rooms were 20mm and in some cases we came down to 15mm copper.

We built upon our work, rather than using different paths, so in most cases we were using the same route for the waste to come down. A slight restriction we had was that no sewage pipes were going onto the outside of the château. It did cause a bit more work but there was no real need to have them outside, so why spoil the look of our château? (Can anyone else hear Angela's voice when I say that?).

The multicore came in 100-metre rolls, which was a godsend as we could lay long runs without having to join pipes. Having put the first pipe in place, we had to go back and cut it and insert 'Ts' at every location where we were going to eventually connect into a bathroom. Again, this increased our workload but it did mean in the future we would not have to drain down the pipes to make connections as they would already be there, ready to go, which was to prove very sensible. Years later, I connected the water for the final bathroom in the château to the pipe and connector we installed on that very first day. I love it when a plan comes together and I raised a glass to Lee and Kyle that evening!

It was not all plain sailing as daylight was very limited and, without mains electricity, everything had to be done by hand or with battery tools. Rather than drilling out holes we put pilot holes through the two-foot-thick walls and then dug out the stones around them; it was not neat and definitely not tidy. Progress was slower than we had hoped but Lee and Kyle had the bit between their teeth and there was absolutely no way they would have left us until there was heating and a hot- and cold-water system working in the château. A hole that could have taken a physical twenty minutes of drilling (the drills are heavy and the walls thick) instead took a couple of hours jackhammering out stones and making a lot of mess that had to be fixed afterwards.

But before we could get any system working, we needed the electricity turned on. The only electrical item we had in the château that was acceptable was the meter. That was a little disheartening, but we needed power, and EDF wouldn't turn it on until a competent electrician said it was safe. Enter Monsieur Manceau.

It took three visits before we got any work from him. The first was to say he would come and look at the job – that was lost in translation, so when he turned up we got very excited, only to discover he'd turned up to look at the job and intended to come back and work the following week. During all this diddling we had no power and no electrical lighting, so in the middle of winter it was very hard to work, which was more than a little frustrating. When Monsieur Manceau and his assistant, who was a very young apprentice and moved with the lack of energy that only the young can show, turned up again, we had a list of tasks for them. Firstly, a socket below the meter; secondly, power to our thermal store and down to the boiler on the Rayburn; then there was a whole raft of simple spurs to give us power around the château.

After a day's work, the two of them had put in one cable and a socket. It was incredibly disappointing because at this rate the total bill to rewire the château would have worked out to be hundreds of thousands of pounds. They had done enough to get us connected and from there it should have been a case of 'don't call us we'll call you'. However, electricians who would come and take your money for working were as rare as hen's teeth, so we had to smile and see when he would come and visit us again . . .

The EDF inspection had been booked in anticipation of some electrics being done and it was not long before we were switched on and had a functioning socket at the château. It was a total game changer: we had electric lights, we had a kettle not flasks, we had a microwave, we had power tools. We had rejoined the twenty-first century. The amount of joy that single socket brought us was amazing. I don't think I'll ever take the flick of a light switch for granted again.

As well as making the work faster, it meant it was possible to have a warm lunch. We always had a relaxing and substantial evening meal back at the gîte complete with wine – we were in France after all – but lunch had been very ordinary with baguettes and some fillings to keep us going.

Now, Lee's wife Val is a legendary hot sauce maker. He always travelled with some and he knew if he didn't bring enough to give us some we'd eat his supply, so he'd come with plenty. The recipe was a closely guarded secret, but there were a lot of Scotch bonnet chillies in there. The word on the street was that Val wore full chemical protection to make it and it was way up there on the Scoville scale (actually between 100,000 and 400,000). But it was a lot more than just heat – the flavour was also very special and, because it was Scotch Bonnet-based, the heat seemed to be worth it for the flavour.

It only took a little experimentation before we developed a soup that is now classed as 'comfort soup' here at the château. In all French supermarkets there are freshly made, or heat-treated, fish soups available. Doesn't sound great on paper, but it's delicious! They are very rich and deep in flavour, ranging from posh lobster-based soups to very basic fish soups. We had tried them and found the one we liked best, which was actually not the most expensive and it was lovely. However, to add a little extra, we popped in anchovy fillets in chilli and oil that we bought in bumper-sized tubs. The hot, smooth soup with the whole fillets in it was lovely, especially with fresh baguettes covered with too much butter.

Then, of course, Val's hot sauce took it to yet another level. This was the fuel that warmed and comforted us on those freezing, short February days, partly because it was so easy, but also because it tasted so damn so good. We loved it so much we even served it at our wedding nine months later. We knew Lee would approve.

It had been days of very physical hard graft for Dick, my dad, Lee and Kyle. They started work before first light and finished well after 9pm. Compared to the team on the ground, my days were easy-peasy and every evening I looked forward to their return, to hear the stories of the day.

I tried to get as much ready as I could during the day, so every night we had a feast. We would have soup, salad, pasta, cheese, some kind of meat dish and lots of fresh baguettes and wine. We had to remember to enjoy this . . . and we did. But at this very early stage there was mounting pressure to get the essentials done and Lee and Kyle were due to go in four days' time.

With the arrival of electricity came the opportunity to get out our truly massive drill. I knew it made short work of cutting a 150mm core through solid granite and, as we still had a fair number of holes to do, we looked forward to the job getting more quickly. Sadly, the château had other ideas. Unbeknownst to us, the walls had been constructed with stone and infill material in exactly the correct configuration to defeat a huge water-cooled core drill. We tried several walls and a couple of different core sizes but no dice, so after a couple of hours of doggedly trying, we gave up and it was back to prising out stones to make our holes.

Heating needs a heat source and, after long deliberation, we had decided to start with a gas boiler that could be augmented by wood burners. To be honest, it was all we could afford, so the aspiration to have a biomass system or heat pumps had to be put to one side as we cut our cloth according to our means. Even though we were limiting our initial 'system' to just one bathroom, the small service kitchen beside the dining room and a bit of general heating for the house, the whole infrastructure had to be laid.

With cold water all the way up to the attic and down the other side, the thermal store had to be connected. Obviously cold water is only a proportion of your plumbing problems: you need hot water and central heating too. When the mains are linked to the thermal store it can then be miraculously converted to hot water to be shipped around the château. This was done via the hot-water pipes. Obviously you need heat going into your thermal store so that meant flow and return pipes to the boiler in the basement, flow and return pipes to the two back boilers behind the log burners in the dining room and salon and, to provide the actual heating, flow and return to the radiators, some of which had to be connected in phase one. Our suite and the salon and dining room may have been the priority but – just as we had done with the first set of pipes – we also had to lay all the way to rooms that would need heating and hot and cold water in the future, and everything had to be terminated (which basically meant isolators to stop all our heating water escaping), so we could fill the thermal store tank, the boiler, the back boilers behind the log burners, the radiators and all the pipes. Trivial really . . . (If you followed that, you probably feel our pain. And if you don't understand what I am even talking about you can probably imagine our pain!)

My feet were getting itchy. I knew being at home and ensuring the kids were happy was my best role at this point but I was desperate to see what was happening at the château. The heating was going in and I knew that today there was going to be a Frenchman called Pascale fitting flues for our chimneys. I have to be honest, I never even knew this was a thing, but I did know it was a huge step in the right direction for getting heat into our house. Plan 'move-in' felt closer. So I asked my dad to stay with the kids while I visited the château. I knew I only had a few hours before Dorothy needed feeding, but I was very excited.

We were all sharing one car, so Dick drove my dad back to the gîte and picked me up to go back to château. But as we left the gîte, he chucked the keys at me. 'Go on!', he said. I laughed, 'No bloody way!' I hadn't driven in France yet and I was really nervous. In fact, I'd never driven on the other side of the road before (if you discount the time I accidentally drove the wrong way down a one-way street, of course). This was a big deal for me. I looked to Dick for support. Poker face. I believe this may have been a tactic to not make a drama out of it but I was truly petrified.

I did it. I drove the seven minutes to the château, but I was shaking all the way. I still remember Dick repeating to me to stay in the lines, but we got there and no one had been hurt. I was delighted and full of excitement! When I ran into the château to tell everyone about my achievement, no one seemed to share in my elation. So I called my mum. If there was anyone who would understand it would be her . . .

I suppose I was a bit insensitive to the difficulty of driving abroad, but I'd lived in Germany on and off for most of the 1980s and after that thought nothing about jumping behind a wheel all over Europe, the Americas, the Middle East and the Far East. To me, it was all about going for it and giving the locals a run for their money.

It never crossed my mind that Angela was seriously nervous. But as with all things that are important, Angela didn't let it stop her for long. She thought about it then just had a go.

As I stood in the entrance hall of the château, I took in all that was happening: there was stuff everywhere, pipes and tools in every direction, not to mention the dust which was thick in the air. Dick has always said our home was going to be like a building site for some time and he was definitely right about that.

It was very cold that day: the grounds were frozen, the trees were as white as the sky, which was vast, and it looked like there might be snow on the way. I was wrapped up warm with a cashmere brown scarf that I had bought for Dick one Christmas. In all this craziness, Dick and I stood outside and watched Pascale as he climbed up onto the roof. As we stood together in that moment, holding hands in silence, it felt like we were watching our house become our home. And when I looked across at Dick and saw true happiness in his eyes, I knew he was thinking the same thing.

For our heating to even think about working we needed to start by lining three of our chimneys with stainless-steel flue liners. Being in a château this involved long and heavy liners going up three different chimneys. We did not have the time or the equipment to do that so, on a recommendation from Jacques, we called in Pascale, our whistling roofer. We didn't think of him as such to begin with, but he definitely earned the title.

It was a very good start: Pascale and his assistant arrived at a good hour, we had the coffee that seemed to be expected and they proceeded to unroll and lay out the liners. The château was a bit of a building site, but we were still taken aback when he popped out to his van, put on his harness and came back through the entrance hall with a lit Gauloise cigarette dangling from his mouth. Before we could say anything, he had disappeared up the stairs, exited through an examination window in the roof and began walking along the apex of the roof, whistling. He seemed to be precariously balanced at the top of our home. It was freezing and the roof still had ice on it but this didn't bother Pascale – he just sat on one of our chimney stacks, dropped down a weighted rope and then proceeded to pull up the liner as it was being pushed up by his colleague. Maybe whistling is a clever French trick to keep your bum warm? Within a couple of hours, he was fixing the *chapeaux* to the chimneys, having attached and sealed the liners. So all we had to do now was connect the boiler, the fires and all the pipes. We were making progress and things were happening thick and fast.

* * *

Life in the first few weeks seemed to revolve around pipes, holes in the walls and connecting things together, but there was more to it than that – we were living in France and it was important that it was not all work and no play. We wanted to truly enjoy the benefits of the food and wine that were now at our fingertips, as this was a huge part of why we had moved.

Angela was at peace that at this stage her main role was to keep everyone sane, keep the children happy, do all our admin and generally look after us, as well as all the cleaning and decision-making that was needed to keep our project on track. And it was a surprise to no one that she was the consummate hostess in the evenings. After a shower, it was slippers on, drink in hand, then some olives, crisps, nuts or nibbles. In the early days, we never really thought of our first drink of the evening as being aperitifs, but now that is just what they are.

Eating, relaxing, having a drink, and at the same time planning the next day, was a stress-free way to make sure we all knew what was happening. There were two separate upstairs in the gîte with a set of stairs going up to each, so Lee and Kyle had their own domain as well as having access to the communal family area. When friends stay as guests it can be a real test of the robustness of that friendship, especially with very long, cold working days. But Lee and Kyle were an absolute pleasure to have with us. Though it is interesting what you learn about people . . . Who would have known that Lee couldn't live with a butter dish that was messy or had a knife mark in it? It provided endless sport. All it took was someone digging into the butter or, heaven forbid, putting some jam in the dish and you could visibly see him twitch. We are not naturally cruel but we had fun for a while.

In the evening, to make up for the paucity of lunch, we invariably had two or three courses, and then we finished with a cheese board. Now, I'm not saying Kyle is odd, but he doesn't like cheese – that's not normal, is it? I'm afraid we are too British to subscribe to cheese (without crackers!) before the dessert, though.

February is the time for warming one-pot food, so we tried to ensure we had something that was slow-cooked, even if it meant trying to cook a day ahead. As we were leaving dishes to cook for a long time, a favourite was *jarret de boeuf* *. It is always well marbled but this means it takes well to long, slow cooking as all the fat and sinuous bits break down and become tender and sweet. Cooked with red wine, onions, tomatoes and root vegetables, it's a wonderfully thick and rich dish that goes brilliantly with baguettes and butter.

If we fancied something a bit lighter, I'd slow-cook pork belly in a 'green sauce'. This dish has evolved over the time Angela and I have known each other. The green sauce is prepared in a blender and is all things loosely 'green' to hand: green chillies, apple juice, lime juice and zest, fresh coriander, ginger, garlic, onions, salt and white pepper. You blend it all together until it is smooth, then

---

* Shin of beef.

pour it over the big lumps of pork belly and then leave in the slow cooker for the day. It's great served with the three-rice mix of basmati, red and wild.

We would normally serve food in waves, never rushing to clear the table, and constantly adding new platters. Grazing is a fabulous way to eat. Savoury rice dishes with lots of al dente veggies were always a winner and Val's hot sauce made lots of appearances too. If we needed something quick, we often turned to mussels or other seafood. It takes moments to get something on the table and it's delicious every time. It is just a matter of chopping some shallots, garlic and herbs and cooking them very quickly in butter, then in goes the white wine followed by the mussels as soon as the wine is bubbling. By the time we had rounded everyone up and they had broken their first bit of baguette and buttered it, it would be on the table.

....

MUSSELS

We made mussels differently every day. It really depended on what people fancied and what we had in. The options are endless, but the process is the same.

Ingredients

Lots of mussels, de-bearded (it doesn't take long if you are chatting while you do it)

Sauce option 1
Shallots, finely chopped
Garlic
White wine
Fresh parsley

Sauce option 2
Coconut milk
Ginger, grated
Fresh chilli, finely chopped
Fresh coriander
Soya sauce or salt (to counter the sweetness of the coconut milk)

Method

Soften your onions or garlic in a little oil.

Add all the rest of the ingredients apart from the chopped fresh herbs – they should only cover the base of a large pan with a lid about a quarter of an inch ajar.

Turn the heat up to fierce. When it boils, toss in all the mussels and put the lid on and leave on a high heat until the steam makes the lid move. Shake the pan to mix. Give it another two or three minutes, then turn it off.

Shake again. Then sprinkle over the chopped herbs and serve.

. . . .

As Dick said, we didn't call them aperitifs at first, but that is definitely what they are to us now, and we bought and tried aperitifs of every colour and flavour. We soon discovered there were many we loved: Suze and ice, Campari and tonic, Aperol and orange juice – the list goes on. And we still keep experimenting, but that is easy compared to the challenge of choosing wine in France.

There are certain wines we know, which are safe and delicious, however they can be a bit on the expensive side. We have always tried to buy local produce and that includes the wines, but with so many to choose from we may have been missing some treats. So we try lots and when we find a bottle we like, we usually buy a reasonable amount so we have some in. Lee discovered a red wine he found 'easy' to drink, a lovely Bourgueil AOC, and now we try to make sure there is some available any time we see him. The only problem is that the shops tend to change their stock, so it can be hard to find. Maybe everyone in France is constantly trying different wines to find the perfect one. Maybe it's the French equivalent of searching for the holy grail. There's nothing for it: we'll just keep trying to see what we can find.

I'd always lived a very social life in London, so one of my biggest fears about moving to France was the distance it would create with family and friends. With the benefit of hindsight, I now know this most certainly is not the case. Obviously geographically it does, but the reality is you carve quality time out for them as and when you can. It truly feels like a treat when we get visitors, or go home to England, and our first year in France saw lots of friends and family coming to help and stay.

Shortly after we started our new life, I received a call at 6am: it was one of those 'out of normal times' calls when you know someone has either dialled you by mistake or they have something important to tell you. In this case, it was the latter. It was news that we had been expecting: my grandad Donald, my mum's father, whom we named Arthur Donald after, had passed away. Naturally there was great sadness, as my grandma, his seven children, his thirteen grandchildren and his many great-grandchildren had all lost someone they adored. It wasn't a surprise but not physically being there to support my mum and our family felt pretty crap. But my grandma, always the caring practical one, gave me strict instructions: 'You are not to come home. You have only just moved. Save your money and buy a new window.' So that was that.

There were definitely a couple of days where I felt particularly sad and helpless, though. Being more than a hop and a skip away from everyone hit home and there were only so many times I could call my mum to see how everyone was doing before I became annoying. Feeling my sadness, a couple of dear friends put on their capes and flew from London to be by my side.

Hazel is my vintage soulmate. We have been friends for a good ten years and both get immense pleasure from rummaging around in dusty charity shops. I first met Hazel at a vintage fair she started. I had just stopped my Angel-A Vintage Experiences in east London and needed a fix, so I popped along and Hazel was taking the money at the entrance. We did not become friends that day but I remember thinking how incredibly stylish she was. Our paths soon crossed again and our lifelong friendship was secured. With Hazel's incredible work ethic, her scent for a bargain and her hunger for life, I knew she was going to be a great asset to the team.

Next on the plane was Alan, another great friend I had met many years before at a posh dinner party. We got on like a house on fire because he had a wicked, if sarcastic, sense of humour and loved food. Alan was a chef and had a degree in French: tick, tick. He even stopped at the *supermarché* en route and spent his entire first day cooking an arrival feast. Despite a tricky few days ahead, we celebrated that night and toasted absent family.

First up was a lamb tagine made with figs and pine nuts: tender pieces of lamb shoulder cooked with warming spices and enriched with just enough fruit to make it the perfect balance of sweet and savoury. It was a very simple dish in essence but the spices make this one special. With an exotic touch of saffron, this filled the gîte with wonderful mouth-watering smells to welcome the workers back in the evening. Another dish which we recall fondly was his classic *boeuf bourguignon* made with local red wine. The delicious slow-cooked stew created meltingly soft beef in a thick sauce studded with smoked bacon, mushrooms and little cara-melised shallots. It was beautifully rich thanks to the cooking liquor being made up entirely of red wine. I remember him using a slightly more full-bodied red on this occasion rather than the classic lighter red burgundy.

The third dish probably won't come as a big surprise, but Alan makes a truly great onion soup. And the one that night really was the bees' knees. A true onion soup takes only a few simple ingredi-ents. Firstly, a mountain of finely sliced onions need to be sweated down and caramelised in butter with perhaps just a little pinch of sugar. This is the important bit and you need to take time over it. It can take a good hour and a half to properly caramelise onions. Then garlic gets added to the mix and, for me, some white wine. The wine is reduced slightly before I add a little fresh thyme and good beef stock. It all simmers away for around thirty minutes and then it's ready to be served topped with little slices of toasted baguette with delicious melted Gruyère.

With my new found confidence in driving and my sidekick Hazel, always keen for a bargain, by my side, we jumped in the car and headed towards a huge *brocante*. Mission: 'find a bath for our family suite'. It was a couple of hours' drive and the rain was pretty heavy. But by now I had fallen in love with driving in France. This came as a surprise to me as I don't love driving normally. But in France the roads are wide and very well looked after. *Petite* rustic villages overflowing with flowers fill me with inspiration and the sight of locals collecting their daily baguettes make me feel calm. Sharing the drive with Hazel added to the adventure and we giggled and chatted all the way there, talking nonstop about our lives, work, families and our latest vintage bargains.

---

* A large shop or market where second-hand goods are sold.

When we finally found it, the *brocante* was the size of a small village. There were barns upon barns of stuff: statues, stones, baths, chairs, iron pagodas, benches, pans, lights, bricks, wood. Everything and anything you could ever have wanted, stretching out in every direction you looked. It was overwhelming. And the rain still came in buckets. It would probably have felt different if the sun had been shining and someone had offered us a drink and baby-care on arrival, but alas. We had to keep our focus on the mission to find a bath but with dozens of chickens roaming everywhere I was distracted, trying to ensure I didn't slip over chicken shit. After a brief (forty-minute) look around one barn, it became apparent that looking in all ten may take a couple of days, so I checked I knew the French world for bath (*la baignoire*) and used by best Frenglish to ask if they had any.

After that, we got taken to the new part of their estate and shown a room full of very expensive baths that had been reconditioned. Our eyes popped out of our heads as we stroked an original 1919 Ritz Hotel bathtub. It seemed like we were in a dream. How could we be in France, soaked through, being taken into a room that was selling a bath from the bloody Ritz in London for €18,000? To add insult to injury, the other baths weren't even that great. There was one solid bath with a nice shape: it was symmetrical with a roll-top and instead of feet the bath was mounted on a solid cast-iron plinth. It was elegant and definitely substantial, but of course it was also the second most expensive one in the place. But at this point, having looked at millions on the internet and knowing the issue was actually getting something delivered to the château, I just wanted to complete my mission and get home to put some dry clothes on. The gentleman selling us the bath made us wait for a further forty minutes as he ummed and ahhed about whether he could deliver it. In the end, he reluctantly agreed for an extra €250 (on the basis we unloaded it from his van ourselves). I still kick myself today at the thought of giving such an arrogant man our money but it was early days and I can assure you I never made a mistake like that again.

While Hazel and I were at the *brocante* with the kids, Dick had dragged Alan to the château. It was all hands on deck and, while on paper, Alan was our team chef, there were more important things to do during the day, like stripping the kids' windows of lead paint.

We had a couple of spare boiler suits so, once properly attired, Dick showed him what to do and set him to work. And he went for it with gusto. Alan has a willing heart and skills that are useful in certain scenarios, but the ability to smile was what we valued above all else. Alan would be the first to admit that DIY was not listed on his CV but his perseverance got that room done and, when we returned to the gîte, you could see the weight coming off his shoulders. And it took no time at all for him to change back into his chef hat and get food and drink on the table. Having lived in France when he was younger, Alan thoroughly enjoyed sharing his love of French foods and wines, and the rest of us weren't complaining – it just made getting up in the morning to go to work that little bit more difficult!

We made many special memories that week, despite the endless challenges at the château – being together with great friends and having the ability to laugh at all the craziness that was happening around us kept everyone going. But I knew that once Alan and Hazel left, Lee, Kyle and my dad's departure was imminent too and, with so many setbacks with the building work, things were far from on track. On top of that, Dick was due to go to America in a couple of weeks. So that evening my objective was to ask everyone to stay a bit longer – you know, just until everything was finished!

Our possessions from the flat in Southend were still in storage and we were keen to get them out to France as soon as we could to save any money wasted on storage charges. After all, we had a château, how hard could it be to find somewhere clean and dry to put it all? Every opportunity Angela got she would be cleaning. It was a challenge, because with many panes of glass missing, the château had become a great place for birds to roost, so each room was filled with dust, dirt and even bird poop. But we definitely had enough space to store the contents of our flat. We decided we were going to occupy certain rooms immediately, even though they would have to be cleared out again at a later date to be worked on. Our logic was to see how we liked the rooms and how we used them and then do the necessary work to make them truly ours.

On 17 February, less than three weeks after we had moved to France, the removal lorry arrived. It was amusing seeing them progress down the drive and then stop and do a double take of the bridge and the gateposts. I'd measured the gap and the very large lorry a couple of times and it was going to fit – there wasn't a lot of room to spare but the driver was a professional so there shouldn't be any issue . . . Still, I don't know who was the most relieved when the lorry pulled up to the front of the château, the driver or me. Despite the work on the plumbing and heating being in full swing, our attention immediately changed to ensuring we put things in the right place and knew where they were. First we provided the team with tea and coffee, then we showed them around the château naming all the rooms, so they had an idea of the destinations for individual boxes or furniture.

I have moved about twenty-five times in my adult life so I fully understood the pain of a messy delivery. There are many ways of doing it but I am a firm believer one person should be in charge – on this occasion it was to be Angela. The removal men were brilliant and their attitude was spot on and Angela was at her post at the front door throughout checking what was being carried in and telling them where to go. I never saw any of them flinch, even when they were told the destination was the attic or rooms on the fourth floor. Most of the rooms above the ground floor didn't have names, apart from our suite, so it was a wonder so many items ended up in the right place. It was a mammoth task and it took over six hours to get it all unloaded. After all those stairs I reckon the chaps would have slept well that evening.

In the midst of all the frenetic activity a van turned up with a very slight French chap who came to deliver the bath for our room. Angela had mentioned the delivery cost was €250, so I was very keen to see him take it up the forty-five steps up to our suite. But I wasn't allowed to be cruel and when I saw the bath I realised if we hadn't got a bunch of burly lads there it would probably have remained on the driveway. From what I could ascertain, Angela had paid by weight: it took six of us to get it upstairs. We were sucking oxygen in our arses by the time we placed it on the landing outside our suite. One thing is for sure, that bath will stay where it is until after I turn up my toes!

The men who brought all our possessions for us were bloody angels. I couldn't believe all our treasures were here and part of me wanted to start opening boxes and making our château lovely straight away. But I knew I had to stay focused – I only had a few seconds to decide where each box was to go and, what's more, I had to remember where they were all going (a château is a big place in which to lose things!). It was like a giant version of *The Generation Game* at the end when you have to remember all the things you've seen!

The long, cold days continued throughout February and the work was never-ending and hard. But the arrival of our boiler was a big day. The pallet with the cast-iron, gas-powered Rayburn was deposited outside the cellar doors. Even if you have never seen a cast-iron stove, it sounds heavy, and ours was 350kg. We knew we wanted gas in our kitchens so the decision to go for a Rayburn was easy; while we waited for our environmentally-friendly plans to come into effect some years downstream, the A-rated boiler would provide all the heat we needed (for some sixteen radiators) and the focus of our family kitchen (when we got to that stage). With the flues, the flow and return pipes and the power all in, all we needed was gas.

Like so many things, when we finally had a visit from our French gas installer (following several earlier appointments when he didn't show up) it proved more problematic than we had hoped. Instead of the progress we'd been expecting, he suddenly told us his certification was out of date so he couldn't actually do the connection. Thanks a bunch! Some phoning around later we hit lucky: a lovely chap came with his wife acting as his assistant and connected our gas, fitted our regulators and did the piping to connect to some temporary bottles outside. Lee and Kyle had the water connected so after that we just needed our installer to commission it and fire it up. We couldn't wait!

With a way of generating heat and getting it to the thermal store, we could then prove the system that distributed the hot water through our hot-water pipes and heating system.* It may sound odd, but when you have a thermal store you don't have a tank of hot water to use. To get hot water you pass fresh mains water through coils that run through the tank of 'stored' heat. The mains water is then heated up. So out of the hot tap comes freshly heated mains water.

It was late in the afternoon towards the end of February when the boiler installer arrived. We had been in conversation (he was

---

* 'Proving' in this case would be seeing if it was watertight and actually worked.

bilingual – hurray!) and he understood how important it was for us to get our system up and running. He turned up and worked away in our dark cold cellar and within a couple of hours we had a fully functioning boiler. As the flow and return pipes ran all the way up to the attic we could now fill our whole system.

It was an interesting evening filling the system – we had installed lots of isolators so we could grow the system a little at a time. After a lot of gurgling, and water being pushed into every corner of the system, we followed each and every pipe to check for leaks or problems. And would you believe, there were absolutely none – which is unheard of in such a complicated system. Well done, Lee and Kyle! The backbone of our whole system was in and functioning. The heating pipes to the radiators in our suite were connected and the pipes that could have a bathroom connected to them were in place as well. We even had a hot and cold tap at the sink in the service kitchen, which would have been without any hot water for years. We'd disconnected the lead piping as part of our initial tidy up and now we were bringing running water back to the château again. It was a BIG moment.

It might sound like our trials and tribulations were over but our gas supply was a still a bit of a problem. We only had the ability to run on the 13kg bottles, which we knew would not last very long, but the system was working and now we could grow it a bit at a time until our home was fully functioning.

In the meantime, we were going to be more reliant on our log burners. Sharing the island with the château is a large and very impressive 'coach house'. Eventually this was going to be home to Grandma and Grandpa but at this point it was just a very big agricultural outbuilding. In fact, the surface area of the three floors in there is actually well over half the floor area of the château. And it was absolutely full of chopped and unchopped wood. It was a mess in there, with years of junk mixed in with cut wood and old planks, but even a conservative estimate would give us log fires for a couple of winters. And that was only part of the story – we also had acres of woodland that would produce more 'free' wood every year. It is a long, laborious process to go from a growing tree to a cut log burning in the stove but if we wanted to be truly sustainable and environmentally friendly we knew this was a brilliant asset and one we could control entirely. So the conclusion to have log burners helping feed heat into our thermal store felt logical and sensible.

Lee and Kyle had been with us for over two weeks by this point and they had worked tirelessly throughout. It had all taken much longer than planned and they had rearranged their diaries to stay on and look after us. It had taken a huge effort but they had installed the basis of our heating and hot- and cold-water systems. Having laid hundreds of metres of piping and connected everything seamlessly, they were now ready to leave us and go back to the real world in east London. Some people are very special.

> *Dear Isabelle*
> *I hope you and your wonderful family are well.*
> *I'm sorry we have not seen you in a little while. We were hoping to have been in the château by now and are desperate to invite you over to our new home. Coming to the gîte is not quite the same but you are, of course, very welcome.*
> *Fingers crossed we do the move this week as Dick leaves for America on Friday for three weeks.*
> *Love, Angel*

I was desperate to get into the château. I wanted to see what the light was like in the different rooms at every hour of the day. I needed time to soak in our new home. There was so much to do: the unpacking, the cleaning, the working out where the furniture would be best placed. But to do this I needed time and the only real time I ever had was when the kids went to bed. I didn't want to have three more weeks while Dick was away when I couldn't be productive. I had made my mind up: I wanted to be in the château before he went.

We had come so far it was now possible to see what it could be like living in our château. But the time for me to disappear to America was fast approaching and I could tell Angela was more than a little apprehensive about me going. Then she dropped the bombshell. She wanted to be in the château before I went to America. I was genuinely struck dumb but her logic was sort of sound. Living in the gîte for the time I was away would be expensive and there was little chance of her getting much done as her world would be taken up with looking after the children. And then there was the big one: she wanted to be in our home. I got it, but we definitely weren't organised enough for her to move in. For one thing, there was no bathroom. They were feeble excuses, though. I may have had reservations but I knew Angela and I knew what was going to happen, so it was a matter of just doing it. To be very honest, I was very proud of my girl. We would both have some serious challenges, but our new life was about to move into the next phase.

Once the decision was made, it was all systems go. We raided the outbuilding where we had corralled the various bits of bathroom equipment we had found around the château, which included a lovely Art Deco sink. The glaze had sadly been stained but the taps were lovely, though we had no idea if they worked, and the plug was a white solid rubber ball on a chain. We'd never seen the likes of it before and we decided we'd make it work. We also found a loo that looked as if it could be recommissioned, but we had to go out to buy some taps for the bath and all the necessary waste

fittings. For two long days we worked on what was to be our bathroom and, when it was time for the children to go to bed, we took them home and had a bite to eat, then Dick would go back to the château to carry on. My evening job was easy: pack up the gîte and clean every room ready to give the keys back to Olga.

Getting the bathroom working was a matter of sorting the basics. It didn't matter what it looked like, or where anything was, it just had to work. We needed a sink, a loo and a bath with a shower attachment if possible. The waste disappeared into a pipe in the wall, which made me twitchy. There was some damp in the cellar that could have been caused by the pipe, but as no bathroom had been used for years we thought it more likely to be a rain issue and so decided to go for it. We didn't have much choice.

There was also a corridor of sorts between our room and the children's that needed sorting – it was currently filled by a plastic shower cubicle from the 1980s. We removed that and made the corridor a little wider by pulling down a flimsy stud wall. Everything else would have to wait.

We moved in and settled the children early one evening. It was very special being in our own bedroom in our own château but we did not really have time to savour it. Arthur and Dorothy were sound asleep in our room and Angela was silently arranging things and making sure I was packed to leave for the US. Getting the bathroom working just had to be done; it just wasn't easy. For example, the waste under the world's heaviest bath had to be connected in the ceiling of the service kitchen on the floor below that was nearly five metres high. You name it and it fought back, so the final completion of the bathroom was more a sigh of relief than a cry of victory. It was late, we were seriously pooped, but we did smile as we fell asleep.

On the evening of 28 February 2015 we finally moved in. I had no idea how anything worked but I didn't care. I was just so happy to be in our forever home. We put the children to sleep in their beds and continued to tidy, clean up and finish the bathroom. The fun was about to begin.

February had been cold and provided us with an unforgiving environment in which to work. What we needed to get done in our first month, in the middle of winter, was challenging to say the least. There are not many tradesmen who would have stayed the course and, from our limited exposure to local craftsmen, we knew it was too much to ask them. Luckily for us, Lee and Kyle were as bloody-minded as we were and they made it happen. Unbelievably, just over a month after we had arrived in France, we had some electricity and enough of a heating and plumbing system in to allow us to get by in our home. We were in.

CHAPTER THREE

MARCH

March was a month of new beginnings and the start of living in our home as a family. For years, the château had been silent but, as its new custodians, our family brought the château children's laughter and fun inside the walls and grounds again.

The old saying is that March comes in like a lion and out like a lamb. That usually refers to the weather, but for us it felt like the whole month was shaping up to be very busy and there was no sign of the pace relenting. We are always being reminded by my mum to take time to 'smell the roses' but we believe she would have forgiven us for failing so badly during our first year. Although we did manage to appreciate the cherry blossoms that appear every March around St Patrick's Day. We inherited some wonderful ornamental cherry trees: one as you turn into the driveway and a couple more at the western corner of the moat. As we were continually popping in and out on shopping trips it was easy to notice the beautiful display of flowers but it took us over a year to discover we also had a massive fruiting cherry tree in the walled garden. It had probably been tended to at the start of its life, but for decades it had grown wild and it was now at least thirty feet high.

Logic has never won me an argument with my gorgeous wife so when she announced on 25 February that she wanted to be in the château before I left for America I knew I just needed to get on with the work that needed sorting. Our family bathroom was far from perfect but by 1.30am on 1 March it worked. There had been a niggly little drip behind the cold water tap on the bath that had meant taking it off and refitting it three times but with that sorted we had the bathroom that served us for the next two years.

The toilet and sink were château originals and showed many signs of wear. Our bath looked wonderful, though, as it was new. It was a bit out of place, with the taps mounted on plywood onto a stud wall that only had plaster on the other side. All of the noggins made a massive shelving unit we got used to and really missed when we eventually boarded and plastered the bathroom side of the wall. We put up a shower curtain on a semi-circular rail that was again attached to the wood of the stud wall. It failed on all levels of style but it was robust and stopped the water from splashing everywhere. We must take every victory with glory, but I have to say there is something very uncomfortable about brushing against a cold, wet curtain when in the shower.

When you have young children, a bath is essential. It was and still is the start of our bedtime routine. We bathe Arthur and Dorothy every night before settling down to snuggle and fall asleep. It is a huge part of family life and the kids know nothing else. On the 28 February they did miss their bath but we made up for it on our first morning.

I was quite well organised for my trip. Angela had mustered all that I would be taking and it was all in neat piles in our room. It was so novel – it was 'our room'. It was spotlessly clean but far from salubrious. There were cracks in the plaster ceiling ('our ceiling'), peeling wallpaper ('our wallpaper') and the tower room was full of boxes and suitcases, but it was all ours. We couldn't have been happier, though my imminent departure meant we never actually raised a glass to celebrate. We were too busy and far too knackered.

Without any lights or sockets, a cable and extension leads were used to bring us civilisation. I don't think our eyes shut properly before we heard our alarms. I was up and showered and then we were bundling luggage and the children into the car before 5.30am to get me to the railway station.

I drove and I can't really remember the short fifteen-minute journey, as it was mainly full of lists and instructions. Angela was so brave and, after unloading and the briefest of hugs with very dozy children and a lovely warm wife, I sent them home. It was a hard goodbye as there was so much to do and so much that was new, but the money I was earning was going to allow us to do the things we had to do over the next few months, so there was no choice.

Driving back through the freezing early-March morning was surprisingly peaceful. The kids were asleep and there were no cars on the road. I kept telling myself to be calm and brave. I know I have a strong and determined spirit but the truth is I'm shit-scared of the dark and it was pitch black. I blame my imagination. I grew up in Essex and I'm a city girl at heart. I love a bit of light pollution.

It started well, the drive was fine and I didn't miss the turning. But when I stopped the car I realised that I was in a truly petrified state. It was so dark and without the lights and security

of the car to calm me I was on my own with my babies . . . even the sound of an owl made me jump! I had a plan: to open the door while the kids were snoozing and then dash in with them both. So I left the kids in the car and, with my hands shaking, I put the key in the door, turned it and pushed. Nothing. Again I tried. Nothing. I started using my shoulder to push the door. Nothing. It is a huge door – to even think I could push it with my weight was hilarious. But I carried on. Full-body pushes. Nothing. Little body launches. Nothing.

Then I started to hear Dorothy crying from the car. I can't help but panic a little when the children cry. Then Arthur, who is a sensitive little soul and must have felt my anxiety, joined in and then he vomited all over himself and his car seat. I was at my wits' end and grabbed the door handle with frustration. Finally, it opened. I dashed back to the car and, at this point it was one kid at a time because Arthur was covered in vomit. I ran with him first, with one eye on the car, just in case a wild boar tried to steal Dorothy, or something. Then I dashed to get Dorothy, keeping my eye on the château, just in case a wild cat, or a huge spider, tried to get into the house.

We were all in – a bit smelly from the sick but in – and we headed upstairs to get clean and warm. Having the luxury of the new bath was unique. This was our forever bath, but like everything new I did not have everything to hand. Towels, bubble bath and cream were all needed – I even managed to find a rubber duck. Even though it was not perfect, it was very satisfying bathing the kids in their new home. It was still only around 6am, so after the bath I took the kids back to bed for some extra sleep. I lay cuddling both children in the darkness and tiredness took me through to first light. As we awoke, everything was perfect and our morning outing felt like a distant memory.

I was away for over half of March on my first trip to make *Dirty Rotten Survival* for National Geographic. First I was off to the swamps of Louisiana, then it was to the wilds of Texas. After a childhood spent camping and exploring the countryside in Northern Ireland, twenty years travelling the world when I served in the army and a couple of decades of TV experience, I was not at all bothered by what I was about to do. I was much more concerned about the fact that Angela and the children were at our château without me. Throughout my train journey to Paris and after I checked in at Charles De Gaulle airport and was waiting to depart, I was writing in my notebook and trying to remember all I needed to tell Angela to make it a little easier.

In the daylight everything is supposed to look better and it did for a while, until I rubbed my eyes and realised that the little heater keeping our room cosy had hatched tens of thousands of flies. Dopey flies that lingered making buzzing noises and then dropped and died. I had never ever seen anything like this.

Luckily Dick was not on the plane yet, so he answered my call immediately. I could tell straight away that he had been worrying about me; family is everything to Dick.

First, I told him about my troubles getting into the house. He went quiet – and to this day I'm still not sure if he was giggling or feeling guilty. After all, he'd forgotten to tell me that the door handle turns in the opposite direction. Of course, it made sense but at the time I was not amused. Then there was the small issue of the flies. He laughed. I told him off for laughing but I also knew partly it was my fault for insisting on moving into the house against Dick's wishes.

Told me off?! I got hell for not being sympathetic. To be fair, I was happy they were just flies – there are hornets the size of small birds in France.

Dick said that they were cluster flies and they had been brought out of hibernation by the heat. There was no real solution as they were in our living space so we couldn't use any sprays or fumes to kill them. I just had to be patient, wait for them to hatch and they would go away and we'd keep them out. So every day I would clear them up, but then the next day there were always more and more. I had convinced myself they were laying eggs that were hatching too. After a few days, I started getting used to the sound of buzzing as we slept, but it was not a nice experience.

I did some research and came up with a plan: first I made a sweet sugar syrup solution, then I placed a bowl of it in the bedroom when the kids went to sleep, with a small side light plugged in a couple of inches above it. Every morning the syrup resembled fly soup. Then, slowly but surely, the number of flies started to diminish.

The next problem was the temperature: it was the middle of winter and the house was bitterly cold. I knew how the heating system worked but I had never lit a fire before. Growing up we had radiators and one gas fire that was turned on with a button. The heating system was run off the gas-fired Rayburn and supported by the log burners. If the log burners produce enough heat to keep the thermal store satiated (it provides the hot water and the heat for the radiators), then no gas is used. I was to discover that we had a big problem – it was so cold the wood burners were not providing enough heat and the biggest bottle we could get (a measly 13 kilogrammes) only lasted a couple of hours.

I foolishly took it for granted that everyone could light a fire. Is it not something we all learn as children? Actually, I grew up in an era when solid fuel (coal) was the normal way of providing heat and, as a youngster, it was unusual for the fire not to need some attention to stoke it up in the morning. The revelation that Angela had no idea how to rub two Boy Scouts together to generate heat and then how to use that heat to make fire and then how to harness it – well, let's just say I hadn't thought about it. Telling someone how to set and light a fire may sound trivial but there is a bit of a knack to log burners and that only really came to me when I was on the way to Charles de Gaulle as she told me about her morning . . .

Dick had ensured there was lots of wood left for me. Putting the wood in the fires felt very exciting and then lighting it seemed rather easy too. I remember Dick saying, 'Keep the door open at the bottom to ensure a bit of wind goes through to the wood.'

The fires were not hot at this point, but I checked and it looked like a fire.

'Once you are happy it's going, close the door and add more wood when it gets low,' Dick had said.

It all seemed very easy, so I closed the bottom door and we went to get breakfast. Going to the *boulangerie* was still a novelty and a bit of an outing for the kids – I guess kind of like going to an old-fashioned sweet shop in the UK. It is just a five-minute drive from the château and is run by a lovely family that live in the village. It's quite small and traditional in design with two counters – one for all the breakfast bits and another for all the patisseries. Then behind the counters there are stacks of baguettes and *boules* and a huge machine to *coupe** your bread. It's a feast for the eyes. On that morning, I got a fresh baguette and a couple of croissants, which would keep us all going – Arthur loved to suck croissants and if I tore a tiny end off for Dorothy it would keep her entertained for ages.

After that it was back to the warm house, which was actually not so warm. To my disappointment, the fire had gone out. But I didn't understand – there were still plenty of logs in there. A

---

* Cut.

little scratch of the head and a search around for any clues later and I stood staring at a big bucket of what looked like rubbish. I realised then that this was my clue: Dick had told me to add something called kindling.

For everyone that knows how to light a fire, it's beyond simple. But for anyone who grew up in a city and didn't pay much attention in Brownies, it's not so simple until you learn. Dick was on his flight by now and I could not remember what he had said for the life of me, so I turned to the internet and discovered that kindling is quite an important part in a successful burn as it gives the logs enough time to light properly and to stay alight. My flames had just been superficial.

I often say the best way to learn is to get things wrong, so round two was much better, so much so that an hour or so later the logs were still burning. But it's not a quick job. I remember thinking that the Bagliones must have had a full-time member of staff just to light the fires!

That evening, I planned to bathe the kids as per our routine. If I'm honest I did not have a clue if enough heat was travelling up to the thermal store from the fires alone and it was cold so I turned a couple of radiators on hoping to take the edge off the chill. The gas bottles are an additional source of heat to the thermal store and a combination of this and the fires should be enough to keep us warm, assuming we only occupy a couple of rooms . . . But a few hours later, the radiators were still cold and, upon investigation, I discovered the gas bottle was empty.

Changing the gas bottle was tricky. To do that I had to go outside, in the cold, with two-year-old Arthur and ten-month-old Dorothy in tow. And the full replacement gas bottle was very heavy. I managed to read Dick's bad handwriting with instructions on how to change the bottle over but for the life of me I did not have the strength to get the new one on.

So, it was back inside to the fire, and now I know it's much easier to keep a fire going than to light a new one from scratch. There was enough hot water for a bath and a quick shower for me that first evening. I was just going to have to take every day as it came. I had thought that once the kids were in bed, I would be able to start work around the château but that would have to wait for tomorrow. For tonight, I would do some research for the interior of the house and that dream led me to sleep very quickly, well, at least until it was feeding time for Dorothy.

Angela and I spoke a couple of times before I got on my flight and nothing was making it easier for me to go – from the flies that had appeared in biblical proportions to the struggles she was having lighting the fires. The fact that the gas bottles lasted a couple of hours rather than a day or two was a major logistical nightmare. We had a supply in but not enough, and how was Angela going to change the bottles with the children in tow?

I was on the aeroplane and had just turned my phone off when there was a commotion at the front. The doors were about to be closed but a deputation of ground crew, security and an Air France flight attendant came down the plane and asked if I was Mr Strawbridge, and could I come with them please? I very quickly put two and two together. My hold bag was packed with all my survival kit for the series. In addition to the saws and half-dozen tools for making fires, including magnesium rods, waterproof matches and a fire pump, I had a collection of axes and knives a psychopath would be proud of. Plus a skinning set, including a bone saw, filleting knives, sheath knives of various sizes, a machete, lock knives and Leathermans. I even had a Ghurka kukri. It was going to be interesting talking my way out of this.

So it was a real surprise when I got to the door to discover it was my other bag that was sitting there and it was making a humming noise. Everyone looked at me, and I looked at them. I then unzipped the bag and turned off my electric toothbrush.

It was dawning on me, the way a light suddenly turned on in dark bedroom wakes you violently, that I should have given Angela a lot more information and briefing before I left. The saying, 'To assume makes an 'ass' of 'u' and 'me',' sprang to mind. What a plonker I was. So, the first of my 'how to' notes were written. These were not just emails, because diagrams were essential, which meant writing them up in my notebook, drawing annotated sketches and then taking photos and sending them to Angela. That would spawn numerous questions and so the 'how to' ping-pong started. Being thousands of miles away, and seven, eight or even nine hours behind, really feels like a big separation. Apart from missing everyone, I felt guilty for not being there to look after them.

The ability to see each other when we spoke was a lifesaver. I couldn't imagine what it must have been like for my parents when my dad had to work away in Libya and the Middle East for long periods to help finance the family back in Northern Ireland. Communication was by letters that took weeks to get there and with a young family it must have been very hard for my mum. I'd never really thought about it before. As children, we had missed Dad but were safe and loved, so just accepted what was happening. It must have been the same for Arthur and Dorothy.

The next morning was exciting as I could call Dick. It had been years since we had not spoken for a couple of days. I'd received a text in the night to say he was safe and we were to FaceTime him as soon as we were all up. So we called, all sleepy and snuggly in our warm room. I could see equal amounts of love and worry in Dick's eyes. But after a while he knew we were fine and we laughed hard about the continued fly problems. But trying to look after the children, surviving the plague of flies and keeping the château at a

living temperature with the very rudimentary system we had was taking all my time and Dick and I had plans for me to get on with the renovation while he was away. I really wanted to start seeing progress. I knew I had to get more help.

Angela was so brave. She was a city girl who was scared of the dark, living by herself in a derelict château with two young children. I can think of very few people who, if taken so far out of their comfort zone, would have survived in a similar situation. If I was staying in a hotel or travelling, we would speak a couple of times a day. I insisted I get my early-morning phone call when the three of them were all bouncing around the bed and chatty. For me it was the middle of the night but it meant I was there with them. On one occasion, when Angela and I were catching up, I noticed an upturned glass on my pillow on the far side of the bed. I pointed it out to Angela, who was obviously very aware that it was there, only to discover that it was a spider that had freaked her out, so it was trapped under a glass until she could work out how to deal with it.

Dick would send me pictures of diagrams in his notebooks and emails with instructions of how to keep things on track. I understood the soppy bits but sometimes the technical bits scared me as I wasn't really sure what language he was speaking . . .

'Gorgeous, I love you and am seriously missing you all,' he started his email on 3 March. Then followed a list of jobs and warnings:

- *Ensure front doorknob is attached*
- *Be aware sockets are live!*
- *Need to strip out as much as possible*
- *Break down walls within the new envelope*

- *Buy insulation and block off the major holes created for the pipes (corner of kitchen, downstairs WC, petit salon and grand salon, our room to honeymoon, our bathroom down to kitchen, fourth-floor bathroom to ours)*
- *Cover and lay on the pipes in the attic*

Looking at it now, it makes sense to me, which is even more worrying! But back then it was incomprehensible.

We both agree that if something is painful it's best to grasp the nettle and change it. We knew we had months ahead of us with long periods of separation, so we had to find a solution – and I knew I needed help. The first and most logical place to turn was to my family. Mum was still running her restaurant while waiting for the buyer to take over but Dad had closed and sold his jewellery business so I hoped he might be at a loose end. Plus I knew he and Mum were missing the children, so the cavalry, in the form of Grandad, was called in. It was such a relief when he didn't hesitate and, within twenty-four hours, he was at the château where he became live-in nanny, chief fire-lighter and remover of unwanted insects.

The Atlantic may have separated us but we still had to keep things moving. On 3 March, I sent a further email to Angela and a translation to our electrician M. Manceau. I felt it was self-explanatory:

Dear M. Manceau,
Thank you very much for coming to commence work on our electrics. Can you please tell my wife Angela how many days you will be working? Please find below a list of tasks. There is a significant amount of work, but the jobs below are in priority order, but firstly we need an earth behind the château.

We need the power distribution to be organised in a more logical way. It would seem to make sense for the power on each floor to have its own fusing and distribution.

We obviously need sockets and lighting on all floors and all rooms.

The routes should use the same path as the heating and water pipes where possible.

We do not want surface-mounted wire, it needs to be chased in or routed behind studding.

Please start with the following (Angela will show you which room is which):

- *More permanent sockets in the children's room (near the corner where the pipes are should be easiest)*
- *Cables through the wooden stud walls please.*
- *Lighting and switches in the children's room and our bathroom. Lights on the stud wall would be easiest – Angela, confirm you are happy?*
- *Lights and switches and sockets in our bedroom. (For our room you may wish to use the route down from the attic through the honeymoon suite – our radiator pipes come that way.)*
- *We will also need some on the other side of the wall in the adjoining room at a later stage.*
- *Sockets and lights in the service kitchen. The power cables to go down to the cellar and then up. Angela, where would you like the power sockets and lights (if just hanging in the centre of the room we can move if necessary)*

As I said, I thought these instructions were clear and unambiguous, but it seems talk of 'earths', 'fusing' and 'distribution boxes' is not widely understood. Angela and I ended up talking about it for some time. We couldn't just leave it to M. Manceau to crack on; Angela had to be there nudging. However, in the end M. Manceau proved elusive, so Angela had to start searching for another electrician.

Dad flew out immediately – Southend to Rennes proved to be an excellent route; both airports are small and well organised with friendly staff. I had to get my brave hat on to collect him from the airport. I can be quite nervous if the kids cry when I'm driving and I cannot soothe them, and although the local roads had become familiar, I had not driven this route before. Arthur and Dorothy were both still in nappies, so there was the normal organisation to do. The day started with no naps for the kids (my plan was for them to sleep in the car). Next I packed the bags. How do kids generate so much stuff? Nappies, wipes, changes of clothes, changing mats, toys to keep them entertained and, of course, snacks were all thrown in the boot. The weather was cold but the skies were blue and, as I drove out of the château, I remember having a sense of relief; when we returned everything would be that little bit easier.

Arthur and Dorothy have always had a very special relationship with my dad. He is such a soft touch with them. I guess that is part of the joy of being a grandparent. Rules and discipline are left for us, which allows them to do all the fun stuff. Being just eleven months old, Dorothy was obviously not speaking yet, but Arthur had got to grips with a few words. 'Mama' being one and 'G', short for Grandad, another; this is how my dad got the name Mama G. They were both very excited to see him.

My plan worked and the kids fell asleep within minutes. I was driving our English car so decided to give myself a little extra time to avoid the motorways and the toll booths. Having to climb over the seats or get out of the car to pay the toll was a small inconvenience I did not fancy today and driving on the slower roads is actually wonderful if you have the time. Even in March the

villages are full of flowers hanging from lanterns: fuschias, lantana, begonias. There were purples, reds, deep pinks and yellows and they all looked like they had been lovingly crafted. The greens of new leaves are almost lime coloured and somehow every tree seems to be a little different. The average small French village has charm in abundance and the daffodils and magnolias were out in full force as well – a lovely reminder that there was lots familiar in our new homeland as well.

It takes just over an hour to get to Rennes this way and the roads are lovely. There must be around fifty roundabouts and a very long road, which always reminds me of a Roman road. On the way I spotted a very large *brocante*, which got me very excited. I could see baths, bricks, statues, pans, lights . . . My hands were getting balmy just thinking about the bargains.

I reached the airport in great time but as it is so tiny I chose to park about fifty metres away in a row of spaces outside a small row of shops and restaurants (I didn't want to clog up the *petite* slip road). It was lunchtime and the restaurant I parked near was rammed and I was starving. I'd packed brilliantly for the kids but forgot to include myself in the equation. I could see on the chalkboard that the restaurant has a *carte de jour* for just €13.50. I could have eaten a horse at that moment!

I decided that this might be the time to feed and change the kids. Arthur was still asleep so Dorothy went first. A few minutes later, the restaurant owner must have realised that I wasn't planning to dine in his restaurant and he let me know in no uncertain terms that this was not acceptable. He was shouting and waving a serviette at me and, although I couldn't translate everything word, I knew he wanted me to leave. There were zero 'No Parking' signs, he was just being a bit of a tosser. What annoyed me most was that I couldn't tell him that in French, so learning a few naughty French words got added to my list of things to do.

I'm not sure I have ever been so happy to see my dad. We hugged and he took the car keys straight off me, as my dad loves driving abroad. Finally, I could relax. When you have two children under the age of two, even having a shower and a couple of toilet breaks in a day can feel like a success. My dad's presence meant that we could start getting things done. It also gave me a new braveness. If I found a huge spider or a bat, or a rat, he was on hand!

Dad had a number of roles. Come bedtime, his first job was to hoover up the flies I could not reach. This meant climbing up a ladder with a long attachment and hoovering the thousands of flies that had appeared that day on the ceiling. At the same time I was on the floor, sweeping up the new ones that had appeared there. We were aiming for 'fly zero' by bedtime.

Dad stayed in the salon, seemingly happy with what was essentially glorified camping. Dorothy slept in our bed. We knew we had created a rod for our own back, but she never slept in a cot. She just loved human contact and I loved the snuggles, especially when Dick was away. Arthur loved his snuggles too but only to get him to sleep, then he wanted his own space to wrestle with his duvet. With the kids successfully settled I would get out my laptop and start work.

One night, I looked up and saw the shadow of a bat on the wall – it was around four metres wide. Firstly, and very quietly (to ensure I didn't wake the kids), I shat myself. Then I immediately called for my dad. Next thing I knew, the bat started flying around our bedroom. I have no idea where it came from, but it felt like I was in a Dracula movie. It must have been huge. Luckily Dad knew exactly what to do. He said there was a net in one of the outbuildings that was made for this, so he dashed out, got the net and a ladder and caught the bat before releasing it out of the window. After that, he really was my hero. I called him Batman for weeks. I don't think my dad ever saw himself as a knight in shining armour but he earned his spurs that night.

*   *   *

The weather in March had been kind. There were some rather cold days, but more often than not we had beautiful clear skies. Our family suite at the front of the house often felt snug from the sunshine that streamed through the window after midday. And as the grounds of the château started to warm up, it was a joy to be outside in the fresh air. I could not get my head around the fact that only weeks earlier we had been in the gîte and it had been freezing. You could feel and hear the thaw happening around you. I started going for regular walks with Dorothy either in her papoose or in a pram, and if I wanted to get Arthur to sleep as well I took our double pram.

I went from the main staircase at the front of the château over the muddy front, through the gate and round to the right, which led me to the path that went right round the moat. A walk round the moat and back again normally took about twenty minutes, but mostly the kids would be asleep by then, which meant I could then use that time to be productive (which sometimes meant just getting the washing done!).

One day, close to Dick's return, I was out on the walk, feeling so excited to have our family back together again. I often daydream when I walk. When the kids were not in the pram, my time was mostly spent ensuring they were safe, feeding them and playing with them. My walk was an escape. It allowed my brain to rest. I would dream what each of the rooms would look like, or what kind of wedding we would have, or how the kids might be in one, three, five years' time. It seemed like a million things entered my brain in seconds.

On this particular day, as I looked up from my daydream, I noticed our cherry tree over on the right of the moat in full blossom! Millions of delicate, dusty pink flowers. It was a visual feast. I stopped immediately and took a photo with the château perfectly placed in the background. What with everything that had been going on in our first couple of months at the château, taking in the beauty did not happen as much as we would have liked. This felt like a special moment – I immediately sent the photo to Dick and felt very excited he would be home soon to see it.

I feel guilty admitting it, but when I wasn't worrying about everything going on at the château, *Dirty Rotten Survival* was an amazing experience. From driving a sixty-year-old Willys jeep that was prone to break down through the swamps of Louisiana and having to build beds hanging from trees to avoiding alligators and poisonous snakes, while eating frogs and crayfish, it was a doddle. Then Dave (a survival expert), Johnny (a builder) and I moved onto Texas to live off the feral pigs (it's thought there are over 1.5 million of them devastating farmers' crops. They basically revert to type, and to all intents and purposes become wild boar within a couple of generations). We trapped and had an abundance of boar. I even showed them how to make bacon, it was great!

The journey home was long and very slow but getting back to Angela and the kids felt wonderful. I just couldn't get over the fact that the children had changed so much, especially Dorothy (three weeks is a long time for a child under one). Thankfully, they appeared to recognise me, as I don't know how I would have handled being a stranger to them – good old FaceTime! I was knackered, jetlagged and undoubtedly a bit smelly, but we all held hands and went for a walk.

I'd left château in deepest winter but had come back to spring. Everything was bursting with life. There were small flowers popping up everywhere, the cherry trees had thrown out their first blossoms of the year. It wasn't even that cold. Within moments, it was as if I had not been away. It was great to be back home; however, we didn't really have time to savour the feeling as returning to the château also meant a walk around to catch up on progress. And, with that, we were fully immersed in the detail of the renovations. There were a thousand things to see, a thousand decisions to be made, and a thousand things to do and of course the clock was already ticking until I had to disappear again in just over a week's time.

The filming abroad was essential for us to be able to afford all the work we had to do to make the château comfortable and launch our business in France but the next few months were to be difficult for both of us as we hated the separation. As a team, we are more than the sum of our parts and we love being together, but on top of that we were undertaking a mammoth task that would have been challenging even with both of us being present all the time.

Dick arrived home late morning, which was great as it gave me time to clean the house and put on a face. Hugs were tight and, within a couple of minutes, we were walking around the château taking in the beauty of our run-down home and admiring the blossom. These few moments were precious, but it did not take long for our brains to start racing off onto the list of things that needed doing.

Despite the fact that you could have fit the three-bedroom flat we had been renting in Southend-on-Sea into just one of the château's five floors, we've never felt it was dauntingly big in the way some other châteaus we had viewed were. One property had doors that were so massive they made you feel like one of the Borrowers when you reached to open them. Whereas we have always felt our château is beautifully proportioned and small enough to still be a family home.

After we'd completed the tasks required to enable us to move in we focused on a number of priority rooms. But ultimately we knew the château was going to have to pay for itself if we were not

to end up working away from home to pay the bills. In the light of that, we decided that we needed to have the reception rooms, at least one guest suite and a functioning kitchen up and running as a priority, so we could start advertising a high-end 'château experiences'. These would fund the work needed to get the château ready for weddings, which we planned to hold in the orangery, which would be our events space. We knew we wanted to offer packages that we would enjoy ourselves, so the first château experience we developed was the 'Food Lovers' weekend', but that was all still a long way off at this point . . .

If anything, our list of high-priority tasks was getting bigger. We urgently had to address the fact our heating was just not practical. It seemed impossible but it had to be sorted out before my next trip to America, so it became our number-one focus. We had intended that the log burners would be powerful enough to warm the room they were in and also pass excess heat via the back boiler up to the thermal store. Even though we had done the sums, the poor glazing, the construction of the outside walls and possibly the fact that the wood was a bit rotten, rather than just seasoned, all contributed to the wood fires not being as effective as we had hoped, so the gas boiler was even more important. Supplying our heating system from 13kg gas bottles was just not viable, so we had to find another way. Our initial thought was to get two 47kg bottles linked together with an automatic switchover, which meant when the first bottle was empty there was a seamless changeover and a quick visual examination would tell us if there was an empty bottle (the inspection window turns red). It would mean if it was cold and we were using the boiler a lot, we'd still be changing bottles every three or four days, but that was better than daily. It was always going to be an interim solution but then we failed to find any larger bottles in our local area. However, research and a nudge in the right direction from a French friend of Angela's showed that Butagaz installed large gas tanks as well as filling them.

Where could we put the tank that would not be too ugly? After devising a cunning plan to screen and camouflage the incoming monstrosity, we contacted Butagaz and arranged for an onsite meeting. Compared to some of the interactions we had had, it all moved quickly. The salesman arrived to talk to us and we weren't sure who was going to kiss him first when he said the 1,000kg tank would be buried so as not to be an eyesore. The deal was sealed when he said the installation was free. Free! OK, we knew there is no such thing as a free lunch, it meant we were to be contracted to them for two years, but we'd get a tank big enough to mean heating and hot water would no longer be an ordeal. We tried to play it cool and said if he could sort the installation as soon as possible we'd sign there and then. March can't be a busy time for gas tank installation because a couple of days later a very nice man and his little digger turned up and set to work.

I couldn't believe the lack of pain getting our large gas tank. When our installer arrived, I immediately joined him for a coffee and he explained what was going to happen. We knew that the tank had to be within fifteen metres of our external isolation tap, but we hadn't been told that the trench joining the tank and the external tap was our responsibility. Bugger!

As the small digger started to excavate, my navvy blood kicked in and I started digging like a man possessed. If I finished on time, he would connect the tank for us. If not, he would leave and we'd have to find someone else to connect our gas. With a pickaxe, a trenching spade and a lot of sweat (which on a chilly March day is no mean feat), I matched his work and by the time he had bedded in the tank we had a trench along the side of the château to our isolation tap. True to his word, we had a connected tank that was neatly buried by mid-afternoon. As our new best friend was so skilled with his digger, I even asked him for a very quick favour and without a quibble he went to our gatepost and gently nudged it back into correct alignment (a delivery driver had failed to look up and the top of his vehicle had caught the granite block on top and skewed it out of kilter). That day couldn't have gone any better!

All we needed now was gas, and again that was so much faster than we had grown to expect. A cynic could surmise that the salesman had to hit a year-end target but who cares, it arrived and life at the château instantly became a lot easier. All our energy was no longer purely going into surviving as hot water and heating were available at the flick of the thermostat or tap. We never had any illusions about how much it was going to cost to heat our home, but it really makes you think about the amount of fuel you are using if you have to replace two gas bottles in a single day. That knowledge reinforced our desire for a more environmentally sound heat source but we also knew we wanted convenience. We were never going to be slaves to our heating again.

As well as being invaluable sources of information on anything to do with the château or the local area, Jacques and Isabelle De Baglion had become our friends. Even though the language was sometimes a bit of an issue, with a bit of sign language and a fair bit of laughter we all generally managed to communicate. One evening they invited us to join them for dinner. This would be our first social evening with them and we didn't know quite what to expect or how to dress. Although Isabelle invited the entire family, Arthur and Dorothy had a much earlier bedtime so we used that as an excuse to have a date.

Dad was looking after the children and the novelty of not being in a boiler suit covered in dirt or sick was already making me smile. Our walk must have been 600 metres round the moat and then a short hop across the countryside and we arrived to find quite a large social gathering. Jacques and Isabelle had very kindly invited a number of local *châtelains*˙ and friends they thought we would like to meet. It was a lovely evening and there was enough English spoken to make for lively conversation.

On arrival, two of the six Baglion children, Jaqueline and Louis, were serving aperitifs: sparkling wine with a homemade kir in champagne flutes. I'm not sure what the fruit was to be honest; it was orange in colour, but the flavour wasn't strong, so it could have been mirabelle. Whatever it was, it was cold, fizzy and tasty, and the fact that the children were serving it on trays (probably for some pocket money) made me smile from ear to ear. Then came some canapés. I was hungry and they were very tasty, so I had to try hard not take one every time Louis or Jaqueline offered, but it was hard. They were mostly little biscuits with a mixture of cheese, tomato or meat, but there was also a lovely homemade cream of mushroom soup shot, which I could have eaten a gallon of given the chance. The gathering was in the very large room next to the kitchen and I could smell dinner.

Isabelle worked the room, ensuring everyone was happy and that the children were practising their English on us. It made me feel very guilty as I knew I needed to practise my French too, so thirteen-year-old Jaqueline and I made an agreement: we would both speak to each other in the other's mother tongue. The gathering in the main room lasted for a good hour. It was lots of fun but it was torture smelling the scents of dinner getting stronger as the evening progressed.

We were really interested to see what food they were going to serve. The menu reflected their connection with the land and their love

---

* *Châtelain* is the French title for the keeper of a castle (or château).

of hunting. Like we do now, they store their squashes over winter, so we started with a simple squash soup. Then arrived the star of the evening: Isabelle's wild boar terrines. There were fourteen of us round the table and two massive, glazed terracotta terrines were passed around with chilled cornichons. This was proof that there were wild boar here as the meat used in the terrine had come from within sight of the château. They served butter with the baguettes, which is not always the way in France, so we were as happy as happy people. Next there was a lovely hearty venison casserole, followed by a compote and cream that ensured no one was hungry.

Jacques loves his wine and that night we were being treated to a 2005 claret that was far too easy to drink, so the conversation was lively and fun. I'm old enough, and have been around enough, to be socially competent. That doesn't mean I don't misbehave; it means I know when I am misbehaving. I have since taught Jacques the joy of Bushmills whiskey, Black Bush to be more accurate, and a friendly rivalry has grown between us. But at that first dinner, he had not yet learnt the error of his ways and still thought the blues, the French rugby team, could be lauded in the same way as the Irish team, but we enjoyed the craic.

However, being British, there are some things that cannot be allowed to pass without comment. Our end of the table was discussing the history of the château and I'm sure I heard someone passing comments about, 'that was when the French drove the English out of France'. I like a bit of history on the side and I'm sure that when the very pious Henry VI married Margaret of Anjou, in the middle of the fifteenth century, he agreed to give King Charles VII back a large part of France (where we lived was actually part of England, the counties of Maine and Anjou as I told everyone) won during the Hundred Years War. I think I may have even mentioned that my son James had a yew longbow. When Jacques said it was in his history book that we had been driven out, I asked who had written the book. And when he said it was in French, I just nodded sagely and declared – case proven! Then I changed the subject and talked about rugby, though still giving no quarter.

We had a lot of fun that evening and also met Gabrielle, another of Jacques and Isabelle's children. She shared with us the Baglion legend of the wolf that lived at the château. The story took some unravelling because as far as I knew they could have been talking about a magnifying glass until Louis started howling like a wolf. Apparently, the old count, who I think was Jacques' grandfather, shot the last wolf in this part of France out of one of the tower windows at the château. It had then been stuffed and spent decades scaring the children by snarling down from the ledge overlooking the grand double staircase. I have to say, our understanding was greatly improved when Gabrielle nipped off and returned with some photographs. We asked where the wolf was now and apparently it had taken residency in a flat in Paris with one of Jacques' sisters. Like any great story, it was told with passion, drama and excitement. Dick could not stop talking about the wolf on our walk home.

We felt very lucky to have caring and thoughtful neighbours like Jacques and Isabelle. We also knew how kind it was of them to introduce us to everyone, but we also knew in our hearts that we would not be part of the château circuit. We have such busy lives, not as *châtelains*, but as simple people who are lucky enough to live in a château.

We had a lovely walk home that night: the sky was so clear that we could see the Milky Way. That was probably the first time we had been outside on a clear evening enjoying the size of our sky. We've done it many times since but I'll never forget that first time. In that moment, I realised how different life was now. I discovered how much I like looking at the sky and the stars. I still love the peaceful feeling of walking slowly beside our moat, holding hands and gazing up above our château as Dick points out Orion and the Plough, and explains how to find the North Star ... We had briefly stopped to smell the roses and we knew just how lucky we were.

* * *

Even though our time together was short and, for the first few months in the château, there was always another trip to America looming large, we managed to talk about everything in that week. There may have been an ocean and thousands of miles separating us when Dick was away but we stayed in touch enough so that we always felt we were doing it all together. We even started to look forward to imagining what it would be like when the targets we had set ourselves for the year were done and we were living in comfortable surroundings. It was in moments like this that a housewarming party was first muted. Our wedding also got a mention, as that hadn't been discussed since we'd found the château and up to that point the plan had been for half a dozen people, or an elopement. That, however, was not the case for long. And, with time flying by, if it was to happen, we'd have to tell people soon.

Somehow we both have a different recollection about what happened from here onwards. I can categorically not remember ever agreeing or knowing at this time we were to have a big wedding. I think I was actually surprised when everyone started turning up, but that's another story. I think I was naively holding onto pre-château comments about small weddings and I hadn't moved with the times. We were going to have a party to celebrate, so our wedding seemed like the best reason Angela could think of to get everyone we cared about together.

The very first moment I had met the château a seed had been planted that we would share our marriage day there with family and friends. For many years now, we had discussed running away and having a very intimate wedding with just the two of us . . . but although I loved the idea – and an Elvis chapel in Vegas excited me no end – I had never really come to terms with not having family there. I had been growing this 'wedding at the château seed' in our new forever home slowly and perfectly. It could double up as a housewarming too. I may possibly be guilty of not sharing the growth of the idea with Dick. However, Dick and I often have chats about things and he swears blind we have never discussed them. But on this occasion I remember his answers and the conversation vividly.

We first met on 14 November 2010 and so it just made sense to me to have our celebration on this date. Neither of us wanted another anniversary date to add to our calendars! When we met, Dick was cooking at a pop-up restaurant in London and I was attending with my TV agent, Sophie Laurimore, and her husband. Sophie was Dick's TV agent as well so she introduced us and we chatted all night, and very quickly fell in love. For 15 per cent, Sophie gave me Dick Strawbridge. It doesn't get any cheesier or more romantic. Neither of us expected that five years on (and two children later) we would be planning our wedding in France, but here we are. You really cannot write the script.

It was the end of March now, so we had oodles of time to plan, or so we thought. And although we had a lot of dog work to do still, as we started to chat about family and food and all the little extras for the day, we both felt very excited. It gave us great focus and a huge fire in our bellies.

After so many years living in the UK, you get used to the fact that shops want your custom and they will try their best to help you, and if you live in London there is a 24/7 mentality that means you can get anything you need at any time. That is a long way from life in rural France. Next to nowhere is open on a Sunday and garages aren't manned unless you are on a motorway. Apart from a few (a very few) convenience stores that open on a Sunday morning to coincide with the bakers that have to open to ensure the masses have bread seven days a week and the *bar tabacs*, Sunday is family time.

A month into living in France and we still hadn't really got to grips with shopping. The supermarkets were not an issue because for the six days they are open, they are open all day. That comment may seem a bit odd, but shops in our part of France close for lunch and many of them also close at least one other day during the week – maybe a Monday or a Wednesday, but obscurely sometimes a Tuesday. Those old enough will remember a simpler time when half-day closing in the UK was normal. There were numerous occasions when we nipped out to pick up something from a DIY store, or electric wholesaler, or plumber's merchant, to park up, walk to the door and discover it was just after midday and they were closed for the next two hours.

How do you respond to this inconvenience? Our first reaction was to be annoyed, but that has absolutely no effect on anyone else. No one will open up, apologise and say, 'Please come in and spend your money here.' In fact, the overwhelming feeling you get when shopping in France is that they don't actually care if you are their customer or not. It took time for this to sink in but we worked out that the world-famous 'Gallic shrug' – that show of indifference where a person's shoulders twitch and they make the facial expression that says, 'And this is my problem, how?' – is not actually someone trying to piss you off or a declaration of war. It is simply them letting you know that this is only work and there are so many more important things in life, so why should I give a f***? In the time it took for understanding to dawn, there were many examples of how slow we were to learn.

One morning, I went out for a list of items that was both long and complicated. After the best part of an hour, I was doing really well and was three-quarters of the way through it when one of the assistants, who had been noticeably absent when I was searching for rubber washers, came up and told me the shop was closing and that I could leave my *chariot* and come back at two o'clock. It is all but impossible to imagine that happening even at closing time in any large DIY shop back home. The real crunch was that we needed everything in the trolley and more and there was no other shop to go to during the next two hours. The choice was to rant in bad French to someone that wasn't invested or to give the assistant the best Gallic shrug I could muster and leave with as much dignity as I could manage. I did the latter, but I think I was still mumbling under my breath something along the lines of, 'As if I give a shit . . . I like lunch too.'

At the start of March, the idea of family lunches was a fantasy we aspired to but not something we were close to achieving, so we definitely had teething problems coming to terms with our new shopping culture. Someone explained to us that it usually took someone moving to France a couple of years before they too were absorbed into the way of life. However, quite quickly we decided it was good and we too appreciated the idea of stopping, eating a leisurely lunch, spending some family time, then going back to work recharged. Though having said we appreciate the idea, we are still waiting to be able to adopt it – while lunch as a family is one of our greatest pleasures it is still probably a bit of a rarity.

But a Sunday-morning trip to the *boulangerie* is an experience we love and the perfect example of French village life. Often on a Sunday morning, I will take the children to get fresh bread and patisseries for an afternoon treat. The village is just over a mile away as the crow flies. For a lot of the week, the streets of the village appear deserted, but on a Sunday morning they are always full of activity. It is expected of you to greet people with a *'Bonjour, Madame'* or a *'Bonjour, Monsieur'* and if you know someone you kiss or shake hands. Not to greet one another is unthinkable, so everyone does it.

What happens next all depends on the time . . . If it is just before the church service, we always meet a stream of elderly ladies who take a moment to smile with the children. Smiling is contagious and our children have always been open to new people so they smile easily. After a bit of cheek-pinching and lots of *'petites mignonnes'* we will reach the queue that usually stretches outside the shop. We only ever see these ladies on a Sunday morning and I had, mistakenly, assumed them to be either widows or living alone, until one day I arrived a little earlier and spotted them walking down the hill with elderly partners. With military precision, the old gentlemen peeled off and went into the *bar tabac* for a coffee, a cognac and a chat as the ladies went to tend to their souls.

The owner of the *boulangerie* is always cheerful and, on leaving, there is always a *'Bon Dimanche!'* to see you on your way. It was all a little confusing for me in those first few months, though, as I could have sworn the owner of the *boulangerie* was pregnant, but then the next time I saw her she wasn't. But that is not something you comment on if your acquaintance is at a superficial level and, even if it isn't, it pays not to speculate. I questioned Angela on this and somehow she knew that the *boulangerie* was, in fact, run by twins and that one was having a baby . . . all gleaned with next to no French?

To queue in a *boulangerie* on a Sunday morning is a mouth-watering experience. The shelves and cabinets are filled with every form of yumminess. It must be years of conditioning that allows the French to leave without a bags of cakes or delicacies, but we were new to this and felt no guilt in yielding to temptation. The cabinet on the right as you enter has chocolates and truffles, all made on the premises, then comes the patisserie and the cakes. It's just not right. They look too beautiful to eat and every single flavour you can imagine will be represented there somewhere. There is every combination of white, milk and very, very dark chocolate, often in layers, to tempt you. Over time, we have tried them all. On those first visits we used to limit ourselves to buying two patisseries unless we had guests, in which case it was gloves off and fill a box! The patisseries with fresh fruit or fruit-flavoured mousses, often with a crisp coating or crunchy praline to add texture, are exquisite and we even found some with 'popping candy' in them, which sounds wrong but really wakes up your mouth to the other flavours.

The gateaux are always perfect. Our region is just south of Normandy so apples and cider feature predominantly in our lives and you can't go anywhere without being near a variant of an apple cake or tart, usually topped with exactly the right amount of apricot glaze to balance the acidity and the sweetness – and being heathens we love them with cream poured over. Even the supermarkets in France always have a gateaux selection that would not be out of place in a very high-end tearoom and somehow they always have perfectly ripe fruit arranged in a way that is surely an indication of OCD. However, *boulangeries* seem to have to go a bit better and be a bit fruitier, or a bit taller, or a bit more exotic. And yet in the shop when it says 'for 6–8', it just never looks enough. Consequently, we always buy too much, which just means coffee break on a Monday is a treat too – win/win!

And all this is just the first cabinet. I haven't even got the bread yet. Guess what? There is so much more to French bread than baguettes. Don't get me wrong, we really love the baguettes that are baked several times a day to ensure they are at their freshest, but they only occupy about a tenth of the bread shelf. There are massive round loaves that are cut up and sold by weight and other breads that we assumed were baguettes too but are actually all very different. We often buy the *traditionale* (the crust is much denser and tougher and the structure inside is much more like a sourdough) or the wholegrain variant the tradi-grain. Lots of other breads fall into the traditional category and they are varied in shape and size but all the bread has one thing in common: it doesn't keep and goes stale very quickly. We were a bit perplexed by this to begin with but it makes sense. The bakers don't use any enhancements to help preserve the bread. People who stay with us often pass comment that they don't feel bloated after eating lots of bread in France. Perhaps that is the reason?

Having managed to make decisions on the patisseries and the bread, we then move onto the pastries that make Sunday breakfast special, and there are a lot more than just croissants. Though it is very hard to beat a warm croissant. We are suckers for them all: *pain au chocolat*, *pain au raison*, Swiss (large folded pastries with *crème patissière* and small bits of chocolate), the little open pastries with half a peach or apricots, some with *creme patisserie* and fresh fruit toppings, and on many occasions we have been seduced by almond croissants (yesterday's croissants filled with almond paste and covered with flaked almonds before being rebaked – rich and so tasty).

Obviously with so many decisions to be made on a Sunday morning, it is no wonder the queue takes a bit of time. What is so refreshing is that no one is impatient or agitated by the speed things move forward, but every once in a while there is spanner in the works (demand outstrips supply of the croissants). This is further complicated by the fact that the croissants can't just come from the oven onto the shelf, they have to cool a bit or they can be squashed in the bag and, of course, this is France, so revolutions have started for less ... We've been there on several occasions when the croissant queue has grown and it's been great. Everyone is chatting away, even those of us who are linguistically challenged, in the sure knowledge we are going home with warm croissants – it's the little things that make life special.

Getting home from the bakery we sit down for the ritual of a Sunday 'French breakfast'. When Arthur and Dorothy were little that involved sitting on a rug round a coffee table and ceremoniously eating our breakfast. With coffee and fruit juices on the table, we started by breaking off bits of baguette. This makes a crunchy sound because the crust is so fresh and the dough seems to stretch as you pull it apart. Dick would be master of ceremony and put on a slice of butter (Bons Mayennais *demi-sel* butter that had been made within a mile of the château, with milk from the *département*) – and it really would be a slice (Dick justifies it as part of his Northern Irish upbringing), topped with a teaspoon of apricot jam. It was always messy, and the children would always end up sticky, but that is irrelevant. We were immersing ourselves in the culture and having a ball. Croissants are made by folding a lot of butter and dough, over and over again. Dick knows that as he was taught how to make them by a French baker; however, in our house, they get eaten with even more butter on them.

* * *

March ended with us all feeling spring was in the air. We'd been through the darkest, coldest part of the year and progressed from the nightmare of a bitterly cold midwinter first night to the joy of sunshine and cherry blossoms. We now had convenient, functioning heating and hot water and some electricity, so the family were well established in the château. With Dad's arrival, multi-generational living had started, though we were still waiting for Grandma to come and join us. It is fair to say we had had a taste for what living our dream would be like, but there was still a lot of chaos in our lives.

The moat on a still day.

Our entrance hall with the pineapple chandelier.

The wolf and the château coming to life with our personality.

Wild flowers and a warm kitchen.

The wallpaper museum.

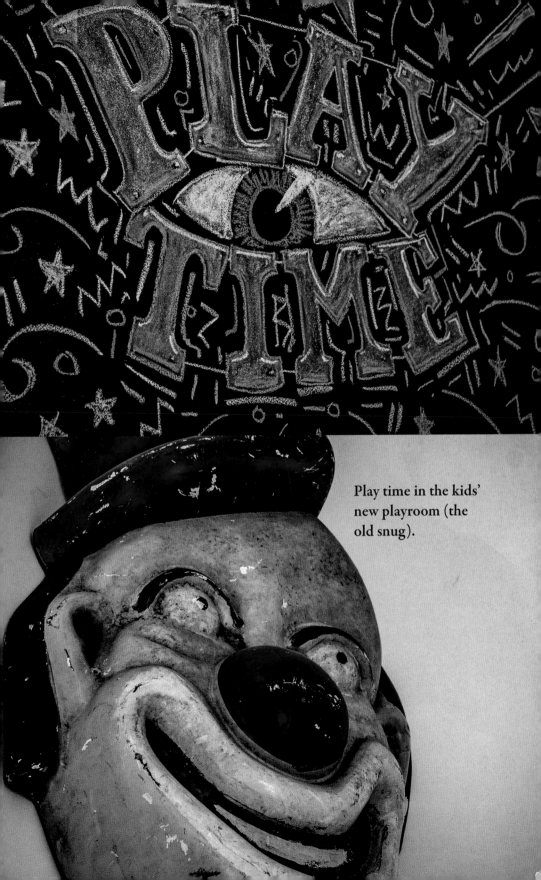

Play time in the kids' new playroom (the old snug).

Dick in America.
Angel in her Emmaus
and being kept busy.

Our new kitchen.

CHAPTER FOUR

APRIL

April is known for showers but it is spring and the sap is well and truly rising. We didn't really know what to expect. It was wonderful. We didn't have the showers that first year and maybe it was because we were still coming to terms with living in our château, but it seemed like spring was even more springy.

There is something very special about 'owning' trees. If you look at the life cycle of an oak it can be said to 'grow for 200 years, live for 200 years and die for 200 years'. Some live a lot longer, but it's a great description. Based on such longevity, ownership is a nonsense. Like with the château, we are only custodians. The trees will be there long after we have gone. Our largest tree is to the south-west of our land. It is huge but you have to get up close to see just how massive it is. On the internet there are calculators that allow you to enter a circumference and it will give you an approximate age.

When we did that for our tree it showed that it dated back to at least the 1660s, to the reign of the House of Bourbon and to Louis XIV, the Sun King. At that time, our château didn't exist. Instead, the original twelfth-century castle would have stood on the island we now occupy. If only trees could talk . . .

When the bare trees start to bud and leaves start to appear, the landscape around us changes from browns and greys to a faintly green tinge, then suddenly fresh and vibrant greens. The evergreens around us cannot influence the landscape to the point that the countryside feels green; it's only when all the native trees come into leaf that the colour palette changes.

The lime trees on the island were in need of pollarding and their thick limbs provided abundant foliage. Around the moat the alders had taken over the banks and, at the far side of the moat, to the north, some splendid sweet and horse chestnuts and oaks dominate the view. Over to the east of our plot, our woods and swamp are full of oak, beech, birch, sycamore and even some walnuts. When the leaves first appear, it is all fresh and it doesn't take long before the château and our little bit of France is surrounded by leafy trees. As we walked round the château, it was wonderful that everything we could see was ours, yet when we climbed the stairs and looked out we had views over miles of beautiful countryside.

The first of everything at the château always felt overwhelmingly exciting, with feelings and passions that came tumbling. I went for many walks with Arthur and Dorothy during the times that Dick was away. The routine gave me comfort and time to breathe, and we all loved the peacefulness of our surroundings and the fresh air.

During April, my regular walk down the drive to the end, back, round the moat and round the château started changing visually daily. Every day there was something new before my eyes. Grasses that I had never seen before: green, brown and purple that looked

like feathers. Wild daffodils popped up around the bank by the moat. One day, they were just there and they gave me a real jolt of excitement: daffodils. Our daffodils. Ours! The big dilemma was if I should pick them and bring them into the house or simply enjoy looking at them on our walks. Wild primulas also sprang up in abundance around the moat. Suddenly there were so many different shades of yellow. One day the bank looked golden. We started to come and have little picnics there under the trees. It became a haven for us, especially when the sun shone . . .

With the seed planted for our wedding party, I had my heart set on having our wedding breakfast in the orangery. The orangery was the château's original winter garden. I had learnt the Bagliones used to host tea parties there, so I had an immediate connection to the building. The windows are Art Deco fan shapes that extend from the ceiling down to the troughs and cover the entire front and right-hand side of the building and the roof is an apex with delicate slate tiles. It is a stunning building to have and I clearly remember saying I would have bought the château simply for the orangery.

We had seen lots of rustic farm-type outbuildings for sale as part of an estate but never an elegant orangery. It was very special and the perfect place to host our wedding breakfast. So one sunny day, Arthur, Dorothy and I took a detour from our routine walk and headed over the long grass to see what state it was in. At this time, the meadow was just that: a meadow of wild grasses and a few wild flowers. It looked stunning to me but there was no path as such. But we still always went the same route and, looking back, I've realised we subconsciously followed the path that Jacques and Isabelle led us on the very first time they took us to the orangery and we shared the harvest of the quince tree. Since then, Jacques has told us the original path was white and it curved up at the edges. It must have been big enough to take a horse, maybe even a carriage.

On this particular day, I could see dense patches of violet all around the Art Deco building. From a distance I truly had no idea what this was . . . it was clustered around the left side of the orangery and under the trees on the right. As I approached it became clearer: it was hundreds, possibly thousands, of untouched, untrodden on, completely beautiful bluebells. They looked like little pixie hats. I'd never been this close to nature and I could not wait to tell Dick. I think Dick was more excited to hear of my excitement than the bluebells themselves – having lived in London I had always been one step from nature, so life at the château meant I was seeing, living and feeling seasonality for the first time.

There was a little fight between me and the doors to the orangery because of the wisteria that had grown over it. It was so heavy over the door that it had curled through every crevice; in fact, it had made some new ones too. Once inside, I quickly realised just how much this plant had savaged the windows and taken over the ceiling. Another job to add to the long to-do list before it caused any more damage. Had it not been for the damage, I may have chosen to keep it – it looked quite whimsical. The walls and the ceiling were dirty white and there was a hole around a metre wide but the potential was all there. Right now, I knew the least we could do, and probably the most we could do, was a little repair, a good paint and an even bigger clean.

Another day while out walking, I got thinking about the wolf (and how I was glad they were not around now!). Beautiful creatures but also a little bit scary – so knowing that the wolf that used to live at the top of our stairs was the last one in this area gave me peace. I also started to think it would be great to bring this piece of history back to the château. Not with a real wolf or taxidermy, but a faux taxidermy replica, so when the kids went to bed in the evening I started looking to see if such a thing existed as a piece of art. I thought I would surprise Dick and give it to him as a wedding present – a nod to the past as we started creating our own Strawbridge story at the château.

I came across a UK-based company that sold unicorns, giraffes, zebras and took commissions, all faux and by the looks of it not bad value. The company is called Broken Hare and it's run by a husband and wife duo, Jon and Katherine. They are based in Wales and make everything themselves in their studio. The following day I called them. Dick and I believe it's always best to call. There is a well-known theory about us all being connected by six degrees of separation – and every time there is a connection outside of the one you are making I always feel happy and believe it's a good sign. On this occasion it very quickly became apparent that there was another connection: I had hosted a tea party for Katherine in Wales many years ago and Dick had even attended to serve tea. In fact, there is a wonderful picture of Dick with feather boas round his neck surrounded by thirty women at Katherine's party. I love the picture so much that I included it in the introduction of my *Vintage Tea Party Year* book. We giggled at the coincidence – what a small world.

Jon and Katherine loved the wolf story and were very excited about working together. How could you not be drawn into this piece of history? Their passion for their craft was abundantly clear and before I knew it I had purchased two unicorns, a zebra, a giraffe and wanted a commission for the wolf. We 'shook hands' and an agreement to deliver the items and come and see the château to discuss the wolf was sealed. It was very exciting. I knew that I was sacrificing something practical for some statement faux taxidermy – we definitely had not budgeted for these luxuries – but I wanted to start making the house ours and for me that meant ensuring I kept my love of fantasy alive.

It was all too obvious that we needed an electrician who wanted to work – or at least one we could communicate with enough to find out why he didn't want to work. We decided to see if there were any certified electricians available within the ex-pat community; we needed someone who could sign off any work he did. When we had been searching for a translator prior to purchasing the château, we had found a lady called Valerie who made a living helping British people living in France to navigate their way through the bureaucracy. She put us in touch with some British 'artisans' who lived north of us.

That is a very interesting differentiation. In Britain we have workers and tradesmen, whereas in France they have artisans. We cannot say how they are perceived in the community – those are nuances we are still trying to absorb – however, we do know that our French friends are always interested in contacting and using anyone we found to be industrious or reliable. It is not possible to generalise, and the quality and work ethics vary greatly by individuals, but we have been told on more than one occasion that the quality of some ex-pat 'builders' or 'plasterers' or 'craftsman' should be questioned. It is joked that many get their qualifications on the ferry when they decide to move to France. There is undoubtedly a bit of truth in it, as people often redefine themselves when they make a move. We have experienced both good and bad. All I can say is a strong recommendation from someone you respect is the best way to find someone reliable. We have kissed a fair number of frogs before finding our current team of princes and princesses, and by that we are not talking about French people!

Although funds were tight, we were always searching for people who were willing to do an honest day's work for an honest day's wage. Sometimes it feels as if being the owners of a château makes people believe you have either more money than sense or are a bit simple. One British builder contacted us and quoted us to supply us with a plasterer to skim a room. It was a couple of days' work but the quote was ridiculously high so we phoned the plasterer up directly to work out why, only to discover that he knew nothing about the job and wasn't interested in it. When we discussed his rates it was apparent that the broker had basically doubled it as commission. Suffice to say, I told him to f*** off and not to bother coming anywhere near us ever again.

There was another occasion when we learnt the true value of being on-hand to supervise work. We had a couple of simple rooms that we felt should be quick and easy to transform. The plan was to make them into studies to allow us to work in a degree of tranquillity amidst the chaos that was our home. We followed a recommendation and employed a builder who had the resources to do the job. It was not cheap as they claimed it required a plasterer and an assistant. Halfway through the job we were surprised to find the both men at the supermarket in the middle of the afternoon buying beer. When we challenged them, they tried telling us plastering was hard work and they were tired, even though there were two of them doing the job usually done by one. Yet another builder to avoid in the future.

With so much rewiring required we were frantic to find someone qualified in French electrics with a reliable work ethic. Luckily Alan and his daughter/helper were available and to our delight were reasonable, reliable and turned up exactly when they said they would.

With seven months until our wedding we had hoped that our list of jobs would start to get smaller. Instead, it continued to grow. To add to our challenges, we decided we needed to sort out another suite upstairs so that we had somewhere for guests to stay with us that had all the mod cons (you know: lights, running water, a loo). This may seem like simple stuff, but the entire house was still running from one socket at this point. Heating wasn't included as it was April so it should be warm enough and I had convinced Angela that we should subscribe to the idea of putting on a jumper if you are chilly. Like our family suite, it was a temporary fix, so not to the same standard as our letting suites. This may appear like a distraction from our main tasks, but it would mean we could have more people come to stay – even if they had to be fit enough to walk up seventy-five stairs.

The suite on the second floor exactly mirrored our family suite on the floor below. The bathroom also looked like a corridor that had been widened and it caused no end of pain. I wanted a 'quick and easy to erect' shower cubicle and so bought one that was meant to be installed in minutes. My arse was it simple! The instructions were allegedly in French and English, though they may as well have been in Swahili. I wrestled with plastic nuts and tubing made from cheese* for hours before I managed to get the cubicle up drip and leak free. It was not of the best quality as it was to be in commission for less than a year and we couldn't imagine it being reused in the château in the future. In fact, its finest quality was that it was the cheapest we could find. That said, it was a shower, and it even had jets that squirted out sideways in imitation of massage jets. The loo and sinks were from our barn of plumbing treasures. We slapped some paint on the walls to pretend it was not an extension of our building site and it was done.

Getting planning permission in a country where you know the language and can understand the system can seem daunting. Try doing it in another language in another country! We had all decided that my parents' home was eventually going to be the rather large coach house on the island, beside the château.

---

* 'Cheese' is a derogatory way of describing a material that has not got any physical properties worthy of credit.

We knew the benefits of multi-generational living but we also recognised that we all needed a little bit of space. Historically part of the building had been used as the cook's house. It is the only outbuilding on our island and, although there were many other outbuildings that surrounded the walled garden to choose from, some already with planning permission, we loved the idea that when the kids are old enough we will be able to say, 'Go run over to Grandma and Grandad's house.' So we set about finding an architect.

Word of mouth soon led us to an English, fully in-the-system, French-speaking man who could do exactly what we needed. My parents' needs were quickly understood and the process began. It took months and many tos and fros to get it over the line. It was not the plans; they were quite straightforward. It was the system in place in the centre of Mayenne that kept losing bits of paperwork (at least, that is what we were told!). But it all worked out well and, a few hurdles later, we were granted permission to get started. Sadly, the roof of the coach house was in a bad condition, so this needed to be fixed before we could commence any other work – this meant we had to park it until our wedding was over, but still dreams of my parents' house started to come together. As always, there was a lot of work to be done, which would have to be done in phases, but it felt within our grasp.

* * *

Though I had spent weeks being excited at every new flower, every bumblebee, every new smell, every new taste, I was not really looking forward to my and Dorothy's first birthdays at the château. Dorothy's birthday is the day after mine – and Dick was missing them both as he was away in America again, while Mum was still in the UK running the restaurant. Dad had been home to see Mum but she always felt happier that Dad was with me when

Dick was away. I love her for this, but that is just my mum – always putting others first.

We always joke that my dad is the biggest kid of all and, after a little chat about what to do to celebrate our birthdays, we decided on a trip to Disneyland, Paris. I knew Dad and I would have a giggle and the kids would probably enjoy themselves too. It did not take long for me to see the positive in this. It's not very often as a grown-up that you get to spend quality time with one of your parents, especially when you have kids – and to be honest Disneyland is not Dick or my mum's cup of tea. So off we went for a couple of days. It was the first time the château had been by herself, and I have to say she never left my mind, but we had a ball and I loved how close we were. I could not wait to get to know Paris like I knew London. There were so many hidden gems waiting for Dick and me to explore.

When we were 'courting' there were many occasions that I'd travel up from Cornwall to London. As there were still chickens and geese at my smallholding, I would bring fresh eggs with me for us to enjoy when we had the opportunity for a leisurely breakfast. I took for granted what it was like to have truly fresh eggs 'straight from the chicken's bum' but it was a revelation for Angela. Life is about enjoying even the most mundane of activities and making them special. I have always loved Angela's desire to make an occasion out of every meal or every drink we have together – setting the table for us always involves napkins and lovely china and glass. It may take a little effort, but it is so worthwhile.

As Angela's Vintage Patisserie business was thriving, and that involved lots of weekend events, during my visits we grabbed our fun when we could. Friday evenings and Saturdays were always busy, preparing all the bespoke cakes, patisseries and sandwiches, and then hosting up to half a dozen tea parties in different locations in the capital. By the time everything had been cleared up and turned round for the next event they were long old days. (Right from our first weekend together in London, I was in awe of Angela's work ethic – despite finishing late she would have her alarm set for an early start so every event had the attention she felt it deserved. When I say early, sometimes it would be 3am to allow her time to bake and prepare for the next morning. That is early in anyone's book!) So if we had a Sunday morning free it was savoured. Breakfast would be prepared together, which made Angela a bit twitchy, as she loves looking after me and allowing me to relax as she busies herself around the kitchen. However, when it was our time together, we would prepare all manner of meals.

When I brought produce up from Cornwall it would be the centrepiece of our meal. Unusually, breakfast would be large and varied. This was ten years ago and mashed, ripe avocado with salt, freshly ground pepper and a little squeeze of lemon juice, served on toasted sourdough, was not yet common, but we loved it – especially with soft poached eggs and crispy rashers of streaky bacon. It's a simple fact, but it's impossible to poach a truly fresh egg badly! Eggs that are fresh hold together and by cracking them into a teacup and then lowering them into gently simmering, salted water, your job is done. A couple of minutes later and they just need to be lifted out with a slotted spoon and served. It's a hangover from my childhood, but I love a little splash of vinegar in the poaching water – there will be some spurious folklore rationale for adding vinegar, but I just like the flavour. These breakfasts are amongst our fondest memories. We were cocooned away from the outside world and revelling in each other's company, and little by little I was seducing this beautiful city girl to the dark side, because she may not have known it yet, but she wanted a life where your chickens provide you with eggs for breakfast that are so fresh that they are still warm.

....

PIPERADE WITH BAKED EGGS (BASED ON THE TYPICAL BASQUE DISH, BUT A BIT MORE BREAKFASTY!)

There is nothing better than eggs for breakfast. Here's one of our favourite dishes, with a French twist.

Ingredients

1 red pepper, sliced
½ onion sliced
2 tomatoes sliced
1 tsp paprika – smoked or hot, you choose
Too much extra virgin olive oil
4 eggs
Salt and pepper

Method

Slowly fry the pepper and onion in the olive oil. Don't spare the oil!

When the peppers are soft, add in the paprika, cook for thirty seconds, then add the tomatoes, stirring until they have broken up.

Pour the mixture into an ovenproof dish, make four egg-sized hollows and then crack the eggs into them. Season well and bake at 180°C for fifteen minutes.

I warn you: you need bread to dip into the unctuous, oily sauce.

....

In mid-April, there were ten wonderful days that Dick was home and my mum was here. We were all together. But before Mum arrived, the pressure was on. It was never talked about but we all knew it was there – the desire for my mum to be romanced by the château and the French lifestyle. The château is large; however, very little of it was really habitable or comfortable in the first year and it still had very few facilities. So we spent a busy couple of days getting the salon habitable for Mum and Dad. First, we gave it a huge clean. Then we made sure their bathroom, in the eastern tower, off the dining room, was functioning. We hadn't been able to find out where the waste went, but it was going somewhere, so it would have to do. There was no time to touch anything else, but the high ceilings and faded blue walls were a great backdrop to a king-sized bed and their three-piece suite, which had been placed next to the fireplace. A few fresh flowers later and none of us could wait to hug Mum.

When she arrived the scrabble to hug her was very funny. Of course, Dick and I stood back and let the kids go first. We knew how much she had missed them. It was a great relief that Mum loved her new room and that evening we stopped all work and ate like one should when you live in a château!

Eating slow, leisurely meals is the ultimate, decadent way to spend an evening talking and catching up. The individual dishes don't have to be complicated; they just have to keep coming.

With aperitifs of sparkling demi-sec *Loire Crémant*, we started our 'welcome to the château' meal with toasted seeds. These are very easy to prepare: you simply toast your seeds in a pan (we had sunflower seeds, pumpkin seeds, pine nuts and even a few sesame seeds). When they are browned you take them off the heat and add soya sauce and chopped chillies to the still hot pan, stirring to coat them. Then serve in a bowl with a teaspoon. The salty spice goes very well indeed with the cold bubbles.

We followed that with a large pan of garlicky prawns, which are incredibly simple to prepare but delicious to eat.

....

GARLICKY PRAWNS

Ingredients

200g butter (yes, 200g!)
4 cloves of garlic, sliced
1kg large prawns – shell on
Baguette

Method

Melt the butter.

Add in the garlic.

After a few seconds (don't let the garlic cook too much or it can go bitter) add in the prawns.

Heat and toss until the butter has become a pinky, garlicky yumminess and the prawns are cooked through.

Put the pan on the table, with a couple of bowls for the shells, and sit around peeling and eating.

When you pull off the heads you have to suck them to get the juices out. Don't think about it, just try it . . . You'll find that is where lots of the flavour is hidden.

....

Our main course was a leg of lamb cooked in white wine over a bed of root vegetables and whole garlic cloves. For dessert, we had our first rhubarb dish of the year, which had to be crumble – slightly soggy where it touches the fruit and wonderfully crispy on top. We could have served *crème anglaise* (custard to us!) but instead we opted for fresh cream.

To finish we obviously had to have a cheese board, served with some of our precious quince jelly we'd prepared from the fruit we had been given by Jacques and Isabelle the very first time we saw the château the previous October. That was only six months before, but my goodness lots had happened since then . . .

We were never short of tasks on our 'to-do' list but we were living in a château and very aware that our lives could not just be graft, so we always tried to spend quality time with the children and not to forget why we chose this lifestyle in France in the first place. Despite lots of very important and urgent jobs, we made the decision that it was time to spend a little more time outside the château. Our overgrown walled garden had been all but ignored. As it was surrounded on all sides by walls, it would take very little effort to turn it into the most amazing chicken run. All we needed was a chicken house and then they could enjoy the whole area to scratch around.

There are three ways into the walled garden: from the château/ moat side there are four steps leading up to some ornate pillars; in the western wall there is an arched doorway with a sturdy wooden door (rotten on the bottom but still solid); and then in the north-eastern wall there is another arched door by a set of old run-down rabbit cages with the remnants of a gate hanging off. Having decided we wanted to make the walled garden secure for the chickens, it only took a couple of hours to knock up a simple wooden gate covered in chicken wire for the 'main' entrance and to patch together a couple of Frankenstein doors Shelley would have been proud of for the other doorways.

All the gates were functional but I could tell Angela was affronted by the very simple, somewhat ugly gate that adorned the entrance that could be seen as you approached from the château. It was a rectangle of various pieces of reclaimed wood (all the pieces were the same colour, so it wasn't too unsightly) with a diagonal piece to force the weight to act through the lower hinge. To finish it off, I covered it in chicken wire. I explained it was only temporary and that there was work to be done there to sort out the very wonky steps, and so when we addressed that we should discuss a gate design that would do our walled garden justice. I'm not quite sure how I got away with it, but I did and, interestingly, that gate is still there today. Though the comments about replacing it are getting more frequent!

I have not spent much time in the walled garden until recently. That gate is most certainly on my list to get done this year!

With over an acre to run around and be free range, all the chickens needed was a coop. This was the subject of lots of discussion; however, we were totally in agreement that the coop had to be cheap as we had so many other pressures on our finances. Somehow it was decided that our chickens could live in one of the outbuildings that appeared to have been a laundry at some time. Decision made, there were several things we needed. Firstly, a way for the chickens to get from their new home to the walled garden; then secondly, an entrance that allowed us to enter the room without the chickens all making a bid for freedom in rural France. And last but not least – chickens.

As the chickens were to be a joint venture we decided to modify the stone building that was to be the 'chicken shed' together. As with every project at the château, work commenced with clearing and cleaning. With our unsung heroes Jenny and Steve looking after the children it felt like a date. The treasures that were not to be used for our chickens' home had to be moved out and whatever remained was to be repurposed – that included the most amazing hand cart, miscellaneous drawers, an old laundry cauldron, various sets of old rickety ladders and stepladders, and lots of old wood.

There followed several hours of construction. It was a bit chilly and, as this was basically a non-essential project, we didn't start until the evening, so it was dark. But I loved it. Who gets to spend a romantic evening doing woodwork with their wife in an old building, lit by battery work lamps, while she looks gorgeous in her vintage fur coat? Not many chaps, right? Despite her attire, Angela got stuck in. I had her sawing up the wood to make our internal fencing and even knocking the hole through the wall to put a doorway for the chickens to access the garden.

We had scavenged some wood and an old gate from one of the other barns. It was only when I went to move it into the chicken house that I discovered that it was so heavy it must have been made from hardwood – it looked as if it could even be mahogany. We arranged the cauldron, the drawers and the cart and filled them with straw to be our laying boxes, then laid the ladder horizontally to provide the roosting space. Indeed, our setup could easily have been home to a hundred happy chickens and the lucky ones that ended up with us were guaranteed a house that was solid stone, slate-roofed and complete with mahogany fittings. We just had to find some chickens.

Research uncovered a market about an hour north of us at St-Hilaire-du-Harcouët. We hadn't explored that area at all so we were really excited to be going off on our expedition. It was around an hour from home and our sole purpose for this visit was chickens.

We left Arthur and Dorothy at the château with Jenny and Steve. All four could not wait to have fresh eggs. Before we left, as parents do, we'd been explaining to the children where we were going. There was lots of clucking and talking about dippy eggs. I think there was even a 'quack' from Papi Steve but we won't go into that . . .

By the time we got there and found somewhere to park, it was mid-morning. Fresh eggs were within our reach and our trip was actually feeling very romantic. The market was full and bursting with people, many with baskets and wonderful baguettes and produce. But initially all we could see were market stalls of goods of mainly plastic 'tat' destined to be landfill. We attempted to get directions to the livestock but only found two different butchers. However, things started to look up as we found lots of stalls of fresh vegetables and artisan meats and cheeses. All was not lost and, although we were there for chickens, I could not pass by without stopping and we ended up with a bag of rhubarb, asparagus, leeks, cabbage, baguettes and some cheese. French markets are not cheap compared to supermarkets but there is an authenticity to buying direct from producers and you know you are being guided through the seasons. There are larger stalls that have obviously been supplied from wholesalers but there are also stalls where it seems as if the produce is the surplus from their garden or allotment.

Contrary to what many city-dwellers may assume, spring is not a time of overflowing bounty. April is actually a relatively barren time for local producers. Most of us are totally unaware of this as supermarkets have undertaken to keep supplying us with cheap and abundant fresh produce all year sourced from all round the world, so much so that the seasons don't really seem to matter. In fact, by April, most domestic winter crops have bolted and gone to seed and the other vegetables and fruit that have been stored are running out. Spring salad and vegetables have been sown but most won't be ready to harvest until May and June, so this period is often called the 'hunger gap' and is a time of slim pickings. That said, there were plenty of cheese and charcuterie stalls to drool over, and more than enough greens for us to fill our shopping bags, so we were already laden down when we found the separate car park where livestock was for sale.

This part of the market contained all sorts of enticements to get you to 'grow your own'. Supermarkets back in the UK sometimes put up displays that celebrate seasonality but it doesn't feel particularly like fruit or vegetables have their moment in the year when they are the stars. It's almost as if seasonality is hidden so you buy everything all the time. In France, we find it enlightening to see what everyone else is using.

As the chance of frost diminishes, it is as if everyone is encouraged to go out and dig for victory. In every large supermarket in our *département*, you cannot avoid the fact that it's time to plant your crops or flowers – when you enter you have to wind your way through the racks of seedlings and plants that you should be taking home and planting. There are the normal rows of packet seeds that are there all year round, but they are now accompanied by rows and rows of young plants that have been put into small pots. They are not exactly cheap, but they are vibrant and ready to go out into your vegetable patch. Maybe, like us, no one else was organised enough or had time to grow from seed but, either through guilt or an overwhelming desire to join everyone else, the trade in seedlings, flowers, shrubs and herbs is a bit frenzied in April. We knew we wouldn't be able to join in and dedicate time to our garden as the château needed us, but the desire was still strong to buy at least a couple of runner beans to grow up our bamboos, or maybe one or two of the courgette plants, but ultimately common sense prevailed and we continued on to the livestock.

I was a little surprised at the cages upon cages of young poultry available to buy. Logic says that the only reason they are there is that there is a demand for them. But as we walked up and down the rows of chicks, ducklings, goslings, point of lay hens, mature ducks and geese, there was a mind-boggling choice and to say it was noisy was a bit of an understatement. I thought I had dampened the mood a little when I explained to Angela that not all these birds were going off to become 'pets' and the bigger, chunkier ones were destined for the pot. But she got it, so we set about choosing our flock. The vendor spoke no English but he was a natural showman, whipping birds out of cages and pointing to their best bits. In the end, we came away with several boxes containing a young cockerel, and a couple each of what I thought to be point of lay Light Sussex, Cuckoo Marans and what looked like a Rhode Rock Hybrid. Even though we would have to wait a little to get our eggs, 'point of lay' is the best age to buy a chicken, as egg production is just about to start and, when it does, it starts with little eggs and progresses very quickly to larger eggs, so for most of the year we could expect them to be laying an egg a day.

When we arrived home, it took only moments to get the boxes into the chicken house. And when we opened them to release our hens, Arthur surprised us all by saying, with perfect diction, 'chickens'. He got lots of praise from his very proud parents and grandparents. And it only took a couple of days until we had the first of many eggs. They were ceremoniously collected, brought to our little temporary kitchen and then soft boiled and served with buttered toast soldiers as our first château-produced, dippy eggs. We may be biased but the taste of buttered toast dipped into soft, very fresh egg yolk is a winner! Arthur and Dorothy loved them from the first and egg collecting has been a part of their lives ever since.

* * *

National Geographic was continuing to provide the much-needed funds for us to continue our work, but that involved yet another trip away. Any couple would find it hard if one of them had to work away from home but for us it felt slightly different, as we needed to have both of us there to provide the necessary horsepower for a project as big as the château. And decisions also needed both our inputs. We really felt the separation. Consequently, getting everything organised before we parted, and agreeing what had to be done in my absence, was manic. During the day, we would be engrossed in whatever task we were doing and at night we would catch our breath and have 'meetings' to discuss deadlines, costs and what we had to do next.

Along with the lengthening days and therefore, what felt like easier working hours, spring had brought with it a sense of optimism. Grandma had arrived and we saw the first swallows swooping around the outbuildings. Even though we had been disciplined and kept the château as our focus we had made a step towards the *potager*, being productive by getting the hens. Unfortunately, I was still commuting to America but . . . needs must.

CHAPTER FIVE

MAY

May feels like summer but is definitely spring. We had not had any rain for a couple of weeks and the temperature had crept up, so the feeling of summer days was there and there were more daylight hours, but as any gardener knows you have to expect cold snaps, even frost, and the need to pop a jumper on in the mornings was a constant reminder that we were not quite there yet. With young children come early starts but being welcomed by eggs from our chickens first thing in the morning always felt like a treat. And going out to collect the eggs meant being able to enjoy the dawn chorus, which is positively deafening here. It makes you think a bit about your day ahead, when every little bird is singing its heart out ahead of a day of working away building nests or feeding young. They all sound so happy. Our lives had been devoid of cuckoos prior to arriving in France, but now every

morning there was one happy bird cuckooing with such convic-
tion that you simply had to listen. We already knew we lived in a
very special place, but now the extent of the natural treasures we
had on our twelve acres was really starting to unfold. The birdlife
was varied and numerous. We knew there were wild mammals
from deer down to shrews but it was only slowly that we actually
got to see them all.

I grew up spending most of my time outdoors and enjoying
nature. Back in the 1960s, it was not considered wrong for a
boy to have collections of butterflies and moths or one of a
wild birds' eggs, each collected after spotting a bird, following
it, locating the nest and then taking an egg home, blowing it
and mounting it. Such fieldcraft gives you an appreciation of
nature and I couldn't help pointing out things to Angela and
the children. I think my excitement must have been infectious
because now all the family will point out anything we see. In
our first year everything was new and, more importantly, everything was ours to look after. There was so much to remember
that I started a book of wildlife: our sightings. It wasn't exactly
a survey but I noted down all the birds I saw, including our
herons, sparrowhawks and even kingfishers.

One time, I was fortunate enough to have been watching a
kingfisher cross the moat (they fly like a vivid blue and orange
arrow from A to B with great determination and no messing
around) when a sparrowhawk swooped to try to take it out of
the sky. The kingfisher dived straight into the water and, within
seconds, had flown out from the same spot it went in, with equal
haste but in exactly the opposite direction. The sparrowhawk had
no idea what was going on. Well done, the kingfisher! I was so
astounded I wrote about it on Twitter and was delighted to have
a response from a gentleman who had been studying kingfishers
for the best part of twenty years and had felt privileged to have

seen a similar escape trick once himself. Our little piece of France is truly magical.

Back home, we know that the grey squirrel is a bully that has driven out the more *petite* red squirrel, which is now rarely seen. I did a double take the first time I saw one of our red squirrels – *we have red squirrels!* That explained what appeared to be a couple of random walnut trees growing in the 'meadows' to the left and right of the drive – unclaimed squirrel caches. My first glimpse of one was in the trees above the marshy area to the east of the château. I was to see them regularly but not often. I only ever saw one at time, above the marshes and then scampering across the driveway to the 'enchanted' woods by the orangery. I did a little research and apparently boy and girl squirrels only really spend time together when they are being . . . frisky. It all made sense

I had really got into my rhythm now. Although my rhythm changed by the second because, with the kids growing, their needs were developing on an hourly basis, and the château's needs were also changing constantly. I suppose change was part of my rhythm. But my constants kept me settled in this hectic time.

Looking back, our life was a little different, but maybe it's like seeing photos of an old hairdo and thinking: wow. Because at the time it seemed very normal. And, in between it all, Arthur and Dorothy kept me very grounded. They needed routine, so my days revolved 100 per cent around them. Every day, after lunch, I would take the kids for a drive in the car. With the two of them strapped in safely, we hit the peaceful roads. Dick loves the rolling hills and on our initial searches it was this that drove us to this part of France. The country lanes have a lovely curvaceousness to them, so with the added whisper of white noise and the counting of crows, Arthur and Dorothy would always settle quickly. At this point I would drive back to the château

and park up under a tree until they awoke. Then I would sit on the steps of the château and get some work done. Every now and again one of them would stir, but then they would see me, feel safe and doze off again. And I was always thankful of a few more minutes to get work done.

When Dick was away, the best constant of the day (apart from the daily trip to the *boulangerie* and the special time with Arthur and Dorothy) was our 6am phone call. I called it my 'Love Sandwich' call:

> *Bread*
>   *Me: Darling, I miss you.*
>   *Dick: I can't wait to see you. How are the kids?*
> *Filling*
>   *Dick: What's on the list?*
>   *Me: Paint removal, scrubbing, painting, shopping and*
>   *getting ready for the wedding. Trying to find tiles, paint,*
>   *lights . . . and fly removal.*
> *Bread*
>   *Dick: The wedding?*
>   *Me: I love you. Have a great day . . . Don't get eaten by an*
>   *alligator.*

Dick says that we never discussed our big wedding in detail. He may be right, because I don't have enough memory of the initial discussions to disprove his outrageous statement, but we both know that I would never have gone ahead with an enormous fairy-tale wedding without us both agreeing and being excited. For a couple of weeks, my twenty to ninety minutes of work that I got done each day when the kids were asleep was spent on our wedding invitation and wedding list. More and more weddings are now paperless, which reflects how we live and work. It's much easier having a wedding website with all the information in one place that you can easily manage and keep track of who is coming – and it's easier for guests too, having access to all the information they need to book flights and hotels. Technology really does make everyone's life much easier. But I could just never come to terms with the idea that our guests would not receive something physical to touch. It's the very beginning of the whole process – the ceremony of opening something and feeling the excitement that you are at the start of a journey. So I decided to do both: an informative website and something beautiful to send our guests in the post.

I have been planning events for over a decade so I was determined my own wedding would be perfect. I wanted it to be magical and for all our friends and family to have the time of their lives. Simply bringing everyone together is magical in itself – this is something I tell all the brides or grooms that get married at the château now – but, as there are so few occasions in life when it happens, I wanted it to be extra special. And I started like I meant to carry on: over the top, handmade and with an attention to detail that made everything unique.

I'd been going to Emmaus* shops for some time as they are great for second-hand bargains. I had recently discovered there was one just thirteen minutes away in Laval. Like most Emmaus, the Laval branch is only open on Wednesdays and Sundays, from 10.30am to 12.30pm and then again from 2.30 to 5.30pm, so when it's open it's very busy, especially if you get there early.

Every Emmaus is carefully and systematically organised. In Laval, you have a kitchen area on the left as you walk in. This

---

* Emmaus is an international charity founded in France to help the homeless. The Emmaus shops in France sell all manner of second hand goods, from furniture to clothes, electrical goods to bric-a-brac.

includes everything from pans to utensils, all stacked high like they will fall. There is no division of quality; you'll find a copper pan inside a tin pan with the handle about to fall off inside a Le Creuset. And shelves after shelves of them. Next there is an entire wall of glassware with over a thousand pieces at any time: champagne flutes, wine glasses, tumblers, dessert glasses, port glasses, gin glasses, whiskey and brandy glasses, kids' glasses, gold glasses, red, blue and yellow glasses, and even tiny glasses. Then there is a central reservation of plates, platters, cheese boards, decanters, butter dishes, teacups, coffee cups, teapots, coffee pots, milk jugs, jars . . . Everything you could ever imagine, in epic amounts and virtually for free. I didn't see anything for more than one euro.

Opposite the kitchen area are the books, which includes maps, vinyls and old magazines. Then food is luckily by the entrance to the kids' area, which is great for a quick dash on the way to what feels like an incredible cosy library. After the kitchen area on the left there is lighting, then a miscellaneous section (which is where Dick always disappears to after the kitchen), then it's toys. On the right after the books are pictures, clothes and linens, and then at the end is furniture.

Who I was with and what we were looking for defined my route. However, whatever route you take, Emmaus has ONE system (and you see the wrath if you get it wrong!): you shop by category. After you've found what you're looking for, you queue at the desk in that area and receive a ticket. Then you pay at the front desk and then go back to that area to collect your goods with a stamped 'paid' receipt. This seems simple, but sometimes I'd find something I wanted in every category, which means you can end up queuing ten times. Not great when you have two small kids . . .

With the wedding approaching, I started going every Wednesday. First, I bought chairs for the orangery. They were around €3 each – for a solid-oak dining chair! As long as I left the prams at home, I could squeeze four in the car at a time. But we needed eighty chairs, so that racked up a lot of visits.

After that I was after linens, for the guests to delicately dab the sides of their mouths after they ate. The clothes and linen section is every crafter's dreams: piles upon piles of French linens, napkins, tea towels, bedding, buttons, threads . . . What made me so happy was that every batch had been starched, ironed and tied with a little bit of string. I could never work out how they would only cost one or two euros. and I had this picture of someone getting total satisfaction ironing them and knowing the likes of someone like me would pick them up and stroke them. Also in this area were the clothes and the kiddies' section was always filled with adorable handmade items from the forties and fifties, and hangers upon hangers of hand-knitted cardigans and jumpers. I always bought everything I saw that appealed to me and added any items that didn't fit Arthur and Dorothy to my gift drawer for our friends yet to have babies. Then there was also a dress-up section. History has shown me that this is where I always find my best outfits: from oriental dresses and kimonos to the perfect Cinderella and pirate costumes.

With my collection of French linens growing, I got inspired by seeing a lovely French tea towel with lots of writing on. It was my 'that's it!' moment: serigraphed French linens. I decided to get a personalised screen cut and handprint all the invites on French linens. It was perfect: all our guests would then have something unique, French and handmade.

To create a screen for print you expose your photo or image to a special emulsion and lamp in a dark room. This basically burns it onto the screen. I had planned to do this myself but watching all the videos I thought it was easier to go with a company that knew what they were doing, even though I usually love knowing the process of things and find it fascinating to learn. I ordered my screen from a company in the UK; when it arrived it was exactly what I was looking for with all the details from the invite burnt out perfectly. The trick to printing (so I taught myself with the help of the internet before I started) is to be firm and even and to ensure the screen does not move on the linen. Dick knew this was his chance to get involved, so a quick trip to his workshop later I had a handy frame that would ensure I got the best outcome for each and every linen.

Somehow I knew about our wedding before the invitations were produced but I don't know when or how the decision was made, and I categorically deny all knowledge of the scale of the planned event. It was probably when the invitations were being made that I realised that the clock was ticking and counting down to a really big party. Angela asked me to help build a frame to make screen-printing her design for the invitation easy and repeatable, so I did. Then she asked me to help iron the vintage napkins that she was going to print the invites onto, so again I said yes (I was taught to iron when I joined the army so I am competent). Then Angela gave me the bundle of napkins and all I could think was, *Shit . . .* There were hundreds of them, literally hundreds. It was then that I knew I was in the poop!

I was quite restrained during our subsequent discussion and Angela made the point that, as we were in France, 'What was the chances of everyone coming?' Duh, I should have known better. Angela was renowned for the events she has staged, so why would anyone not come and see us and celebrate?

I used black ink for the printing for maximum contrast and the first one came out even better than expected. It felt very exciting! But after twenty or so prints the screen was getting a bit clogged, so I decided to wash it. What was I thinking? I immediately lost all sharpness. I ended up having to order another screen. But, as I always say, the best way to learn is to make mistakes.

On many of my walks I would daydream about our guests opening up their invites. What was going to put them in? A Jiffy bag? I'd put so much love into them. I did not want to fall down on packaging. A quick rummage later, I decided that all the linens would be wrapped in envelopes made from the old newspapers found amongst the treasures in the attic and sealed with a wax seal with our initials and the date of our wedding on it. So then I had to look for companies that make these seals. I vaguely remember Dick saying: 'Just get them out.' But I wanted them to be perfect.

It added a month on to sending them out, and lots more work, but I really enjoyed the process: the smell of wax, the way it flows onto the paper and the fact that each was different, sealed with a delicate detail. I was very proud of our wedding invitations and I also happen to know that all the guests kept them. But thank goodness for the website.

By the second week in May, Angela's mum Jenny had wrapped up her affairs back in Essex and she and Steve were ready for their next big adventure, which involved moving lock, stock and barrel to France – a country they didn't really know, hadn't spent much time in and where they definitely couldn't speak the language. The latter was going to be an issue as they are both independent and wanted to go and explore as well as help us. But it didn't take very long before Steve was conversing with the best of them in a wonderfully English way, which involved him pointing at his chest multiple times while saying very slowly, 'Inglesi, no understand.' It was almost too stereotypical to be believable but because he always smiles, and is so gently engaging, no one seemed to mind – and nine times out of ten he got what he wanted as the locals invariably found some fragment of English in their memories and understood what he was asking for.

Every morning, before the kids were up, I got a small window to catch up on work. I would grab a coffee, sit in bed and check my emails. Love letters and to-do lists from Dick were the most exciting thing in my inbox, but on one particular day I received something else exciting: a picture of the first version of the wolf. Jon is such a talented artist. He had created the wolf in clay first and, although it clearly was not the finished article, it got me very excited that this was happening.

Many months earlier we had narrowly avoided Jacques clearing out the attic and the outbuildings before we moved in. The exact scale of the disaster that had been averted became clear over the first year in the château. If ever we needed inspiration, we'd go and look at our collection of goodies; if ever we needed any materials to make or decorate something, we'd have a rummage around. It is almost unbelievable the number of items there were left in the château, but if you imagine collecting anything that is no longer used, wanted, serviceable or required over a period of more than a century and tucking it all out of the way, that is what had happened here. There was no rubbish collection in our part of France and it came as a bit of a surprise to us both that there still isn't today. Obviously, there was less consumerism in those days, and we would expect those running the house for the family to be frugal, but still the Bagliones would have been materially wealthy. The collection of magazines alone was impressive and showed that as family they were creatures of habit. There were complete sets of informative magazines dating back to before the First World War, and from after the Second World War there was an abundance of fashion and ladies' magazines, and even collections of hunting magazines.

There were numerous items of furniture that had migrated five floors up to the attic and were heavy enough that no one had any desire to bring them down again. There were bed frames, daybeds, huge wardrobes, broken armchairs, bathroom furnishings, religious artefacts ... the list goes on. And then there were many other bits of real treasure: a side saddle, old books, pictures, Victorian clothing, even the remains of French muskets that could easily have dated back to before the battle of Waterloo. And there's actually a whole corner of the attic that we have not even cleared out yet. Angela gets quite excited thinking about all the treasures that are still hidden up there.

And it wasn't just the main château that had relics of the past tucked away. Every outbuilding was also full of items left behind and, like the attic in the château, there are still some areas yet to be explored.

The owners of the house would have lived in the high-status rooms. Everything above and below would have been occupied by the servants working and living with them. It is not difficult to imagine that in the liberated post-war years, when servants were no longer the norm, it would not have been easy to carry lots of unwanted items back down the ninety-two steps from the attic. It would have been much easier just to leave everything where it was and ignore the fact it was there unless someone wanted something.

The attic always felt like my special place and not just because of the endorphins running through my veins by the time I got to the top. The light was hazy up there but it was the one floor that I had no issues with being full of dust. In fact, in the right light, the floating particles looked like fairy dust.

One afternoon, when Arthur was playing pirates with my dad, Dorothy and I went for a nosey. I had been up there a number

of times before, but never for long enough. Dorothy was in a papoose, so was very content, and I had time to explore. The first thing that struck me was how dry it felt in the attic. Considering how long things had been sat there for, nothing felt damp. As you walk around the final staircase with the lovely cast-iron rods still featuring intricate details, you approach an old grey wooden door. It always squeaked – I suppose you would expect that – and it still does even now.

The ceilings in parts of the attic are twenty-feet high, and the same shape as the château below, which is breathtaking. The attic has a couple of workrooms as well as these high-vaulted spaces. When you look up, you can see the thousands of pieces of wood put together once upon a time to make the roof. I can't but wonder at the craftsmanship that went into this, with none of the technology we have today. It's beautiful. The first thing you notice in the room is the very large storage wardrobes. They are most certainly twelve-feet tall and made in hardwood; they were built to last. The wardrobes were full of old clothes, Victorian underclothes, sailors' outfits. I was fascinated by the wonderfully shaped hangers. A couple of them looked like they were faces. I had never seen anything like it and the variety was exceptional.

Next to the large wardrobes is a wall cabinet, about six-feet tall. This end of the attic was only ever used for storage as it was darker than the others because it only gets light from one small window that is used to access the roof and a few holes that were soon to get fixed. A heavyweight cloth was draped over the cabinet. I approached it, both excited and nervous to find out what was underneath. There is nothing like some adrenaline to get you going when you're about to uncover something in a quiet, calm attic.

I could feel my heart beating as I pulled down the cloth. There in front of me was every unused scrap of wallpaper left over from the château's 150 years, all in impeccable condition. I knew at that moment what this meant: we had the design history of the château in our hands. It made me shudder just thinking about Jacques putting this all on the fire. With Dorothy on my hips I could only take five minutes to see if I recognised anything. The first thing that jumped out at me were leftovers of the paper from the entrance hall. I did not even want to touch them until I came back equipped. I was treating them like I had found a family of endangered dodos. This was a priceless find and I knew it.

Half the battle to get a job done for us was understanding the system and the processes in France. Artisans don't just come and do a job. They visit, discuss the work and then produce a quote. The quote then has to be countersigned and returned before they will even put the job into their diary. That is all very simple compared to getting a new sewage system for the château and coach house. For that we needed a survey. Having sought some advice, we were directed to Monsieur Jean-Luc Bechu (the man who did surveys). We booked him to come and visit. He came and visited. And when we accepted the quote he then arranged to come back and do the survey. We knew that the coach house would one day become a residence for Jenny and Steve, so we had arranged for the survey to cover both properties, partly to save time downstream, but mainly because it was much cheaper than having two separate visits and documents produced.

On the day of the survey, I ensured I had time to shadow M. Bechu so I could fully understand the options and make an informed decision as to which solution we would commission. After the obligatory cup of coffee and niceties we discussed the occupation of the château and the planned number of bathrooms, toilets and kitchens. To an extent, it was educated guesswork; we knew we would be living in the château all year round and that during the wedding season we would be having about a dozen weddings, with guests staying in our suites and other rooms, but we were not sure of the numbers that might be coming for the day of the celebrations. We also expected to host guests for gourmet weekends, but we didn't know how many and how often. Actually, to coin a phrase I use when troubleshooting in industry, it was all a bit of a PIDOOMA* when it came to the numbers. We had talked about our business a lot, but we still had no idea what shape it would eventually take. So I decided to err on the cautious side, as it would not be good if our guests generated too much poopage!

We walked around and discussed options. It was very interesting, in the way that only a conversation about dealing with sewage can be, and M. Bechu and I agreed the best way forward. He then went away, promising to get me everything in writing as soon as he possibly could as he knew I could do nothing until I had copies of his report to show the mayor's office, the installer and the wonderfully named SPANC†. Sadly, it was to take another three months to get the reports we needed, but apparently that was not a terribly long time.

During my London years, one of my favourite pastimes was going for walks along the Regent's Canal. Often to meet friends, then with Dick and, in my last couple of years, pregnant and then with a Silver Cross pram. I was always fascinated by the wild flowers and

---

* Pulled It Directly Out of My Ass.
† I have never tried to find out what the letters stand for. It is enough for me to know that it's the local government department responsible for sewage works and that they would be coming to visit to check our installation was everything it should be.

foliage that grew along the banks. It was beautiful and natural and was the closest thing to nature I had. The water calmed me, and Dick and I always said we wanted to be near water. But, like many, I was living to feed my busy life and pay my bills, so my walks were not as often as I would have liked.

I never imagined in my wildest dreams that we would have our own 'canal' sanctuary one day. That we would have the freedom to walk with the family every day, twice, three times . . . more! When Dick was away, this became a part of my daily rhythm. The closeness to nature was soothing and gave time for my mind to breathe. Spotting a new wild flower could make my day. There were lots of 'first time I saw' moments and when I spoke to Dick on the phone I could hear him getting excited by my excitement. That May I discovered for the first time that we have foxgloves on the left bank of the château – they tower tall and elegant with their purple trumpets that spike at the top. I had never seen wild ones before! On the right of the château, on the island bank and opposite it, were thousands of oversized daisies. I later found out these were called oxeye daisies. And next to these, buttercups . . . in the millions. I picked one and held it under Arthur's chin to see if he liked butter. Then I spotted bishop's lace with its beautiful white delicate flowers – though it actually smells horrid when you pick it! And then there were grasses and ferns.

Spring was joyous and seeing the grounds transform before my eyes felt enchanting . . . Everywhere I looked there was an abundance of shades of green. I saw wild flowers I had never seen before and foliage that I would have paid a fortune for in Columbia Road Flower Market. Dick claims to not be a flower man but he has so much knowledge compared to me. Maybe not as much as he has about other stuff but still enough to impress. I often wonder how he retains so much information . . . It seems to rattle around inside his head and pop to the forefront of his mind when he needs it.

I loved watching the bare branches of our lime trees turn green. They were lush and gigantic and gave me and the kids shelter from the sun. Most days we would take a little blanket and play in the shade of the trees. Arthur was into dinosaurs and building blocks, water and sand and Dorothy was just on the verge of walking . . .

In between filming blocks, Dick flew home to be with us and move things along. There was pressure to get as much done as possible but we also had to make time to be a family. One afternoon, we were all sat together on a blanket under the trees. Dick and I had our feet touching, with our legs stretched out in a V shape that made a diamond. Dorothy was clambering over us both, and then she realised that she had safety walls. Dick held her up and steered her to me . . . and she walked. It was only a couple of steps, but it was her first couple of steps. And then it was her smile, stretching from ear to ear, and the joy in her eyes, the kind of joy that makes you wish you could capture that moment and wrap it up, just in case the memory ever becomes less. That's why it's great to write these moments down. I was elated that Dorothy had taken her first steps when Dick was home. As a biased mum I put it down to her knowledge and understanding of what was going on.

National Geographic had been keeping me busy again with trips to the mountains of Nevada, the forests of New Jersey, the Great Lakes in Michigan and the wilderness of Ohio, but every time I came back we tried to do some exploring of the area around Martigné. The town of Mayenne was no longer the main city in the *département*, that responsibility had moved to Laval, so we felt we should get to know it. Where better to start than the Saturday-morning market, followed by lunch in a small bistro.

The market allegedly starts at about 7am and goes on to 2pm. We have never been there first thing in the morning so have not seen the stallholders set up, but what we do know is that we have also never seen them stay and work all the way through lunch. It's just not French. In the years that we have been going, we have learnt to ensure we have finished our walk around before 12.30pm as the city square very soon becomes empty of stalls.

The first time we arrived in Laval, we really struggled to find somewhere to park. All the car parks were overfilled, with every gap that could take a car being taken, regardless of any marking on the road or the signposts. You do get the feeling that the French don't like rules, despite having so many. The big problem is, as a visitor, or someone new to living in France, you just don't know which ones are taken seriously and which ones aren't so you feel you have to obey them all. Not knowing the local parking etiquette, we kept driving around until we found a small, really convenient, car park with a couple of free spots. We parked up and couldn't believe our luck. I popped my coins in the machine, paying for enough time to walk around and have lunch. Soon after, we discovered that, in our part of France at least, you don't pay to park over lunchtime. Why would you? Everyone civilised is having a two-hour lunch break so there would be no traffic wardens.

The walk from the car park passed the old city walls and went along cobbled streets that must have been one-way if cars were allowed at all. The houses on either side were obviously old, with the wooden frames we would call Tudor, which actually is not accurate, as this part of France, the county of Maine, had gone back to French control in the last decades of the Plantagenets.

In the couple of minutes' walk to the square, we passed a small bistro that was obviously full of locals, as it had absolutely no airs and graces, plastic chairs, Formica tables and a proprietor who could have come out of a sitcom. ('Chez Martine' has since become our café of choice to grab a coffee or a beer.) Just round the corner, we entered the square. It's on a hill and at the bottom is a magnificent 'château', which is actually a modern set of government buildings with the truly historic château tucked away off the corner of the square with ramparts from which you can look over the River Mayenne a long way below.

The market occupies the car park below the cathedral and is loosely organised, with the more 'stall-like' vendors at the bottom of the hill and those selling their own produce, which though gnarly looked really tasty at the top. We set about filling our shopping baskets with a week's supply of vegetables. To our delight, globe artichokes appeared to be in season as most stalls had some. We really enjoy eating this massive member of the thistle family as they cannot be rushed if you are to savour every bit. We peel the top couple of inches of the stalk and then trim it off along with the pointed end. The artichokes are popped into a huge pan of salted, boiling water with half a lemon squeezed into it and the lemon skin tossed in for good measure. It's then a matter of up to 45 minutes simmering until they are cooked. Just before we take them out of the boiling water, we whip up a very quick hollandaise sauce. The so, so rich, bright yellow, velvety sauce is a tad naughty but definitely worth it. Though it's not for the faint-hearted, as by the time you have finished eating the small bits of tender artichoke off each of the individual leaves, one at a time, each dipped in the sauce, and then cut away the inedible seeds to liberate the heart to be sliced and eaten with the remaining sauce, you have been eating and talking for the best part of an hour . . .

....

HOLLANDAISE SAUCE

Enough for two artichokes

Ingredients

3 egg yolks
3 tsp lemon juice
170g salted butter

Method

*Heat the butter in a small pan until it is bubbling. Put the egg
yolks and the lemon juice into a blender. When the butter is
hot, whisk the yolks and lemon juice for about 15 seconds, then
slowly drizzle in the butter. The butter effectively cooks the eggs
and they thicken into a wonderful sauce.*

Serve immediately (preferably with some globe artichokes!)

....

Having filled our baskets, it was a matter of finding somewhere
for lunch. So, with absolutely no idea what was good and what
wasn't, we set off to find a little restaurant. We found La Braise
down a side street and soon the four of us were seated at a table.
As always, we chose different dishes so we could explore the menu.
Arthur had fish from the children's menu and Dorothy nibbled
on what she could reach and delicacies from our bag, while we set
out to try some of the traditional dishes.

One dish stood out, not because it was unusual, but it was special
in its simplicity. The terrine of the day was wonderful. It was obviously pork-based but, as we were to discover in many restaurants,

unless there is some special ingredient like wild boar or venison, there was no more details on the menu. We were to accept that it was *their* terrine – it was like saying 'trust us'. As it was served, the waitress produced a pottery jar with a set of wooden tongs in a little holder on the side. It was ice cold and in it was a mixture of cornichons and small pickled vegetables. With the rich, slightly peppery terrine they were excellent, and we knew we had to get one, so we put it on our list of things to find. We write lots of things down, so we don't forget tasks, inspiration, ideas or even just things we want to eat. It took a trip to Emmaus before we could cross off our cornichon pot but we got there in the end and now we have a collection.

May was a month of sunshine and saw the arrival of summery salads and vegetables in the shops. Tomatoes and strawberries tasted the way they should and we were starting to look forward. We had started planning our wedding and it was growing in size and importance. The sewage system was the last very large task to complete the infrastructure for our utilities, but at least it felt like that was underway now the survey had been done, which was a weight off our shoulders. Though we didn't realise then it would be several months before we even got the results on paper, let alone could start work.

CHAPTER SIX

JUNE

In this month of long days and short nights, we do not have the same heat we can expect in July or August, but everything feels alive and fresh and the productivity of nature has kicked in. This is the time to buy local salads. We were a long way off growing our own produce in the first year, but the supermarkets were starting to fill with locally grown soft fruits, salads, courgettes and aubergines, so we were able to enjoy the seasonal produce even if it wasn't ours just yet.

We didn't see any frogspawn that spring, however, come June, our island was covered in tiny toadlets around a centimetre long. As a family, we started calling them this only to find out it's the real name. There were hundreds if not thousands of them all over the place, all heading in different directions. Arthur was fascinated, so we put one on the palm of his little hand. It tickled him, he smiled and that was the start of a fascination with all sorts of small creatures and bugs. Unfortunately his motor skills still weren't very refined so we had to discourage him from picking them up. It got interesting when he named one Timmy, but luckily they were all called the same thing, which made talking to them easy. The 'plague' of toadlets doesn't happen every year, but it is proving to be a semi-regular occurrence in mid-June, so we tend to keep our eyes open when we walk around just in case. For one day, no ground surface is free of little Timmys. Our part of France is full of wildlife and we were very aware of how much there was to teach the children about nature – but for now the best thing was just to be engulfed in it.

I'd now finally got the first batch of our wedding linens sent, which was twenty-five perfectly formed packages. It was definitely a moment when I wished I was not such a perfectionist. There were still another sixty to be done (so I didn't actually use all those I got Dick to iron . . .), but for now at least our immediate family and friends had theirs. I'd also managed a visit to our local village post office for the first time. The post office is just five minutes away luckily, as it took three trips to successfully send them. The first was on a Monday, when I discovered they are closed all day. Next I went on a Wednesday morning only to find it did not open until 2.30pm. Then I finally I had success on a Friday afternoon. The queue was rather long, and my French was pretty bad, but something must have made sense as a few days later I got calls to say they'd arrived. Although at €4 a pop I was glad we had decided it was to be just one tea towel per family!

Our château is in an area of France that is within striking distance of the UK; however, it is still half a day's drive to Calais or at least a couple of hours to the ports in Normandy with their slightly longer crossings. The English Channel that has kept invaders away for almost two thousand years means most people think twice before heading off for a quick trip to Europe, but such considerations didn't seem to put off anyone we had invited to the wedding. The replies came flooding in. It was obvious we were in for a real party!

I reminded Angela often that before we found the château, we had decided we wanted a small wedding, either with just our parents or eloping overseas. But whenever I said it, I got, 'Well, a girl's allowed to change her mind,' or, 'We didn't have a château then.' Which are hard points to argue against. I would never admit it to Angela, but I was actually very excited. This was to be a gathering of the Strawbridges that was seldom matched.

I come from a big Irish family: I have two older sisters, two younger sisters and two younger brothers, so there are seven of us altogether, plus my mum and dad. We didn't have masses of money growing up but we lacked for nothing – and we were all incredibly close. My love of family and adventure comes from my parents and we used to go on lots of trips. We definitely knew how to have fun. But we'd probably only been all together two or three times in the last couple of decades and, with my older children James and Charlotte also attending with all their families, it was going to be very special. It did, of course, mean that we had a hard deadline. The invitations had gone out and the clock was ticking. The second weekend of November was looming.

I was on the hunt for baths again, but after my earlier very annoying and expensive bath saga I was definitely looking for items that 'needed work'. The savings to be made were huge and France is bursting with gems in need of love. On a previous trip to Rennes I had spotted a *brocante* that looked very exciting. It's always hard to say until you get close, but from the roadside I could see pallets of bricks, statues, lights, baths, pans, iron gates and railings. A bit of everything, in fact. It looked like they had cleared out some old houses and that was exactly what I was looking for. With just over four months until our wedding, I wanted to ensure that the honeymoon suite was ready and looking good.

First, I needed a bath, and I had a romantic vision of a cast-iron roll-top bath with ornate claw feet. It was to go on the left-hand wall in the bathroom, next to the shower and looking out through the six-foot-tall windows onto the moat. One of the biggest problems with all the visual eye candy you can now find online is that you always see the 'one' but often then find out it's an old photo or a one-off item sold in auction twenty years ago for thousands of pounds. I find it nearly impossible to find 'the one' and then find it for sale, so Dick and I have a rolling shopping list of items to keep our eye out for. We have been searching for a Rouen duck press for six years. I knew I had to manage my expectations. If I found a cast-iron bath of any kind I should be happy, I said to myself as I drove to the *brocante* that day.

Arthur and Dorothy were with my parents that day as I wanted time to look around. *Brocantes* are different from Emmaus. In these markets, the jewels have already been selected and for that a premium is put on the price. I had dreams of it being like Spitalfields antique market in east London. I had spent many a Thursday noseying around Spitalfields and I knew many of the traders got their stock from France – and now I had direct access. I couldn't wait.

On arrival, I drove through a big cast-iron double gate with ten-foot statues of lions on either side (I had a quick word with myself to check this was not something to add to my shopping list. It was not). Next I drove past pallets of terracotta tiles, bricks and parquet flooring – there must have been upwards of fifty pallets. All good to know for the future. On the right, there were layers upon layers of cast-iron gates, fences and outdoor seats. And in every direction there were statues: angels, chickens, roosters, pigs and more lions. The place was gigantic and full, so the parking was minimal. There were spaces for just three cars and a tiny circle to turn round in to exit. I knew this would stress me out later but for now I just wanted to get inside.

In front of a charming two-storey stone building, I found a thrifter's paradise: tens of chipped enamel jugs and bowls, cutlery, benches, a whole row of sinks, toilets, vases. This was beauty. I could not wait to peek inside, but for the moment I had to keep my focus: I was looking for the perfect bath.

Dick's mum Jenny has two sayings she always repeats: 'The harder you work, the luckier you get,' and, 'If it's meant for you, it won't go by you.' I'm not sure which was in play that day, but just as I arrived, right by the front door, I spotted a spectacular bath. It was rotten and rusty, but it had the most beautiful roll-top and 30cm cast-iron claw feet. I couldn't believe my eyes. The claw feet were more ornate and perfect than anything I had ever seen. I knew it needed work but that didn't matter, the shape was perfect and big enough for two people (it was going in the honeymoon suite after all!). I quickly ran inside.

As I entered the small wooden doorway, I was relieved that the kids were at home; every square inch of space was filled and piled high with china, glassware, linens, religious artefacts, guns, lights, pictures, mirrors. Every cabinet that was displaying the wares was for sale as well as every item inside them. It took every ounce of my focus not to stop. Eventually, I found the lady in charge, boxed in behind more glass cabinets. I waited by the counter for her attention. Every second that passed felt like an hour. First she was writing something, then she finished . . . and I waited. Then she put her pen back in the drawer and moved some bits around . . . very slowly. At that moment I couldn't be quiet any more. Maybe she just couldn't see me past the cabinets? '*Bonjour,*' I uttered in a very cockney but happy tone. She looked up slowly and smiled.

I tried to change my pace to suit the lady and softly asked if the bath was for sale (well, at least, I think that's what I said). Dick and I have been told that it takes two years to change your pace when you move to France. Five years in and I'm sure we are quicker than ever, or we try to be, but I know for sure I definitely wasn't operating at French pace that day. We finally got to the bath after much gesticulating and it *was* for sale – and the best bit about it: it was only €125. Luck was on my side that day!

Mission completed, I had time to peruse. The *brocante* was fascinating and full of so much similar stuff to that which we had inherited in our own château: magazines, newspapers, enamel jugs, daybeds, cots and clothes galore. I tried to buy the bits we didn't have at the Emmaus because they were so cheap, but this place had everything we could ever need, plus lots more that I never knew we needed!

And then I spotted the *globe de mariage**. I had seen one of these once before in Spitalfields. It was selling for £500, which I could never have afforded, but I'd always dreamt of finding another one. And this one was just €85. Bargain. I had to have it.

Then, on my way out, I spotted another bath, not as nice as the first but still very elegant and ideal for one of the other future suites at the château. With that, my shopping was done and I even managed to get delivery of the baths arranged for the following day.

It can be argued that there are very good reasons why cast-iron baths are no longer the norm for a modern bathroom. None of those reasons are about the aesthetics. They do look good and there is a

---

* A *globe de mariage* is a traditional French wedding gift that was popular in the mid-nineteenth century. Originally it was used to collect the bride's wedding bouquet. Later the beautiful glass bell jar became a popular way of containing and protecting other wedding souvenirs.

The orangery.

Welcome
to
Angel
&
Dick's
Wedding
Celebration

ANGEL
&
DICK
15 NOVEMBER 2015

Arthur ready to party.

You are about to witness

DICK &
ANGEL

Tying the knots.

Our wedding day, 13 November 2015.

The wedding party.

Overleaf: With our mums and family.

degree of permanency, as they are built to last – even if the last fifty years of the bath's life may be spent outside servicing the animals, after the enamel is no longer acceptable for human bottoms. When Angela found the first of her old baths, I know categorically that she did not even think about how it would be restored, she would just have had a vision of it completed and looking wonderful. Of course, knowing how much we had to pay for the bath in our suite she rightly assessed that there was a lot of scope to pay for restoration and still save money on a new cast-iron bath. Even lower on her list of practical observations would have been how to plumb it in, get a matching plug or get it up five or six flights of stairs . . . I did get my own way in insisting we move it the minimum distance until it was restored and its final destination was known (and that didn't mean a rough idea of where it was going. It meant knowing where the plug and taps were going to be and the exact position of the beautiful claw feet).

We managed to manhandle the bath into what was going to be our kitchen in the *sous sol*, just the two of us. Obviously, it would have been impossible for the two of us to carry the bath, but by setting it on a remover's blanket and with a lot of pushing and pulling, and lifting one corner at a time, we got it into what was to be our family kitchen.

As the centre of activities for the staff of the château, the floor had become worn, where for over a century working feet had moved between the stove, the hand pump for water, the large sink for preparing vegetables and the pantry and cold room. Like every other room, it had been cleared out and brushed down so all that was left was the bare bones of the room. We had been very excited by the original solid-fuel stove we had found in the kitchen. The firebox would have taken wood from the estate and it would have been used for cooking for every function at the château. It had a lovely stamp on it saying it had been made in Laval and, though it did look very tired, we had great hopes for it . . . Sadly, when we cleaned it, it disintegrated. It had truly been held together by the thin layer of enamel. All the metal had rusted into nothing and wiping it caused it to crumble. We couldn't even lift it up as the top came away and the four sides imploded, so it had been shovelled out and replaced by the Rayburn. The chimney recess that had housed the original stove was conveniently situated near the dumb waiter that would rush up dishes to the service kitchen adjacent to the dining room. In an older plan, it looked as if there was a bread oven in the pantry behind the stove, but we found no evidence of it.

The layout of the château had been well thought through and one of the things we found to be very special was the fact that everything 'flowed' so well. If you consider any activity we may wish to conduct in the château, certain facilities are required, and these facilities have to be relatively close to one another or it all becomes very difficult. For example, if the main reception room is separated from the dining room it becomes awkward when moving from one to the other after aperitifs at the start of the evening or to retire from the table after eating. Similarly, food has to be served at its best so the kitchen and dining room need to be thoughtfully situated. We had it all and even though not a lot was functioning, we could clearly see what was going to be in the future.

At this point, our kitchen, which we would need to have fully working before the wedding, was an empty shell and we hadn't even allowed ourselves to talk about the design as we'd had other priorities. However, it was the perfect location to work on bath restoration as it did not have many people pass through it and it was spacious. It was just important for it to be clear in plenty of time to get the kitchen done.

* * *

My trips to America finished on a high – I had been mining for gold in Oregon and being a lumberjack in Washington State. And yet returning to the Mayenne was like being granted my freedom. All I had to do was work on the château for the rest of the year – after that, who knew what would happen. It was great to be home, especially as I knew this time I would not be leaving again. I was able to walk around and fully appreciate how beautiful the setting was and how lucky we were. With Dorothy on my knee and Arthur cuddled up beside me, Angel produced a couple of wonderful mugs of tea and we sat down to simply enjoy being together.

As every Brit knows, tea abroad tends to be an abomination. In America they don't quite get it, and lots of people drink it ice cold with flavouring added. In France, when you order a *thé* they bring it with lemon and if you ask for milk they look at you as if you are a little odd. They then seem to really want to give you warm milk – what is that about? It also never quite brews into proper tea. Maybe it's the tea in the actual bag? It gives the semblance of being British by using English words, but maybe the water is not hot enough? Or maybe it's because they tend not to use a teapot? Maybe it's the milk that they put in too early – is it actually milk? Whatever the reasons, we learnt very early on that to have a good cup of tea you need to make it yourself with tea imported from home! We like tea and have many different makes and blends in stock, as you would expect in a château housing a notable tea party hostess. We also have a supply of Tetleys or PG Tips at hand that runs into hundreds, if not thousands, of teabags. We sometimes have cups and saucers with a teapot and milk jug but if we are working we opt for fine, straight-sided, bone china mugs. It tastes different and, interestingly, neither of us like the mugs that flare wider at the top (little details like this allow us to believe we were made for each other). We discuss lots over a cup of tea and from a very early age both children have joined us with a weaker, cooler, sweeter brew, that allows us all the opportunity to conduct the ritual of tea and cake – or, now in France, *thé* and patisseries.

With the family united in the château once more, it didn't take us long to discuss what we had achieved and where we were in our restoration. We'd done so much and, amazingly, we'd managed to keep the momentum going despite the separation. We had the infrastructures for our heating and plumbing and electricity in. We knew what was going where and the routes of the electric cables; waste, hot and cold water and heating were all established. There was lots more to do but we had the skeleton of our system sorted. It was messy, though. In many rooms we had holes in our walls that looked like huge rock-boring rats had been making themselves at home. The routes for the electricity had been chased out of the walls in many rooms, though we had limited the number of sockets in an attempt to minimise the devastation. Our family's suite was functioning and safe. And we also had a couple of functioning rooms upstairs on the fourth level (called the second floor).

The whole naming system of the floors in the château appeared to be there to confuse you. The basement or the *sous sol* was basically three steps down from the level of the land – all very sensible. When approached from the outside, the second level was up a sweeping set of granite steps; fourteen on each side leading to an amazing front door. This level, the *rez-de-chaussée,* was the ground floor. The next level up, the third, was the first floor. After that, four levels up, was the second floor. Then on the fifth level was the attic, or the *grenier*. Then, just to make it all very clear, the sixth and final level was actually an attic.

The entrance hall, the salon and the dining room had all been stripped of unwanted paint and wallpaper and some of the electricity was nearly ready to connect. There is always a low point before you start to reconstruct. Unfortunately for us, we hadn't even reached the lowest point and we hadn't been hanging around. Making good was going to take a lot of effort.

We were sitting looking at each other, trying to concentrate on the positives and our achievements, when the penny dropped: the clock that had been ticking was halfway to our wedding deadline. We didn't actually panic but there was a very definite, if unspoken, 'Oh f***!' There was nothing for it – we would have to cut back on our sleep, which is not easily done as we had young children who slept like a nocturnal tag team. The candles would be burnt at both ends.

I was jumping daily from feeling really motivated and focused on a project to feeling frightfully overwhelmed. The trick was not to think too far ahead as the worry halts you. Instead, you need to focus on the project in front of you. In practice, this worked. Dick often says, and I'm sure he will mention this once or twice in this book, 'You eat an elephant a bite at a time.' I really under-stood this, but the issue was I did need to think ahead because I had to order bathroom suites and ensure things were planned. I'm an organised list person but the pure scale of the messy jobs that still needed to be done was terrifying at times. Dick could hear my frustration. We were just so far off starting any pretties. If I started anything, it would soon be trashed – the grubby work was still in full flow.

We took control of this and a 'grubby' worksheet was started and attached to each door. This allowed Dick and I to see exactly where we were on each of the suites, but still the seed was sown: what we initially thought in January would be done by now would obviously not all be completed in time for the wedding.

We needed to know where we were in our work in each room. Now we had taken stock of what had to be done, it was just a matter of doing it all. Sounds easy, but most of the château still felt like a building site and the mess was positively wearing.

On the more positive side, summer had arrived, we had enough baths – even if they weren't good enough to use yet – and my days of working in America had finally come to an end so all of our efforts could now be dedicated to the château.

CHAPTER SEVEN

JULY

Through our first spring and summer in the château it hardly ever seemed to rain. There was definitely very little between April and October. We had moved south but we didn't know how hot it would be. We had spent some time during summer visits much further south and were very aware that it was hard to work and remain productive with temperatures in the thirties or forties. When the temperatures reached the thirties in London, we found it nearly impossible to breathe as even the buildings were giving off heat. With all that in mind, and particularly now we had focused on what we really had to get done before the wedding, we were a little anxious about what it would be like come summer. Plus we had the moat – were we going to be overwhelmed by mosquitoes and midges?

Thankfully, the heat has never been truly debilitating at the château. The same mechanism that makes the château hard to heat up keeps it cool. The thick stone walls are slow to respond to the vagaries of the weather. In addition, the shutters really do help. On the south side of the château, there are slatted external shutters that can be closed to keep out direct sunshine, but with the windows open inside the shutters there is movement of air that, even if it is not cool, is welcome. If it all becomes too much, then a trip to the basement, where all the floors of the *caves* (the wine and cider cellars) are rammed earth and therefore naturally regulated, will soon help you cool down. None of that helps, however, if you have to work.

When it comes to our fear of mosquitoes and biting insects, we have been very pleasantly surprised by the complete lack of a problem. We are fortunate enough to have an ecosystem that seems to be in balance. We do have plenty of insects but they have lots of predators. In the larval stage when the insects are in the moat there are lots of fish – and let's not forget that we have toads and frogs too. When the insects leave the water, they are subjected to an aerial bombardment day and night. Swallows, dragonflies and other 'hawkers' are abundant during the daylight hours and as dusk arrives so does a cloud of bats ... We love them all. Dragonflies have been surprisingly wonderful as they patrol above the water to pick off the emerging flying insects – with colours so vibrant you have to do a double take to see what is there.

* * *

At the beginning of July I realised that we hadn't taken any time off just for ourselves. The château and my trips back and forth across the Atlantic had been all-consuming. So Angela decided to fix that by organising a short break away for the four of us while the château was being sprayed and treated to ensure no woodworm or boring creatures would be dining on our structure. The idea was wonderful – but a relaxing break to ... *Disneyland*? There are very few times that 'relaxing' and 'Disney' work in the same sentence and to make it even more interesting and a 'home from home' experience, after my survival series in America, we stayed at a log cabin in Davy Crockett land.

In the end though it was very special being together without the list of jobs hanging over our heads and we had a great time. We tried not to do too much – though the park itself is an endurance test. That said, we had a ball. Looking at the magical world of Disney through the eyes of our children who believed everything and loved it all was so worthwhile. After the park, we would go back to the log cabin so the children could nap and then to the swimming pool for hours, followed by more eating, then sleeping, then up and out again. As we were staying at one of the resort hotels we had early admission to the parks, so we would get in early and have fun on the teacups and then maybe go around the Small World ride a couple of times. I had never heard of the Small World ride but by the end of day one the song was inside my head, to stay for ever. Disney definitely know what they are doing!

We returned to our version of reality surprisingly reinvigorated and ready to tackle our to-do list. Which was lucky, as we had recently come to realise that there would be at least 150 guests for our wedding! Catering for them all meant we were going to need all the crockery, glassware and cutlery that had been safely put into storage when we packed up all the kit from Angela's vintage events company. As storage costs are high, we had made the decision to send everything to Northern Ireland to be stored in the recently reroofed outbuildings of the Strawbridge family home. It saved us a fortune and we knew it was safe but the only slight issue was getting the many treasures to France. For once, we had time on our side and, after some research, we put the task onto a 'man and van' website, allowing people with an empty vehicle on the way to France but a load coming home to bid to bring us our load. It was surprisingly easy and reasonably priced as the van was taking the ferry from Ireland to France anyway and would practically be passing us. Though, typically, not everything ran smoothly. The van was not quite as big as advertised so when the team turned up to collect everything it was obvious that it would not fit . . . The Strawbridge ladies came to the rescue and we inherited the old family trailer that was hooked onto the back of the van loaded with all the items that would not fit!

When the van arrived with all its contents it was like a Christmas party. Everything was unloaded into the tack room in the stable block as it was dry and clean and in good condition. There were toolboxes of hair and make-up equipment, cast-iron vintage tables with display cases full of vintage ornaments, magazines and displays of memorabilia going back to before the Second World War. There were urns, top hats, feather boas and hundreds of vintage teacups, side plates, teapots, milk jugs, sugar bowls . . . the list went on and on. The Vintage Patisserie had come to France.

I was smiling and remembering the hundreds of hen parties and celebrations I had hosted over the years in London. I hadn't forgotten how lovely all my kit was, I just hadn't remembered how much wonderful stuff I had. We didn't have time to get everything out but while we stacked it away, I was making mental notes about what was to go where. Thinking about the future celebrations that would happen in the château was an escapism I loved. The first would obviously be our wedding – what a great way to start! But I was also picturing Arthur and Dorothy's weddings here one day . . . It would all look beautiful. All my kit would be clean and organised and I would know exactly where everything was. I could almost taste the laughter and it made me smile.

Back in the real world, our November deadline was fast approaching and there were a number of longer-lead-time items that needed sorting. As we were going to get married in France we needed to do all the paperwork well in advance. We left ourselves

what we thought was plenty of time and after a quick visit to the *mairie* we started to pull it all together.

I knew I was going to be responsible for this task, so I accepted with only a little bit of chuntering. We booked the date with the *mairie*; he was going to marry us on 13 November, exactly five years after what we consider to be our first date. That could be classed as romantic but for me it was efficient as it meant we just had one date to remember! We chaps are always getting ourselves into bother by forgetting something important, so it was completely irrelevant that the date was Friday the thirteenth . . .

The file of paperwork grew very quickly with requests for information (in French, obviously). The next months were filled with a steady to and fro, getting information then getting it translated by a court-certified translator. It wasn't slow, it wasn't fast, it was just a relentless grind ensuring every document was found and processed in good time. One of the challenges was to get a certified-copy of an entry of my birth from the consul general at Rangoon from 3 September 1959. How many people can say they have a French version of their birth certificate from Burma? Angela needed forms to say she could get married: a '*certificat de célibat*' and a '*certificat de capacité matrimoniale*'. I was worried about the certificate of celibacy, but in the end it was meant in the past tense. The list was endless: from my divorce documentation in French, to the '*déclaration des témoins*', which was a full documentation set for each witness. As we wanted my mother and Angela's parents, Jenny and Steve, to witness our marriage, we had to fill out lots of different documents for them too, including proving that our witnesses were alive. That was a novel challenge. My mum was all for speaking to someone and telling them in no uncertain terms she was alive and kicking! Being new to the village, I felt that was probably not a great thing to do.

We were also introduced to France's Napoleonic inheritance laws and were advised that we needed to sort out a prenuptial agreement. I had no idea about the Napoleonic Code*. Amongst other things, it sets out rules in relation to divorce, inheritance and property ownership. The idea was to get rid of privilege based on birth and to establish universal property rights and freedom of religion. The code imposed a uniform civil law on France, which previously had had more than 400 separate legal codes in the different regions. Because of piecemeal amendments, the laws are sometimes unclear and inconsistent, which goes a way towards explaining our feeling that the French legal system is complex and impenetrable. It would appear that real estate in France was governed by French succession laws dating back to 1804, which include compulsory inheritance provisions. It is not all bad. It's just confusing. For example, children are 'protected heirs' and cannot be disinherited, they receive a certain proportion of the estate, depending on their number and on the existence of a surviving spouse. As we are a modern family, with my older children and grandchildren, we had to understand the system and the implications for us.

I have always used notebooks and they often end up containing lots of valuable information, but a subject can be spread over several months or years so the info can be in several books. In an attempt to understand our new life, I dedicated a notebook to 'The System' and have collected information about the many taxes and payments made through the year. There are lots of websites that help to explain life in France, but it was only when I started writing down what was to leave our bank account and that I started to come to terms with how it all worked. Without even trying to navigate running a business over here, we needed to ensure we kept paying our *ordures ménagères, eau, foncière* and *habitation* taxes as

---

* The civil legal framework of France, established in 1804 by Napoleon Bonaparte.

and when they were required*. We managed to stay on top of our commitment to the *commune*† and to the government and, over the next months, collated many documents and processes.

As the wedding approached, the demand for documentation grew, despite having a what I believed to be a definitive list that I was working to. Our parents' 'witness' dossiers were almost as thick as ours and it was when, the week before our wedding, we had a request for Arthur and Dorothy's birth certificates in French at the last moment that enough was enough. My head popped a bit and I explained in that slow and rather menacing tone that says 'this is the end of any patience I may have had', that they were not getting married! After only the briefest of pauses the administrator collating our documentation just shrugged and replied, 'OK'. Which immediately raised the question of whether or not I should have pushed back weeks earlier and how much was actually needed.

Our experience of doing all that was necessary to get married in the French system and get our *Livret de Famille*‡ reaffirmed the plans we had had before we left England: that we should only host wedding celebrations at the château and not attempt to do official civil ceremonies. We now knew first-hand that the paperwork, and the requirement for bride and groom to be resident in France for more than forty days, would preclude this from happening.

* * *

If we were to do all we needed to before the wedding it was important that we complete some of the projects as soon as possible, but

---

*   If you own a property in France, you have to pay waste collection tax, water tax, ownership tax and residence tax.
†   A *commune* is a local administrative unit. There are 242 *communes* in our *département* of Mayenne.
‡   A *Livret de Famille* is a family record book that is issued when you get married in France.

it was proving very difficult to get to the stage where we could decorate and then close the door and say a room was finished. Across a very wide front, we were making progress but also causing a mess. We tried not to chase out the walls to hide the electric cabling and instead looked at positioning switches and sockets so that the path for the cables would be behind panelling or, in the case of the rooms on the main ground floor, we took the cables through the cellar and then popped them up where necessary. And it is fair to say we were erring on the side of less rather than more when it came to sockets. But even with the minimalist approach, there were still many holes in the walls and lots of floorboards lifted up. Next we had to address one of the major tasks in our quest to get the ground floor ready for guests: to plaster and decorate the main staircase and the walls around it.

The stairway and landing above must have been cold during the winter months so, at some point, someone had decided to install a wood-burning stove beside the stairs. We deduced this from the sheet of metal on the floor beside the stairs; the hole in the wall in a beautiful ornamental alcove that sloped upwards and was about the diameter of a flue and finally, the tar dripping down the inside of the wall of the main entrance hall. But that wasn't all. If you looked up through the two-foot-thick hole in the wall, you could see another hole cut through a stair on the final stairway leading to the attic and, through that, a charred hole (the flue must have been hot!). Then if you looked up a further thirty feet you would see a very badly patched, slightly burnt hole in the roof. All the evidence suggested that it must have been a sizeable stove complete with a bare metal chimney that went up through four floors and out of the roof. It would probably have been effective, but it definitely wouldn't have conformed to any modern regulation!

We had not been successful with plasterers previously and decided once again to try to find French artisans to help us, as they should have the expertise to patch and tidy up the eight-metre-high ceiling and large expanses of wall. We found a company who came recommended and were based just under an hour away from us. We had a visit from the owner and discussed what was required and agreed that it was mainly patching and skimming over the walls, so he headed off to get us a quote. It arrived quite quickly but it just didn't make sense. As they were nearly an hour away, hotel accommodation had been added so the poor little poppets didn't have to drive. This accounted for €4,000 of the total bill. When you added the €6,000 scaffolding hire they had included for the two-week job, the total bill was over €20,000. OK, the ceiling was high, but this was taking the mickey, so it was back to the drawing board.

But it did motivate me to immediately start looking for scaffolding on *Leboncoin**. Within a week, I had a trailer and roof rack full of *échafaudage*† and a plan to build an island in the sky. Then the roof could be plastered by anyone with plastering experience. The plan was simple: from the first landing I would raise scaffolding to within two metres of the ceiling. I would then take that as my level and build scaffolding up the other two secondary flights of stairs and across the upper landing. So I would end up with a square of scaffolding round the edges that could not fall inwards because it was all connected and couldn't fall outwards because of the walls. All that left was a great big hole in the middle. After a little head scratching, I had a chat with Jacques and asked where I could get some seven-metre beams from. Serendipity to the fore and Jacques pointed to the eight he had lying in his barn. There followed some humping and dumping. And, to cut a long and slightly painful story short, I had the beams screwed down with plywood over the

---

*   A French buying and selling site similar to Gumtree.
†   Scaffolding.

top two metres below the ceiling. We had an island in the sky. Over to Angela to find our plasterer . . .

The monstrosity that Dick built to allow us to plaster the stairway was definitely strong. I watched him test it by bouncing right in the middle with a pile of 40kg bags of plaster. What didn't seem to register with him was the fact that the scaffold also came halfway up the door of our suite and blocked most of the stairs. Access was definitely an issue, especially with the children in tow. To give him his dues, he did smile as he gave me one of the Gallic shrugs that annoy him so much when other people do it.

Before I started the search for a plasterer, I wanted to assess our decorating options and ensure we needed one. The original wallpaper in the entrance hall was yellow, green and brown. The pattern was regal and very attractive but the colour felt heavy and depressing. It didn't have the light airiness that one would expect when one enters a château. This wallpaper continued all the way through to the back of the grand entrance and under the stairs and because of the shapes of the walls here, it made your eyes go funny. I can't lie; there was a part of me that loved it, but it was not right for our wedding venture.

The second big issue, apart from the black tar damage on the walls, was the dark green geometric wallpaper that covered the grand staircase, all the way to the high ceiling. Again, I quite liked it, but it was far too dark and depressing for the staircase and it was also very tatty. I could not see how to bring this back to life.

Julian, a local ex-pat handyman, had stripped most of the wallpaper in the rooms now – a terribly messy but satisfying job. I love stripping walls of their paper. It's something that you can't rush and it always gives me such satisfaction when a piece comes off in a big roll. But there were weeks and weeks of work to strip our château, so where possible we had to find grafters that were

on our side. So now Julian moved on to the entrance hall and the staircase.

The uncovered lime-plaster walls were a thing of beauty. The patina was like a work of art. I actually loved it and quickly imagined the woodwork round the windows looking glossy to frame the 'art'. I was also falling in love with the natural light that reflected from the walls once the dark paper was no more. The whole château felt different. Calmer.

The salon also really suited the lime-plaster look. With its high ceilings and gold plaster coving, it was a visual feast. It felt inauspicious to cover it up with new plaster. Dick and I had a several words on this matter. When I looked at the walls, I saw history and the pattern of history. Dick saw unfinished walls.

One of my favourite haunts in London is Wilton's Music Hall. It is located in my part of the city, Whitechapel, in east London, and became a music hall around 1850 when John Wilton turned a row of houses into the Great Music Hall. Many of the original features still exist and the hall is stunning. I particularly love that, in parts, it is really dilapidated. The hall is still going strong with concerts, plays and weddings, but I always thought if someone had covered its history and got rid of its Constantine furniture it would have lost its magic. I felt the same about the château. But Dick still stood by the walls looking unfinished.

The compromise came one evening when one of our friends called. He was Dick's friend actually, an artist called Dhirmad. He has been commissioned to do lots of rather amazing projects – he sculpted the bronze Peter Pan and Tinker Bell sculpture outside Great Ormond Street Hospital, for example, and he was currently working on a design for a restaurant owned by a famous chef. I knew if anyone would understand my vision it would be him, so we FaceTimed and I showed him around. Now, I quote: 'Dick, I'm getting paid millions to create the look of age and cracks you have naturally inherited.' And with that information, I managed to retain that natural plaster look on the undamaged side of the salon and under the stairs. For the rest, the search for a plasterer began.

I am a member of an ex-pat business advertising site and this is where I spent a great half hour contacting everyone under the heading 'plasterer'. That was how we found Steve. His wife Denise answered when I first called; Steve was working away at the time but she said he would get back to us by the weekend and, just as promised, he did. The following week, he came to have a look at the work and we knew straight away that he was the right man for the job. 'I'm a real plasterer,' he said when I told him the horror stories of our previous plasterers complaining their arms hurt. I burst into tears and hugged him. He didn't seem that comfortable at my outburst of appreciation but I knew he was going to play a massive part in helping us meet our deadlines. Steve was the knight in shining armour we needed.

The first task Steve did for us was to plaster what was to be the children's playroom. The installation of the wood burners with back boilers had meant the pipework associated with it had come out of the back of the fireplace into this room that was described as a 'chambre' on the plans, but was what we would have classed as a 'snug' off the main sitting room. We had routed it behind the wooden panelling to the corner of the room and from there it headed up four floors but also downwards to the basement, in case we needed to connect it to a future biomass system. As the room was now to be a playroom for the children, the heating pipes needed to be boxed in and boarded over. We also decided to remove the marble fireplace and board that over and then the whole room needed to be skimmed. The task was made more interesting by the ceilings being the best part of five metres high. But with no fuss, and a good work ethic, Steve cracked on and, within a couple of days, we had a room with walls ready to decorate. The woodwork needed more attention but it was a major step in the right direction.

After passing the first test with flying colours, the dining room was next on Steve's list. Only two walls required his attention in there and we booked him in immediately. Thereafter, we employed Steve whenever we could afford him and over time he has become a bit of a fixture at the château.

My mind was so full of château renovations that I had to pull my focus away and get my head around who was going to host our wedding. Never have I, or will I, be in a position where I'm not watching over the details at an event, but Dick and lots of our friends and family had already spoken to me and asked that I please step down from being 'me' and just be the bride for the day. It's actually harder said than done and I knew the only chance I had was if I called in my A-team: my beautiful and very talented hosts from the Vintage Patisserie days. With years of experience of being charming and making and pouring cocktails in teapots, I knew I could trust them to be my eyes and ears on the day and then maybe I'd have a chance to relax. Sharon, Fleur, Sophia, Bethany, Lucy and my first-ever hostess Leah came to the rescue and front of house was covered.

Next we had to organise the kitchen and I knew Dick was not going to let anyone leave without being fed delicious food from the château kitchen. For that we booked our chef friend Alan. We knew we would have lots of family on hand to help but we also called in the support of a couple of other working chefs. With just over three months to go, our wedding was starting to feel real.

With activity in the château reaching fever pitch, it was time for a quick break and a family outing to Mayenne. This beautiful historic town, ten minutes to the north of the château, had been the centre of the administration of the area before the prefecture moved to Laval, the much larger city to our south. With the move of all the administrative posts a lot of employment has gone, so now it is a fairly quiet town on the banks of the river that shares its name. If we need to pop to a supermarket we go to Mayenne, but we'd never really explored the town itself. We decided that lunchtime was the right time to see what was on offer and, rather than going straight to the centre, we decided to look along the riverbanks. There is an old saying, 'I'd rather be lucky than smart', and we hit pay dirt on our first outing. The Beau Rivage is a lovely little hotel on the banks of the river on our side of town. By 12.15pm it was busy, which was a good sign, and the four of us managed to get the last table there.

The décor could only be described as in need of a bit of updating but the huge windows overlooking the river made up for it in a spectacular fashion. We looked outwards and the children looked inwards as they weren't interested in the slow-moving water and the occasional person walking along the towpath. (There are locks on the river as it's navigable so we assumed that's what the pathway was.) Looking the other way, Arthur was fascinated by the grill that occupied a large part of one wall. It was a vertical grill and various meats and fish were slowly rotating under their own momentum and cooking.

A quick check showed a selection of different menus and specials of the day. It was obvious that an evening meal at this particular hotel would have ended up being quite expensive but even the most decadent of lunches was less than £20 per person. Arthur and Dorothy's healthy appetites were soon satisfied as their dishes arrived quickly and, as we had come to expect, were mini versions of grown-up food. We cut up the moist chicken breast for Arthur. This was served with a creamy tarragon and wine sauce and rice with vegetables. Lovely! After a quick check that there were no bones in Dorothy's fish, and a little squish of her boiled potatoes, they were off. Angela and I didn't need to mention to each other that we both looked forward to 'helping' them finish their plates, just to ensure the plates were returned to the kitchen empty to show our appreciation, of course.

We have it on very good authority that the *foie gras* our region is well known for is no longer produced through force-feeding, so we went for that for one of the starters. It was the most memorable part of the meal. We half expected a chilled solid block of the liver; however what came was three slices of warm, seared *foie gras* along with a fresh, warm fig chutney and some spiced bread. We have learnt from experience that cooking *foie gras* is not for the faint-hearted. As it is expensive, the slices tend to be thinner, so if your pan is not very hot, instead of a seared and slightly caramelised piece, you end up with a pan of fat and no *foie gras*. It just melts to nothing. What we were served that day was delicious and completely melt-in-your-mouth (rather than the pan) yumminess. The chutney and bread were perfect with it, as there was a slight acidity to the chutney to cut through the fattiness of the liver and the almost Christmassy warm spices in the bread paired wonderfully with the other flavours. As is our normal practice, we shared every dish and as it was so rich a little went a long way. It may be cheesy, and a little soppy, but when we share food it is almost a competition to give each other the prize morsel.

The trout that had been grilled vertically was lovely too, particularly the crisp buttery skin. Though getting the flesh from the bones took some effort, it was so worth it, as it allowed you to savour every little bit that you salvage from the ever-growing pile of debris.

Whenever we have a lunchtime menu in France the dishes always appear to be quite small but somehow by the end of the meal we are satiated. Maybe it's the fact that we eat slowly over a longer period of time or maybe the plates are huge and it just makes the portions look smaller. Whatever it is; we don't usually end up hungry by the end of it, though on this occasion it could have been because we practically licked Arthur and Dorothy's plates clean for them . . .

* * *

That very first job I ever did at the château of making the entrance safe had only ever been intended as a quick fix. There was still a need to do it properly once and for all, and it was pressing to have this sorted before the guests arrived for our wedding. Nearly every one of the tiles needed to be taken up, the mortar removed from the bottom and sides and then replaced. Not a trivial job as the mortar was a hard mix that needed to be laboriously removed with a grinder. There is an old military saying that a volunteer is worth ten pressed men. To the rescue came Angela's dad, Steve. He is the first to acknowledge that he has not got a lot of DIY experience but he is a willing volunteer! So started dozens of man hours grinding tiles. The tiles were worryingly easy to get up but the sides and underneath needed to be ground smooth so they could be relaid flat and neat.

After a discussion, we established a tile-grinding area to one side out the front of the château and we also made up a jig for holding the tiles. It was then down to the very noisy, dusty task of grinding off the mortar. Thank goodness for the one-year guarantee on power tools.

My initial fix had involved slates and angle brackets but now it was time to replace the joists. There was a hole in the basement ceiling from my initial investigations, so now it was a case of attacking from above and below. The beams in the house are so seasoned and solid that they feel like they are made of concrete rather than wood, so replacing the joists was a matter of removing the old ones and putting in and levelling new ones. After a couple of weeks, there was a pile of 'as new' tiles, the plywood that had protected everyone from falling in the hole that went down to the basement floor was taken away and the threshold was brought back to life with the beautiful 150-year-old tiles.

It always sounds easier than it was when I write it down, but admittedly this task was reasonably straightforward and very satisfying because I knew that, once the joists were in and level, the insulation packed around them and the tiles laid, the floor of the entrance would outlive me. So that was a task well and truly crossed off.

* * *

From the very start of our renovations, there have been a couple of huge jobs hanging over us. The roof needs to be replaced quite soon, the render on the outside of the château needs to be redone and then there were the windows . . .

Our first objective was to stop the elements entering the château, so many of the rotten/rotting windows were screwed shut. In a couple of cases, the shutters had been screwed shut so we couldn't see the windows – out of sight was out of mind – but that wouldn't be acceptable for our wedding celebrations. Things needed to be sorted. The glass had been replaced where necessary but the panes were not just rectangles of glass, the corners were curved and of course they were all different sizes. The windows were not mass produced and bought off the shelf – each had been handmade by a skilled craftsman to fit the opening left by the skilled masons who had made the walls. We did have some new windows in the château – about eight out of sixty had been replaced by double-glazed UPVC or aluminium windows. From a distance they were not terrible to look at, and most importantly they worked, but there was something very special about the original windows. The panes are not completely flat and most have a sort of ripple on them, so when you look through them the world outside almost moves and shimmers as you turn your head. They must have been the best that could be made 150 years ago.

The windows were another an ongoing discussion between Angela and I: she wanted the double-glazed ones replaced first but when lots of our windows didn't work at all, it made no sense to me that we would start by taking out the best ones. Therein lies the difference between us. My definition of 'best ones' and Angela's are poles apart. It's the difference between functionality and form. I have to concede that the wooden windows with their lovely metal catches are much nicer to look at. Indeed, even the way they were built with one side being convex and the other concave so they come together and provide a draft-resistant join is very clever, but the fact they are so ornate with curved corners makes each window a significant task. In today's world, I'd expect to just take a measurement and send it off to get a high-performance, admittedly UPVC, double- or triple-glazed window to be installed in the opening and in the process reduce our ongoing heating bills. Not only could they be bought and installed in batches but performance is important to maximise the efficiency of our home.

Then, at the end of July, we spotted another double-glazed window, to the right of the front door, complete with ornate metalwork. It looks exactly like all the original windows but someone had made it thick enough to take double-glazed panels. In that moment, my argument was completely undermined. I had nowhere to go other than to say yes to wooden windows, as long as they performed. Having produced a spreadsheet of what was required to sort the ground-floor windows in our reception rooms, I headed off to buy the seasoned oak for the frames so we could at least start this mammoth task.

France treats its oak trees as a natural resource and there are sawmills all around us, so I set off full of confidence, only to be wrong-footed almost immediately. A very helpful chap showed me the stack upon stack of seasoned planks of every size, really happy that he could do exactly what was required to give me the wood I needed. The downside was that delivery would be mid-September at the earliest. We appeared to have a slight problem and it didn't take long to discover that this was not an isolated issue. We didn't know that most of the firms we would be dealing with for our renovations shut for August, plus or minus a little depending on what day the month starts on, and obviously the lead-up to August is busy, so a bow wave of work forms that takes most of September to catch up on. It was back to the drawing board and we needed to make some decisions about what we actually thought we could complete in the next three months.

Summer saw us enjoying the type of heat that encourages you to relax. Every day was a pleasure, though many of them we did not enjoy as fully as possible as we were deeply entrenched in preparing rooms for electricians or plasterers. The light in the evening was very special and we learnt the meaning of the golden hour, when the sun starts to set, bathing the front of the château in beautiful light. We took to sitting on the stairs and having a drink together. It couldn't have been classed as an aperitif as we had eaten with or soon after the children, but neither was it a nightcap, as when we retired upstairs to our suite, we continued working, making lists and sourcing materials and fittings. We thought of them more as our moments of sanity and intimacy and we came to treasure them.

The seasonal fruit and vegetables encouraged us to eat healthily and we made lots of salads or chargrilled vegetables (aubergines, fennel and courgettes – though we begrudged buying courgettes as they are so easy to grow and each plant is so prolific, but that would have to wait until next year . . .) soaked in olive oil with lots of salt and usually served as bruschetta on chargrilled bread (not toasted!) that had been rubbed with a raw clove of garlic.

The children's playroom had been plastered. We had tackled our majestic staircase, it was plastered and painted, and even the ceiling looked like new. And with the entrance floor once more as strong as it had ever been, it felt like we had finally made some progress. The decision whether or not to try to tackle the windows had been taken out of our hands and we had sent in rafts of paperwork to ensure we could actually get married. We even had enough crockery, despite the growing numbers anticipated at the wedding. All we were missing was our suntans.

CHAPTER EIGHT

AUGUST

August is the height of summer and in Mayenne the temperatures are high. The colours are starting to lose their vitality and the grasses have yellowed. Driving around, we were surprised by how many fields of sweetcorn there were and the cobs visibly fattened through the month. When we asked Jacques about it, he explained that it wasn't 'sweet' corn as we may think about it. It was maize for the dairy industry, which is apparently higher in protein, to help feed the milk-producing herds over winter. We made a note to ourselves that it obviously grew well in the *département*, so when our garden was up and running, we would have to plant a bed of sweet sweetcorn. It may appear negative, but the days start to draw in throughout August and you have to enjoy every chance to spend an evening in the sun. The long, sunny days continued to heat up the steps of the château and we were often drawn to sitting on them in the evenings so we didn't felt like we had missed out on the beauty of the day.

I cannot bear the idea of the children waking up and one of us not being there, so I tended to work at an ear-range distance. We had invested in the best possible baby monitor and apps that worked on the WiFi or 3G, but none managed to battle through the three-foot supporting walls of the château. I mean, what if there was an earthquake, or lightning struck our suite, or a bat flew into the room and into one of the kids ... Dick tells me the probabilities are nearly non-existent, but mums don't take risks. Our suite was comfortable, so I spent most of my evening hours working in what is now known as our 'horizontal office'.

I love putting mood boards together. The colours, textures and order of it all makes me smile. Since a young age, I'd put together boards of ideas, even if it was just a school project. It's like a creative plan that helps bring your thoughts together and lets you see what elements do not sit well on a page. I find it helps my very busy mind stay focused and not be wooed by tempting distractions (such as another colour of paint that is also nice!). But, like every plan, it's there to be deviated from.

I was still working on the décor for the ground-floor rooms and with this particular project my enemy was a dark horse. I had been struggling with the costs of everything in France, from the second-hand items to DIY products. Paint especially was criminally expensive. Or at least it appears to be after you have spent thirty-five years living in England. For a 2.5-litre pot of a well-known brand of paint you will pay around €40 in France. To make it worse, the quality also appears to be different. It's very runny and always ends up looking patchy. We did not have many people we could ask simple questions of, but we had our ex-pat handyman Julian, who was happy to tackle any odd jobs, and then there was plasterer Steve. When we quizzed them we realised that this was a just a thing you had to accept; consequently, they normally brought ten-litre tubs of white paint back from the UK. This sparked an idea.

I had a plan for the entrance hall based on something I had done in my Vintage Patisserie in London. It involved using 3D details to add a burst of colour to an otherwise light and relatively simple space. In the Vintage Patisserie, I had butterflies all over the walls attached with little pieces of polystyrene to give them their 3D effect. It worked very well and I always loved it. I wanted to recreate this magic in the entrance hall.

For the moment, I had to keep my focus and find foundations to get the right feel: I wanted the walls to feel smooth and velvety. If the colour and texture were right (light and matt), I knew the 3D details would look amazing, so I decided to mix my own paint. With this design, less was more – so it would also save us lots of money.

Normally Dick loves a money-saving idea but in this instance he was more than grumpy because he (rightly) said I would never be able to rematch the paint – it's an art that even the most complex machines struggle with. So to make sure that didn't become a problem I ended up making lots of extra, which, of course, then needed to be stored and, by the time the wedding came, it took over a third of Dick's workshop. I feel a tinge of guilt writing this, but then a girl has to do what a girl has to do.

Then there was the second issue that in August everything shut down. The big DIY shops stayed open, but for the taps, beds and general décor I needed more individual shops. This came as a surprise and an annoyance. Even the local bakers and restaurants closed for most of August. Dick and I discussed that we were the ones that had it wrong (a month-long holiday is a lovely thing, after all), but that did not help the situation. For some of the necessities – such as the bathroom fittings and a bed for the honeymoon suite – I ended up looking on UK sites.

The messy work was still overwhelming but with Dick home and the focus on items that were not utility-based, I felt calmer and was finally able to allow myself some real creative thoughts. I work best when my mind isn't too clouded with problems and mess. This was when I had my idea for the turret in the honeymoon suite. The Bagliones had always used the turrets as functional spaces: either as washrooms or very basic facilities rooms, and most had storage space for clothes. Originally Dick and I talked about putting a bath in there but it seemed a bit gimmicky.

I had to think about how this room could be used for our wedding business and I thought it could be a useful room for the bride to hang her dress in, out of sight of the groom. I imagined it as a space she could then sneak into if she wished. For this it needed to look special.

I had also been wondering how I could showcase the wallpapers I had found in the attic. I had seen examples of patchwork walls with leftover wallpaper before. There was something in this but often the walls began to look too much: the shapes and sizes were wrong or they were all different. None of the images I found were quite the look I wanted. I sat on this idea for a couple of weeks and then realised that if I made the shapes identical, the designs would shine. I've always loved the Harlequin print and that was how the idea for the 'wallpaper museum' was born.

First, Dick helped me measure the circumference of the turret. Then he made me a stencil guide to start cutting the diamonds of wallpaper. My first job was to bring the wallpaper down to the honeymoon suite. I used gloves for this and carefully picked up the rolls of wallpaper like they were little babies. It was the first time I really saw what was what and how much I had of each design.

It was fascinating unravelling decades of design history. Once they were all down, I started organising it into collections. Straight away I found around six rolls of the yellow and green paper from the entrance hall. The texture was thick and it felt robust. Then I found four rolls of a pretty floral design with a swallow on it. On investigating, I found out this particular one was designed by French wallpaper designer Paul Dumas. The Bagliones clearly loved his style as there were a number of designs by him. Originally the swallow paper had been on the walls of the snug, which later became the kids' playroom. As a family we were split on whether to keep it or not. But it is never a good idea to design by committee, so in the end I decided it needed to go and that room is now covered with Arthur and Dorothy's own paintings. It did however earn a place in my wallpaper museum.

That afternoon was magical for me. I spent hours matching cuttings with the rooms and discovering new wallpapers I had never seen in any of the rooms: from deep purples and greens to oranges, blues and golds. I found geometric wallpapers with gold foils, the kind of designs that have inspired many modern-day interiors. It was a feast for my eyes as well as my soul. My favourite bunch were very thin and delicate but rich in colour. They looked like they had been screen-printed by hand and then hand-finished with a stencil, and they must have been done at the turn of the nineteenth century. I couldn't get over the vibrancy of the colour. The Bagliones were people after our own hearts. They clearly did not like throwing anything away!

The next stage of this was to cut diamonds out and paste them to the wall. Dick let me use his fancy electronic leveller to get the rows horizontal and off I went. I have often cut up old magazines and papers and some people have gasped in horror, but I see it as giving a new life to something. It's more powerful than putting it in a box and leaving it out of sight. It's something I am a strong believer in. I'm not afraid of using valuable things. Yes, they may get broken, but at least they live again.

* * *

With so much still to do and so many design details to finish, I was missing my London-based crafty girlfriend Sarah. Sarah used to work with me at the Vintage Patisserie. She was my support and we loved working on projects together. I even managed to persuade Sarah to be one of Vintage hostesses. During the years the Vintage Patisserie ran, I wanted all my team to follow their personal dreams too, so when my event space was not being used, they could use it to host their own events. Sarah used to host taxidermy evenings in the space and actually stuffed our first canary, Gerald, for us. I always feel bad saying this, but Gerald never looked better; he still sits proudly in our entrance.

In mid-August, an SOS call to Sarah was made and out she came with her then assistant Sam for a working holiday. They helped with a bit of everything: painting, wallpapering, invites, butterflies. But the five days flew by too fast.

August was also the month that we had to claim our salon back from Mum and Dad to get it ready for guests arriving in November. I was worried about Mum, though – we knew she would struggle with the stairs up to the vacant suites. In a fortunate stroke of serendipity, we were invited to a barbecue at Jacques and Isabelle's house around this time. With so much activity at the château, our only outings were to the shops to get essentials, so it was joyous to spend the afternoon in someone else's world.

We dined together for hours and lots of franglais was spoken as we all righted the world and drank *cidre*. Lunch consisted of fresh baguettes, cornichons and tomatoes picked from the garden. It was simple but wonderful. This was the life that we had heard rumours of.

After lunch, we were given a guided tour of Isabelle's crops and I could see how happy this made Dick . . . It was an inspiration for our future. They kindly leant us some extra chairs for our wedding and even offered to help find some essential items like gravel (I had been struggling to find anywhere open that sold it). But the absolute best thing that came out of that lunch was the offer for us to rent a part of their house. It was the original part of their house before they had an extension added on. We had actually stayed in it once ourselves so knew it well; it had a nice bathroom, that lovely fireplace that we all drank bubbly around when we signed for the property and another room out the back that obviously has lots of things that are special to the family. The only thing missing was a kitchen, so Dick offered to fit this as a gift . . . The arrangement seemed to work for everyone: Jacques and Isabelle would receive some rental income and Mum and Dad would be able to unpack some bits and avoid the stairs in the château. They knew that as soon as we could, we would have them back on the island where they belonged.

To be able to launch our business and have paying guests we needed to have at least one suite we were happy to use, to say this is who we are and what we are offering. Our criteria has always been, and will always continue to be, it needs to be good enough that we would want to stay there (or eat it, or do it), so our first suite (the honeymoon suite) had to be exciting for us. We had a plan that involved what would have been the master bedroom, but having started putting the electrics and heating in place, there was a discussion that changed our direction somewhat . . .

I knew we had to do something to make the honeymoon suite extra special. I couldn't work out why this room didn't feel 'wow'. Then it dawned on me: even with the quirky wallpaper museum and the

vestibule outside the bathroom, it just wasn't grand or big enough to host a bride, bridesmaids, friends, family, hairdresser, make-up artist and photographer. Sometimes you could have over twenty people in the room at one go. The room needed to be bigger . . . All I had to do was convince Dick.

OK, I'll admit Angela's idea to join the upstairs salon where the master and mistress would have 'met' to what was the master bedroom was a brilliant idea. My girl was thinking about what happens on the morning of a wedding and how to make it as wonderful an experience as possible. To be fair, I hadn't had much insight into this part of a wedding; as far as I could work out, the chaps all disappear and turn up wearing what they are told. The wedding seems to be all about the bride, so having a lovely place for the bridal party to get ready and enjoy the build-up to the ceremony seemed very sensible. Unfortunately, in order to make this wonderful space we had to connect two rooms currently separated by a two-foot-thick stone wall and, as if that wasn't interesting enough, there were fireplaces and chimneys in the wall as well.

I made all the 'it's too difficult' noises but when it became obvious they weren't going to work, I changed tack and said Angela could make the hole if she wanted it that badly. She did and she did. The location of the 'arch' sort of selected itself (there were no other choices) and so it was a matter of getting on with it. The first thing that was needed were lintels above where the entrance was to be. That was really just a matter of being sensible. The principles are quite simple: if you remove a stone from a two-foot-thick wall it doesn't all fall down; the force acts downwards and outwards from any given point on the wall, so it spreads out and down diagonally. So if your wall was a bit dodgy and you removed a particularly important stone, the stones below wouldn't move, it would only be the stones above that could suffer. The ones at the side would also stay in and support, so in the worst case a triangle of stones could topple out. All I had to do was ensure the least number of stones possible were disturbed and immediately put in a lintel and rebuild above it as quickly as possible.

With a set of lintels from one side of the wall to the other and the spaces filled in above them, I felt it was safe to let Angela loose with a jackhammer. We had some old mattresses on the floor so we could allow rocks to fall and out of the window was a chute that we could use to empty our debris. Work started two metres up and we worked down to the floor level. If you do some sums, assuming the density of the rocks is somewhere between 2,000 and 3,000kg per cubic metre, we had to move over two tons of rock! When the effort taken to move them was combined with holding up a heavy old jackhammer for more than three hours, it's no wonder Angela slept well that evening. And with all the jiggling from the hammering she was also very pleased that I had advised her to wear a sports bra . . . Just saying!

With the rooms now joined together the 'honeymoon suite' was born. It was a long way from being finished but we knew where it was going and what was required and it was already obvious it was going to be very special.

We have always wanted to keep as much of the history of the rooms in the château as possible, but the condition of the wallpaper and paint has tended to mean that we had to strip everything back before we could start making it lovely. When we removed the wooden panels from under the double-glazed window in the honeymoon suite, they were so badly rotted that there was nothing we could do but burn them. Initially, we thought this meant we needed to get some replacement panels – until we stopped and looked at the back of the cut stones that had been underneath the panels. They had been handmade over 150 years ago and you had to marvel at how interesting they were – bear in mind this is the back of the stones, not the face exposed to the world. *Why not leave them on display?* we thought. But that then opened a whole minefield of problems: there would be draughts, dust, moisture and all sorts of things getting in. Then we had a cunning idea for a see-through 'window' below the window. It worked and is lovely, so now it's possible to see the stonework from inside the room.

Armed with this wonderful solution, we tackled our old wooden panelling with renewed gusto. The panelling under the window in the tower felt very 'spongy', which even the uninitiated know is a bad sign, so we decided to pull it off and see if anything could be saved. I'm going to let Angela tell the story from here . . .

There's no denying that after only six months of living in the country I was not the bravest when it came to wild animals and spiders, but in my defence I come from Essex and it's pretty tame there. And on this particular hot day in August I was not prepared for what happened. As we removed one of the spongy parts of the panelling from the tower of the honeymoon suite, the room filled with a cloud of black flapping bats. Dick says I screamed, and though I'd like to pretend I didn't, it's probably true. I also nearly wet myself. All I could think was what if they got caught in my hair? I was so flustered that I couldn't really work out how to get away from them. They were everywhere. Whole families of them. It felt like I was in a Harry Potter movie! Though I love him, Dick's laughing did not help at all. I could happily have throttled him. We managed to film a bit of the magic on our phones and then, almost as quickly as they emerged, they all seemed to disappear out of the open windows. Looking back, it was incredibly exciting.

After the drama of that afternoon, the honeymoon suite very quickly came together. There was even a loo in the salon that we managed to connect to water and the proposed sewage route.

There are some jobs that give you real satisfaction and putting a toilet into the little *cabine de toilette** was one such task. We managed to save the beautiful linoleum and fit a tiny sink in the room. The honeymoon suite is directly above the entrance hall so the options for the sewage to leave it unseen were not many. With a bit of sleight of hand, I took the waste through the main wall and into the back hallway where the staircase is. I then disguised it by boxing it in and taking it through another main wall and across the service kitchen at ceiling height, and then finally, to finish off the subterfuge, I put in a false ceiling in the service kitchen. No one has ever commented on it – I doubt if many actually care where the poopage goes – but it works and, personally, I find it satisfying that I worked out a route to take the waste from the middle of the château's most salubrious rooms at a 25mm-per-metre gradient to the western wall, down a couple of floors and then out the eastern wall to settle and be pumped under the moat to the filter beds. I'm sure there must be others who are similarly pleased by such things . . .

With the electrics wired in and the sockets in place it was time for decorating and making things beautiful in all but the bathroom. However, before we could skim the walls and make good the new archway, we had one last job. We had to take up the solid-oak floorboards in the salon to rewire the chandelier in the main entrance hall below. For some unknown reason, the cabling went forward to the front of the château and then down through the wall past the front door to the basement before making its way, surface-mounted, to the rear of the château. To follow that route would had meant destroying the walls in the main entrance hall to put in new cables, and that was unacceptable. Anyway, we now had power distribution in the basement, the ground floor

---

* A *cabine de toilette* is basically a room with a jug and a basin in it.

and the second floor, so it was a matter of finding a route to the nearest board, which ended up meaning we had to follow the loo waste pipe.

Sustainability comes in many forms and buying quality that lasts is one philosophy that we subscribe to. But the cost of quality bathroom fittings can make your eyes water. And we had the added problem of sourcing what we wanted. When you go to a large DIY shop you will see displays of every sort of kitchen, bathroom, bedroom or living-room item you could ever want; however, a large proportion of what you see is not actually available to buy there and then – you have to order them and it can take weeks for them to arrive. Such a process was alien to us, and our tastes are such that our choices were already limited, so when we found bathroom fittings of quality that could be delivered to us at the château reasonably quickly, we had little choice but to pay. They were not the most expensive by a long way, but neither did they fit into the budget category.

Having spent eight months in the château, I now had a much clearer vision for the rooms. Sometimes my thoughts had not fully developed until I had the blank canvas of the 'prepared' room to look at. Now Dick said this room was mine to play with. The bathroom in the honeymoon suite was so important.

I'd won the first major argument and the sink was going to be on the 'wrong' wall – or should I say a wall that meant it wasn't as easy to get the water waste down. I did pay attention to these practical considerations but I also wanted what I thought to be best aesthetically and what felt right for use. The shower cubicle had to be spacious enough for two. The double sink, the toilet, the mirrors, the bath and the taps all had to be perfect. It took many frustrating hours sitting in bed searching on the internet before I found the perfect answer. It was a company called Arcade. They

were inspired by the *belle époque* and their forty-seven-inch double basin literally made me shiver with excitement when I found it. Its graceful lines and refined elegance made me very happy and they delivered to France. Unfortunately, the price was such that I felt I'd better not tell Dick . . .

I knew how much Angela had been struggling to find the right fittings and fixtures for the château. I did not interfere when it came to décor, but gas hobs or thermostatically-controlled showers and sink fittings – anything even a little technical – we discussed. Neither of us are good at compromising so we were each given the power of veto. This meant that only goods acceptable to both of us were bought. The results were excellent and we have been really pleased with our buys . . . Although I now know to avoid asking the price, as it is obscene how much you can pay to kit out a bathroom and I think my mental price list is set somewhere in the twentieth century.

In the midst of all this work we also had a wedding to prepare for and I was more than a bit excited to be going home to see my family and friends for my hen party. This was my first trip back to London. I could not wait to give my grandma a big hug as I had not seen her since my grandad passed away. But I was also slightly anxious. I had never been away from Dorothy, ever . . . Mum had booked an overnight ferry from Caen to Portsmouth on the Thursday and then back again on the Sunday night. Caen is a couple of hours from our house and I wanted to take the slow route so we could enjoy the drive, so we set off in the afternoon. The roads are windy and beautiful, through lots of floral villages. Mum and I had lots to catch up on so it was lovely to get this time together.

Once home, there was a lot to fit in and this was made worse by my decision to pop in to visit a dealer of original fairground memorabilia. Wolfe Antiques is run by a young lad called Jack. I actually found him on eBay when I bid for a couple of scary clown heads for the playroom. I had agreed to swing by and pick them up en route to my hen party. The problem was, when I turned up at his warehouse, I discovered it was full of amazing fairground treasures: there were original metal signs, a penny arcade muto-scope, parts from old rides and even ornate coving from carousels. It was my dream to have fairground treasures filling the walls and I knew I would regret not buying more (a plan was already forming in my head for the wedding). Firstly, I got the clown heads in the car, then I went back to talk. I knew I could fit nothing else in the car, but I managed to persuade our plumber friend Lee to find space to bring some things with him on his next trip, so I also purchased two fairground signs and the old penny machine.

After Wolfe Antiques it was straight on to my grandma's for a family hen party filled with hugs. That night I celebrated with my mum, my grandma, five aunts and seven cousins, plus lots of Greek cuisine and laughter. The next day I was off to Hoxton in east London. The party began with a corset fitting by my friend Katie. Then I got my hair and nails done (for the first time in months) before heading on to a meal and a party with all my nearest and dearest friends. We danced till very late to our favourite songs and drank far too many cocktails. Then on Sunday we headed to a brilliant pub near Kings Cross for a big farewell lunch with friends and family, including my ninety-three-year-old nan. There was just time for lots of hugs and 'see you at your wedding!' before Mum and I had to drive back, having not taken a breath.

When Angela headed off to London for a couple of days for her hen party, I had the opportunity to burn the candle at both ends and get the service kitchen sorted. When we first moved in, we didn't know how we were going to use the kitchens in the château. The service kitchen by the dining room would originally have been the 'receiver' for the cooking done down in the main kitchen in the basement. We were in discussions about possibly putting a spiral staircase in the tower to join the dining room and the main kitchen below rather than using the servants' stairs at the rear of the chateau, though that would have to be a later phase, but luckily the dumb waiter was a thing of beauty and still had life in it, so would continue to link upstairs and downstairs. The kitchen is the heart of most homes and we planned to make the main kitchen somewhere for the family to cook and eat, with the ability to also 'supply' the service kitchen if we wished to dine more formally.

However, we also saw breakfast and possibly simple lunches being catered for in the service kitchen. It was handy to the main living rooms and, after using it for six months, we had proven it was big enough, even if it was not somewhere to gather. When we first managed to get water to the old sink in the service kitchen, one of our first purchases was a simple €100 gas cooker that had four rings and an oven. That, with some cupboards, a fridge and some make-do work surfaces, had been a lifesaver and was what had kept the family and troops fed until now. However, it did need to be given a significant amount of love.

We had done our research and found the work surfaces we were going to use both upstairs and downstairs. As this was our forever home, we invested in work surfaces that had both function and form. When we saw Dekton we both agreed that was what we wanted. It is made by fusing quartz porcelain and glass under high pressure and temperature, which means it is stain and scratch resistant and you can put very hot pans on it without worrying. It would probably still be there if the château ever suffered a nuclear blast. It also came in lots of colours and finishes. With the work surfaces, sink, taps and hobs decided, it was now just a matter of putting it on our priority list and doing the work. We had deliveries piling up in the basement and were putting in the time to get as much done as we could. With Angela and her mum away in London, this was my window to get the service kitchen sorted.

Steve was dispatched to IKEA to collect a carload of carcasses and miscellaneous kitchen items. We hadn't decided on the doors yet but everything else was ready to go. We always try to plan ahead so we had mains gas and electrical power points available in the service kitchen, hot and cold water and waste with enough slack to reach the destination of our final sink and even water and waste for a dishwasher, should we ever decide we needed one in the little kitchen. As Angela and Jenny headed to Caen, I had space to spread everything out.

First the kitchen was stripped out and usable, unwanted items made their way to an outbuilding for future use, if required. I have an aversion to flat-packed furniture, but when you buy the carcasses and shelving at IKEA you know exactly what you are getting and they are as good as anything else. The floor in the service kitchen had seen significant activity. We love it but it is worn and uneven, so the best thing to do is to ignore it and use the adjustable feet on the units to absorb the variations.

My mum had bought me a laser level and it has been invaluable. It only took moments to mark up where the metal supporting rail and brackets for the hanging cupboards were to go, but that's when it got interesting. It quickly became clear that one of the walls in the service kitchen was made of cheese. If you can imagine putting screws into cheese and how effective it would be you will understand my metaphor. The wall was nothing more than a single layer of skinny bricks, on their edge, supported between vertical wooden planks. Such construction is how stud walls have been put up in the past and they were never frightfully strong. I could knock most of them over in the château, especially if I was grumpy. The cupboards above the work surface needed to be hung on the rail and would undoubtedly be filled with crockery, which is heavy, so they needed to be secure. I put in more wall fixings than could have been expected and screwed into the wooden supports wherever I found them, but as a final belt and braces and piece of string I drilled holes and bolted supports all the way through. I do not want to tempt fate but the only way for the fixing to fail is for the whole wall to come down.

Starting with the corner unit with its revolving shelves, I proceeded to put in all the units and screw them together. Installing the work surface was not as straightforward as I had hoped, but you have to be thankful for small mercies as the 'cheese' wall was at least flat and the surface sat on the units very easily. The outside wall is an interesting shape and, consequently, I had a choice of waiting for that part of the work surface to be recut with a bow in it or remodel the wall. No prizes for guessing that a cold chisel and hammer made the necessary adjustment.

A new day saw a new burst of energy and, once the children were up and safe with the world's best childcare (Grandad Steve), I was straight back into the kitchen. It's a rule of DIY that everything takes longer than you thought. I seemed to spend an inordinate amount of time under the sink connecting the waste pipe and stopping it dripping but eventually the sink was functional and drip-free and the four-burner gas hob was working as well. With the extractor and lights above the hob in place it was just like a real kitchen. It's funny what small things make a difference in your life: our original gas cooker required a lighter to ignite it whereas our new hob just needed to be pushed in and turned – progress!

We had opted for a fold-down, wall-mounted table and it all but doubled our surface space. The shelving was simple to install, though we had a fair number of the pull-out tray shelves that took a while. I did feel a bit guilty making decisions on what went where but then I caught myself on and realised that Angela would just come and change everything anyway. Even without the cupboard doors, this was a fully operational kitchen. It needed to be decorated and finished so it looked lovely but all the functionality was there.

I can't tell you how happy I was to be home after the weekend. The drive was much longer on the way back. It's a thing, right? It was lovely to be met with lots of hugs and, to top it off, Dick made me some tea in our remodelled service kitchen. I couldn't wait to tell them all about our trip but first there was a little bit of unpacking to do: clown heads, large inflatable penises that the kids thought were balloons . . . just your normal hen party trip away.

With the service kitchen sorted, the main family kitchen was the next priority. This was a very important room for us. The Rayburn had been in and functioning for months but, apart from that, the main kitchen had so far been acting as a workroom and the centre of bath renovations. We had the infrastructure laid to it and the piping and radiators were in place, but we still needed to sort out the lighting and where to have sockets. The tower had a huge sink and an old cow-tail pump in it, but as we imagined the tower would be our link to the dining room it did not have to be recommissioned.

We had discussed the kitchen a lot and the plan was quite mature. There is a very important triangle when you consider kitchen design and it is all about the routes between the cooker, the pantry or fridge and the sink. The Rayburn was fixed due to the flue, but we knew our kitchen was to be sociable as well as functional, so we had decided that we wanted to be able to cook and chat. We had aspirations to put on 'Food Lovers' weekends', which meant our guests would also be spending some time cooking and eating informally in this kitchen, so we decided we needed an island to allow us to cook and face the family, friends or guests. We also needed to ensure there was enough space to cater for weddings, though the details of what we were to offer still needed to be ironed out between us. The kitchen has windows overlooking the front of the château and the moat, so one of our criteria was definitely going to be met – we both agreed that we wanted a good view while we washed the dishes!

Our research had turned up the most amazing style of kitchen that was exactly what was required for our château. It was called La Cornue. We both knew this was what we wanted as soon as we saw it, but it was really hard to find the price, which rang warning bells. Perseverance produced a figure that made us both stop and look at each other. There was no way we could afford the tens of thousands required for a cooker and the work surfaces, but it looked so good. There is something debilitating when you find the one, then learn it is totally out of your price range. What it does, though, is push your ability to think laterally. Eventually we came up with the answer. We'd have the same look but make it ourselves. La Cornue is a quality product and each item is bordered by brass . work, which gives it a unique look and also resilience. We decided that we'd take a normal high-gloss door and attach brass plates to each side like a frame. That, combined with brass handles, would give us the look we were after. It would take a fair bit of effort but was definitely much cheaper.

To allow us a reasonably large kitchen table, the island was to be on the same side of the room as the Rayburn, but the island needed gas and electricity. That meant there was a need to lay pipes under the floor, one of the most remarkable features of the room. But there is no point in delaying what has to be done, so the first brick tiles were removed and off we went. At the same time, Angela was still working on her two baths in the kitchen. To be honest, they were getting in my way, but she had to work on them somewhere and no one wanted to move them until they were ready to go to their actual homes. But it was a reminder that there was still a lot of parallel activity happening and a lot of mess being produced.

We knew we would need an electrician in to connect the island electricity to the distribution box but everything else we could lay and prepare. Making as little damage as possible, I used the nine-inch and four-inch grinders to remove the mortar round a couple of rows of the herringbone-pattern floor bricks. I had some spares that would match but I wanted to replace the bricks back exactly where they came from. To do that, first I took photos on my phone, then I set them four feet away in the exact order they came out. There are few jobs in the château that you can say went smoothly but this was one. The main reason was that under the bricks and a thin layer of screed was . . . nothing. Just a rammed earth floor. I knew the *caves* were earth floors to help with the humidity and temperature control but I'd expected the workrooms to have some form of a foundation. I didn't fret for long, though, as the rooms weren't damp and had obviously been fine for 150 years. I dug down and placed the electrical conduits in (complete with strong string in them to pull the pipes and cables through – that's a mistake you only make once!), then I refilled and packed down the returning screed. And with that we were just about ready to start rebuilding.

With the position and size of the island sorted, and the relative position of the surfaces, lights and switches all decided, it was possible to do the first-fix electrics, which is basically sorting the routes for the cables and laying them in place. Thereafter it gets exciting as the room starts to improve around you. Plasterer Steve was reboarding the ceiling and boxing in an exposed beam. After that, he skimmed every bit of wall and ceiling that would be on show and that didn't move. While he was busy plastering, waste pipes, electrics and plumbing were all put in place and the basement hall became a kitchen-carcass-modification centre. Angela and I worked out the cupboard configuration: how many would be on each of the two outside walls and which would be drawers and which would be shelving. Then the island units were agreed and the footprint was centred on a line in the middle of the window overlooking the front of the château and the centre of the Rayburn. This all sounds very logical and sensible; however, our windows are recessed in 'reveals' that were not made to 'fit' standard kitchen carcasses, so we had to put a mixture of carcasses into each, centred on the window frame, and then we made others fit into the spaces we had remaining on the left and right.

I chopped and customised about a dozen carcasses and their associated shelves, still working around the baths . . . When fitting a kitchen, you expect to tweak some carcasses a little, for example where the sink is lowered in, but in our kitchen probably only one of the fifteen units was not butchered. For example, I made a 600mm-deep carcass 450mm deep and then the next 400mm carcass 300mm deep. The result was not bad as the front of the units all aligned where necessary and, after a little bit of feet adjustment, they were all horizontal and firmly fixed in place. The backs were not as impressive, in fact, it was properly Heath Robinson, but none of that mattered because the work surface would hide all imperfections.

Our main family kitchen was starting to take shape and this made Angela put the baths on her priority list.

I had not been ignoring the baths. It was just I had so much on my to-do list every day that the baths never made it to my urgent list. In my mind, as long as the bath for the honeymoon suite was taken upstairs in time for our wedding everything was OK. But actually everything had a knock-on effect. I needed the baths out of the kitchen to allow Dick and Steve to finish in there.

In France, there are so many cast-iron objects that all the DIY shops have a huge range of enamel paints and resin sets in a variety of colours. It's a brilliant alternative and much cheaper way to reglaze your bath. The finish will never be as good but the zero you knock off your price tag makes up for it. Like everything, the final finish depends on the amount of preparation you do to get your surface as smooth as possible. I sanded and sanded and buffed those bloody baths. Dick had a few attempts, Julian had a go or two . . . I think my mum even went for it. But we got to the point that enough was enough and I went in for the paint. It was a euphoric moment; the paint slid on beautifully and the baths instantly looked brilliant. The tubs come in a set size so I had purchased one for the honeymoon-suite bath and one for 'the other bath that would go somewhere'. I finished the first bath, but would you believe I ran out of paint when I had just a couple of square inches left to do on the second?

So the next day we ran to shops. Once the kids were in bed that night, it was back downstairs to do the remaining square. But then it was the wrong colour! At first I thought it would dry lighter, but the next morning I was back at the shops again for my third-time lucky . . .

The next day the company in Laval supplying the work surfaces for the kitchen came and did a measurement check, cut out the sink and hob profiles and then shortly after came to fit the tops. I was properly excited. With the plaster on and drying and the units in we were getting very close to having our dream kitchen. I was clucking around a bit like a mother hen when the fitter arrived. Any 'accident' with the surface could have meant weeks of delay and the bits with the holes cut in them are more fragile than the long straight runs. Despite my complete lack of 'work-surface-laying French', I think he understood that he was not allowed to make a mistake and, despite the process being tortuously slow, there were no problems, and he even complimented us on the accuracy of the installation of the units.

With all the plumbing connected, the sockets attached to the walls and the bloody baths out, we were nearly operational. We still had lots of decorating to do, but first we spent an evening on our hands and knees scrubbing the floor so we could remove all the restoration grime and henceforth any mess would be ours.

With all the practical stuff in our main kitchen finally sorted, it was time to get creative. I had got very attached to an image I'd seen of a small but very rustic kitchen with hanging copper pans, a wonderful La Cornue oven and beautiful blue Delft tiles. We actually had the making of this look already but if I could source the tiles it would bring it all together.

A crash course in Delft tiles later, I realised the amount I needed was way over our budget. For a kitchen our size it would cost £10,000 upwards. We were planning on hosting our wedding for that. I found companies that printed tiles on demand, but it was still a big investment. But problems like this always lead to solutions that are better in the long run. My solution came from a company called SawGrass that specialise in sublimation printing machines. They had a starter kit available for about £500. Sublimation is a chemical process that transfers ink onto a new surface (in my case, tiles). You have to use special tiles, which aren't particularly cheap and worked out at about £1 each but it's very clever and easy to do. The only other thing you need is a heat press, which is a handy investment if you do a lot of craft (mine has lasted more than ten years and paid for itself many times over). If you can use a printer, you can print a tile. It's that simple. My next task was to work out the designs. I wanted them to nod to the Delft style but undoubtedly be ours. For this,

I used my illustrations from our wedding invitation, broken up into different tile designs.

The kitchen was coming together but it was still a long way off being ready to use. It is amazing how much work has to be done to move from the skeleton of a kitchen to a fully functional, decorated and beautiful room. There were several days of work left finding all our kitchen utensils and putting up shelves and hooks and organising the room to make it work for us, but that had to be left as we had many other projects in other areas of the château all maturing in parallel that needed attention.

* * *

With September looming, the château was actually really quiet. We all had our own tasks to attend to and you could feel the focus and see the hard graft everyone was putting in. We had not got over the hump yet, but with only ten weeks until our wedding I personally could not think too hard about what was ahead as it made my head hurt. Steve was methodically plastering all the rooms, which meant the next step for me was painting the walls and stripping the doors and window frames.

With the decision made to concentrate on the ground floor for the wedding, it was my mission to have the woodwork finished. Of course, my original plan had been to strip, prime and then repaint all the doors and window frames, but good wood paint is very expensive and also cracks and chips over time. There will always be some maintenance needed. When I started work, I quickly discovered that I actually love the look of a stripped door. The Bagliones had clearly painted over the château doors many times, but when the paint was stripped back it revealed a really interesting, natural pattern that looked stunning (in fact, I've been asked many times how we achieved the look!). This really suited Dick and me as it saved both time and money, and in my opinion it looks great.

August had been hot and sticky but, after months of not actually *seeing* progress, in a single month we had lots of work coming to fruition in lots of different areas of the château. In addition to squeezing in a hen party and a shopping trip we had reached the stage where some decoration of the château had started. Holes had been knocked through walls, bats braved and the honeymoon suite was finally a suite, complete with the wallpaper museum turret room. We had a service kitchen and a wonderful main kitchen. They were all rooms that had both functionality and style, though we did not underestimate how much more work was still required to bring them up to what would pass as 'completed'.

With two kitchens, we should really have made more of the opportunity the seasonal produce afforded us that first August but we were working lots more than we were cooking. That said, we did squeeze in a few delicious dinners with our locally-sourced produce. Most salad, fruit and vegetables were readily available by this time and we were spoilt for choice.

Figs are sold by the tray in August and we would cut a cross in them and squeeze them open, arrange them on a small baking tray, sprinkle them with walnuts and crumble amazingly salty Roquefort cheese all over, then a drizzle of honey and bake them for 15 minutes. While they were in the oven, it was a matter of pulling together the rest of a meal. As life was busy, we would always try to have a fridge full of tasty morsels so we could dip in and quickly fill platters that allowed us to eat at leisure.

As well as lots of salad with different dressings and cheeses, we would marinade olives, chillies, garlic cloves and sundried tomatoes in herby oils with orange zest. The charcuterie tempts you every time you go into a shop in France. The cured saucisson and the smoked cured pork fillets and duck breasts are not cheap but go a long way. And to accompany a pot of ice-cold cornichons we would often knock up some of our own sweet pickles.

SUMMER-SWEET PICKLED VEGGIES

Ingredients

Seasonal vegetables (peppers, carrots, fennel, cucumber,
cauliflower, red onions, radishes, courgettes, salsify, broccoli)
– the more colourful the better
Vinegar
Sugar
Water
Aromatic spices (optional)

Method

*Start by finely slicing your seasonal vegetables. If in doubt, try
using a potato peeler to give you long thin pieces.*

*Meanwhile, in a pan, bring a mix of ⅓ vinegar, ⅓ sugar and
⅓ water to the boil. Feel free to add any aromatic spices that
take your fancy.*

*Once simmering, take it off the heat and add all your
vegetables and stir them around.*

*Leave the vegetables to cool in the pickle or, if you prefer, fish
them out after five minutes. It is really up to you to decide how
long you wish to keep your veg in the pickling liquor. As you
could eat all these vegetables raw, this process doesn't need to
be long, but leaving them in the liquid until it cools gives a
different texture and allows you to store them in the fridge in
the liquid.*

CHAPTER NINE

SEPTEMBER

The start of September reminds you that there are only a few weeks of summer left. You can usually feel the heat slowly leaving, prompting you to get ready for the autumn and winter ahead. In our first September at the château, it felt like summer was definitely holding on. We had very little rain and the temperatures were warm. Fresh produce was in abundance as this is the traditional start of harvesting and laying down stores for the winter. The sweetcorn around us was being harvested and a trip to the supermarket showed a wonderful array of apples and pears. Interestingly, some of them looked far from perfect but they were more expensive than the 'perfect' normal fruits.

Apples can be thought of as being very ordinary but it is amazing how the flavour varies. In France, there is still a market for russet apples, which appear to be no longer as popular back in the UK as the rough texture of their skin puts off people who are used to smooth, shiny, perfectly skinned fruit. This russeting is caused by cork cells developing in the skin tissue and does not affect the flavour or the eating quality of the apple. It does however mean the skin is more permeable to water and this can account for apples being slightly drier and sweeter. They will also not store as well as the fruit tends to shrivel. They are therefore only available for a relatively short season and this limited availability is prized and probably explains why they hold their price.

September also sees the end of the summer squash season – that's the soft-skinned squashes like courgettes and pattypan – and the tougher winter squashes that can all be stored start to come to maturity. I've grown them several times and love the fact that they will keep in a cool dry place for months, indeed all the way through winter. I was delighted and a little confused at the selection that met me in our local supermarket. It was normal for us to see a whole area that had been covered in lettuce and salads. Yes, there is a chill cabinet of clean bagged leaves but over the summer there had also been a large unit that was intermittently misted with cool water containing lots of different, real lettuces (the ones you have to clean!) and endives, bunches of watercress, radishes and other things that look like they have just come out of the ground. However, now the salad space had been compressed into a quarter of its usual size and alongside it was a display of squashes that were beautiful in their colours, shapes and sizes. I only recognised about half of them, which made me want to buy everything I couldn't identify. I was only a little reserved and bought a fair number that we simply cut into pieces, removed the seeds, drizzled with olive oil, seasoned well and slow-roasted to concentrate the flavours. An hour at 160°C is all it takes. They were lovely hot or cold and it was fair to say we enjoyed them all. They are really good with a sprinkling of the toasted seeds with soy sauce and chopped chillies that we nibble with our aperitifs. Squashes are hearty food and if they are stored properly can last for months and are a great standby to have in.

* * *

From the moment the swallows arrive in early spring they are a constant presence here at the château. The outbuildings have panes of glass missing and holes in the doors, allowing the swallows to make free with the accommodation we have offered them. They are the symbol of summer as much as our first cuckoo of the year heralds spring. It is lovely to see their season progress. By summer, the young fledglings have to learn to scoop up drinks from the moat, which involves flying and dipping in their lower beak. The first couple of times you see them trying they are so near to disaster it makes you flinch, but by the time they have to leave us they are accomplished aeronautical acrobats, swooping and diving and catching the little flying insects that may otherwise want to bite us! It is amazing to think that they will be visiting us every year all the way from South Africa, so we cannot begrudge them somewhere to build their muddy little nests, even if they do leave piles of crap below them. With a bit of luck, some swallows can live up to sixteen years, so those raised during our first year could keep coming back and be here when Arthur becomes an adult . . .

Every year in September there is a day when all the local swallows congregate and fly around the moat, swooping down to take a drink. We have seen dozens of them diving at a time, but it only lasts for a couple of hours and then, at some unseen signal, they all disappear in a matter of moments, not to be seen again until the following spring. It's spectacular to watch but quite a sad moment as it marks the end of summer.

By nature, I am a very clean and tidy person. However, living with a constant building haze, and the natural disorganisation that comes

from the continuous moving of items when you're in that zone, is all part of the fun – you just have to embrace the chaos. But once through that phase, I was excited that organisation and the big scrub was within my grasp. Dick and I had decided that the outside area just had to slip off our to-do list for now. It was so much work and, to be honest, we could not make a dent in the time frame. I did sign up to this but the sandy ground was niggling me . . . it was continuously being brought into the house on people's shoes and until it was covered that was going to carry on happening.

Dick was not impressed by my worry and said if I wanted to sort it, then I should do it. I noticed Jacques and Isabelle had very neat grey gravel outside their house, so when we were at their house I asked where they had purchased it from. Within a couple of days I had visited the gravel merchants. The space outside the château was thousands of square metres so I signed up for 75 tons of the gravel. At €20 a ton it was going to cost us but I thought it was a bargain.

With just two months until the wedding we knew we had to start sorting out the party itself. Somehow the guest list had grown to just over 200 people and they were all going to need wining and dining. There was a sommelier in the next village so we decided to go and find the perfect local wines for our weekend celebration. Even with our limited French we thought we made it clear that we wanted local wines, but that message seemed to be very difficult to get across as we were given wines from all over France, and even some Italian and Spanish wines. Our definition of local was much closer to home. We were thinking no further than the boundaries of our region, the Pays de la Loire, to try to minimise food and wine miles. We purchased a number of bottles to sample, purely for research purposes, of course. They were all easy to drink. Some we liked more than others but we still didn't feel that we had addressed our desire to try to source truly local wines.

It was during a trip to a supermarket in Laval that we hit the mother lode. Browsing through the Pays de la Loire region in the wine section, we found an amazing selection of sparkling wines from Saumur, which is just an hour and a half south of us. Using our well-trusted technique for wine selection, we made our choices and took them home to try. I am old enough, and have drunk enough wine, to have a fairly wide understanding about the different wine regions, but for us it's more about liking what we like rather than searching for named châteaus. I tend to make a decision based on the region and, depending on the occasion, I will either go for a good cru or a reasonably priced bottle from an AOC I know and like. Angela, on the other hand, will look at the bottle or label and see what she thinks looks the best. We both have similar success rates, so we don't dismiss each other's choices, but with a decision as important as our wedding wine we took several options home to try.

Our final decision was based on taste but the bottles and labels were also lovely, which negates any wine snobbery in our house. We found several excellent sparkling whites from the Ackerman vineyard, one of which even came in magnums, so we immediately ordered those. They also had an amazing sparkling red, a 'Royale Rouge', that was far too easy to drink, so we added that to our list. Whites from the Loire are easy to find, as are rosé wines. In both cases, the samples we took were similar in taste and quality and were very drinkable, so we went for the prettiest bottles, which was a white from Touraine and a rosé from Anjou. The reds were more of a challenge, but we found a pleasant *Chinon*. Our region does not do the heavier wines you find further south, so we thought we'd celebrate that rather than ignore it.

Tasting wines can be quite taxing. We could not finish each bottle we sampled, so instead we had to leave what was left or give it away. We were just too busy to drink a couple of bottles of wine a night – even a couple of glasses would send us to sleep at the same time as the children. Luckily, we had some friends coming to stay that were happy to help us.

Next on our list of long-lead items was the music for the big party. As well as dancing, we had decided we wanted to ensure the entertainment was very French. Now, that probably conjures up different things for different people. Maybe some Edith Piaf or André Claveau? Nope. For us it had to be a bunch of middle-aged blokes with accordions and keyboards.

I didn't know exactly what I wanted but I had a picture of a classic French band playing on the landing of our stairs. I wanted something so authentic that there was no mistaking what it was trying to be. Music that makes you tap your feet, move your body and feel elated . . . Basically, I was after a local and reasonably priced Georges Brassens. The search was not easy. I even put the feelers out to my French friends Alex and Marie, who live in Montpellier – they know everything and everyone. My search turned up lots of very good bands, but for me they were all missing the *authentique* Frenchness.

One afternoon, I was on the way to *La Poste* when I saw a poster on a lamp post for a tea dance. Firstly, a tea dance in our small village was very exciting – even though I knew we were so time poor we could not go – but, secondly, and more importantly, there was mention of a live band. Emilio Corfa was the singer of a five-piece band and they were the perfect combination of *authentique* and cheesy. I contacted them and Emilio came to the château. He was a true gentleman and he'd brought along a CD with a number of English covers he wanted to suggest. His enthusiasm in telling me did a great Gloria Estafan cover won me over, even though I then spent the rest of meeting explaining to him I wanted classic French music that would get people dancing.

My theory: a great beat to music no one knows is better than any potentially bad covers. We couldn't afford the whole band at nearly €3,000 so we went for the three-piece: Emilio on the accordion plus two other band members, one on the keyboard and one on the saxophone.

With alcohol and music ticked off the list, I had a very positive 'whatever state the château is in, our wedding is going to happen' moment.

We were always open for visitors but there were a few simple rules: they had to be prepared to get stuck in; catering during the day is usually smash and grab; and when it came to making a brew, ask around and see who else wants one ...

Johnny had been on the National Geographic survival series with me and had stayed in contact, so when his wife Nadine had business in Paris, it seemed logical that they would pop down and see us for a couple of days. Johnny and Nadine had met and fallen in love on the American soap *Days of Our Lives*. They were playing opposite each other and after falling in love on screen realised that they were actually meant for each other in real life as well. As well as being a Hollywood actor, Nadine ran her own fashion company, and Johnny presented a very successful DIY series, so when they said they were coming we immediately produced a to-do list for them.

With just two months until our wedding, a lot of our effort was going into decorating and cosmetic tasks, so I envisaged them helping finish off one or two of the rooms. But Angela had other ideas and sprang on me that the room that was to be the children's playroom was not sufficiently playful ... It's a simple fact of life that when you are up to your ass in alligators it's not the right time to build a helter-skelter, however Angela was fretting that the children had been neglected in our work on the château. My first thought was to buy them some colouring books and maybe some new crayons but I was hardly going to get away with that. I'd never have dreamt up the idea of a helter-skelter in a month of Sundays but with Johnny coming to stay somehow I was convinced it was a reasonable thing to do.

Angela knocked up a simple sketch and I came up with a very rudimentary plan and then bought the plywood and four-by-two wood for the frame. The longest plywood I could buy was 2.5m so that was to be the length of the sides. I made them such that it was possible to get two pieces out of a single sheet. By making the construction an octagon, four pieces would make main body and a couple more for the slide would ensure that I had kept the price as low as possible. But I grew to hate that bloody thing.

When Johnny and Nadine arrived, I instantly loved the pair of them. We had spoken often via Dick when they were filming together and they were full of energy and had a passion for life. We gave them a quick guided tour. Both were charmed by the history and elegance of what they saw, despite the fact it was a work in progress. Even though they had just flown in from Los Angeles, both wanted to get stuck in. And we didn't ever look a gift horse in the month, so we issued them with coveralls and off they went. Nadine was straight up a mobile scaffolding tower painting the playroom walls with white emulsion and Johnny and Dick were marking up sheets of plywood for the helter-skelter. From what I could gather, the plan had evolved a bit – Dick and Johnny were discussing complex angles and downward forces. Nadine kept popping up and down refreshing her paint tray and adding more to the ceiling and walls. Most of the time she was smiling and shaking her head as our men debated how to build the thing of beauty that the children would eventually play on. I thought the best thing I could do was keep a low profile and intermittently provide mugs of tea.

Angela's plan was for a fairground-style ride that children climb to the top of and then slide down on a coir mat. I knew it was not a trivial build and so to keep things simple I produced an octagonal structure with posts sticking out that the slide would attach to. The construction was so heavy it had to be built in situ and that meant cutting out and bringing the elements from the cellar. Day one finished with lots of bits of wood cut and arranged in the playroom.

We love spending time with friends, and eating and having a glass of wine is an easy way to pass time. However, with the wedding looming, we didn't have time not to be productive, so after a day's work our aperitifs were all contenders for the wedding, namely our sparkling wines. Accompanying the meal, we had a selection of wines, to see what we liked rather than being decadent (covert wine tasting). Even our meals were usually test dishes for the wedding. So Johnny and Nadine had a taster of what was to come.

Johnny and I were happy in the kitchen while the girls sorted the children and did whatever they had to do before supper. I'd done a lot of the cooking on our survival show and Johnny loved trying new things so he was keen to see how I made my rabbit stew. Rabbit isn't very popular in the UK or the US, whereas it is available in most supermarkets over here. One rabbit was enough for a main course for the four of us. The meat is tasty and quite lean. You can buy it jointed but normally you just get a whole carcass complete with head (you also get the kidneys and heart so it's good value for money). I'd eaten a lot of rabbit and even cooked it when I was competing on *Celebrity Masterchef*. It needs to be cooked enough but not too much. In the stew the legs get a lot more cooking than the saddle as it is a shame to let the small tender loins dry out. The kidneys we cut in half, seasoned and flash-fried as an additional *amuse-bouche*.

Johnny helped prepare the carrots and parsnips and carved them into torpedo shapes. Then we cut the larger back legs into two pieces and gently sautéed all the legs portions in butter (this is a northern dish so none of your olive oil) with onions before I added the vegetables for a bit more cooking. Then we added the loin and the ubiquitous garlic. Cider was added next – dry not sweet (the carrots and parsnips are sweet enough). Twenty minutes later, in went the salt and white pepper, cream was stirred through, and the dumplings were floated on the top. After another twenty minutes, the dumplings had risen, their bottoms were soggy and their tops were crispy. The stew was ready to serve. Johnny and Nadine gave it the thumbs up. The dish is surprisingly sweet so enough salt is essential but the cider and cream sauce just shouts out for a bit of fresh baguette to dip in and there is no excuse for leaving any of it on the plate.

Day two was the day of the helter-skelter's erection. We had two octagonal frames: a large one for the base and a smaller one for the top. Each corner had a 'vertical' post so after a fair amount of balancing and swearing in Irish and American we had a frame that was far from solid (the rigidity was always intended to be provided by the sides). We added a couple of sides to reduce the wobble and started to screw on the slide supports. A couple of hours later, we had something that looked a lot like a helter-skelter that was just missing its slide. You could see where it had to go but it was far from finished. Nadine had finished painting the room and she and Angela between them had decided on the itinerary for the rest of Johnny and Nadine's trip. The long and short of it was I had to finish off the slidey bit myself . . .

First, I spent another day cutting out cardboard and fitting templates. Each section of the slide was different as the supporting structure was tapered, so the slide went down, round and out – it was a pain in the proverbial ass! Having cut out each a piece of ply, it then had to be attached and a guard rail fitted. The curve of the slide was far from a perfect but it was very helter-skelter like and even unpainted it was impressive to look at. It's just a pity it wasn't on my to-do list so I could cross it off after three long days' work!

* * *

It seems ridiculous that we had been living at the château for seven months before we discovered the Fromagerie du Bois Belleray, a cheese factory right at the end of our road. We had seen the occasional milk tanker go past but we'd never actually turned right out of our driveway to continue to the end. We were still sourcing things for the wedding and hoping to keep it as local as possible. And suddenly the penny dropped – at the roundabout where we had turned off the main road hundreds of times, there was a sign that said, *'Vente Directe'*. They had a factory shop! We went to explore.

We discovered that the family-run business had been going since 1912 and had 130 employees, turning out over 100,000 cheeses a day from the milk from over 200 farmers from the *département*. For months we had been going to the local supermarket, but they were making thousands of cheeses at the end of our road. Since we discovered the little treasure we had right beside us, every menu for every event we have ever put on has featured butter and cheese from the fromagerie. No food miles at all so everyone can have as much as they want.

As September came to a close, there were lots of areas of the château nearly ready to finish off, but lots of chaos too. With just over six weeks to go until our wedding, it was all hands on deck. Grandma and Grandad had been our mainstay when it came to looking after the children, but they also wanted to get involved so we asked if they fancied getting the orangery party-safe and ready for action.

After years of neglect the orangery needed some love. Insects of every size and shape had taken up residence and the wonderful

wisteria had grown in from every angle: through the eves, the missing windowpanes, even the roof. The first job was to reclaim the orangery from wilderness. This had been on our 'to-do' list since we first saw the château, but now it was urgent. With the growth cut back, next on the list was cleaning, then removing broken glass panes and measuring for new ones. Fortunately, all the arch-shaped windows were intact, so it was a matter of measuring lots of rectangles.

The glass in the orangery sits in metal frames with one sheet on top of another, all held in with putty. Most of the broken panes were low down, which was convenient, but did beg the question what would happen when the broken glass and old putty was removed. We had visions of all the glass above cascading down. With gloves, safety glasses and a selection of old chisels and wire brushes, Mum and Dad soon had the old glass and putty dug out and thankfully there was absolutely no sign of any of the other bits moving. So when the replacement panes were delivered, the most difficult part of the whole task was matching the correct size glass with the correct hole. With more than twenty panes replaced the orangery was no longer draughty, so it was time for them to start making it beautiful.

Some basic patching was required of the wall and ceiling, but the main objective was to refresh it and the answer for that is buckets of white matt emulsion. After months of sending DIY shopping lists to visitors who came out to see us, our paint store had an admirable supply of white emulsion. So armed with rollers, dust sheets and a set of steps, they set to work and the orangery received a couple of coats of white emulsion. It made a huge difference.

The brick troughs round the 'window sides' of the orangery are rather unusual. We debated tanking them and turning it into a water feature but ultimately common sense prevailed and we decided to convert them into plant pots. They were huge and

Our wedding menu.

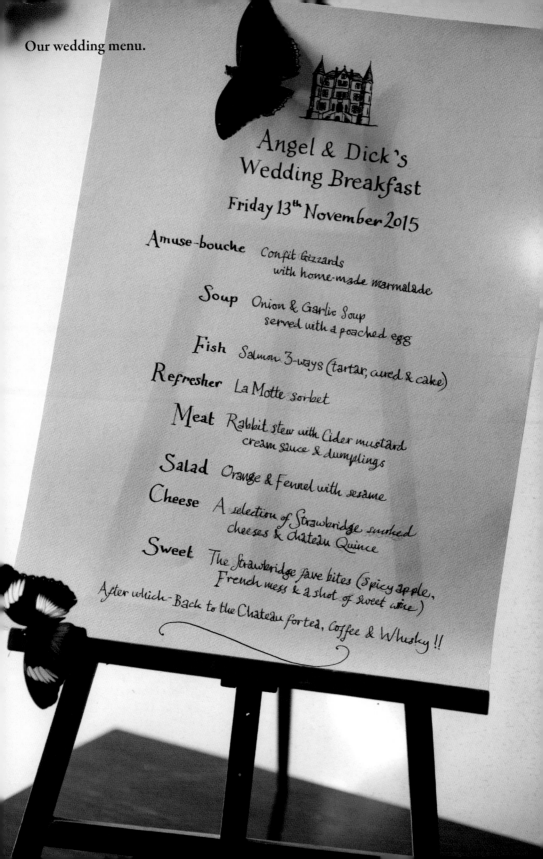

Angel & Dick's
Wedding Breakfast
Friday 13th November 2015

Amuse-bouche Confit Gizzards
with home-made marmalade

Soup Onion & Garlic Soup
served with a poached egg

Fish Salmon 3-ways (tartar, cured & cake)

Refresher La Motte sorbet

Meat Rabbit stew with Cider mustard
cream sauce & dumplings

Salad Orange & Fennel with sesame

Cheese A selection of Strawbridge smoked
cheeses & chateau Quince

Sweet The Strawbridge fave bites (spicy apple,
French mess & a shot of sweet wine)
After which - Back to the Chateau for tea, Coffee & Whisky !!

The wedding breakfast.

Family, friends . . .

. . . and Emilio!

Our first Christmas, 2015.

filling them with compost was going to be expensive, so we lined the bottom of the trough with all sorts of polystyrene packing that had been congregating in the outbuildings awaiting disposal. Several carloads of compost later, it was just a matter of a couple of well-placed palm trees to finish the look.

The days were drawing in but our first September quietly slipped into autumn without us really noticing it. The trees started to change and the horse chestnuts on the far side of the moat seemed to lead the way. After a little breeze, we would notice leaves on the water but rather than it feeling messy, the colours changing seemed to make it even more beautiful. Even now we still pinch ourselves when we look out at all the trees that are ours. They are special at every time of the year and we love them – but, just to be clear, that doesn't stretch to full-on tree hugging . . .

We had made a start on getting ready for our wedding – the orangery was ready to open for business, the menu was coming together and we had the refreshments sorted. The playroom was done and we had a helter-skelter. But there was still so much more to do . . .

CHAPTER TEN

OCTOBER

After the equinox on 21 September there is less day than night and we really have arrived in the season 'of mists and mellow fruitfulness'. Keats' argument that autumn is every bit as beautiful as spring is very difficult to disagree with when you look out of the window of the château and see so many amazing colours: from golds to reds, deep greens to yellows; even the trees that have lost their covering are striking. The château has the most beautiful views from every window and the higher you go, the more the surrounding trees dominate. By the time you are four floors up you are level with the treetops and in October that means you can see for miles and the amount of woodland surrounding us is very apparent.

The horse chestnuts are one of the earliest to come into leaf and also one of the earliest to lose their leaves, but by early October it is the sweet chestnuts that are the most obvious. It's hard to remember seeing sweet chestnuts at home that produced 'nuts' worth eating but everywhere we went in the Mayenne there were large fallen sweet chestnuts nestled in their very spiky husks. A pair of stout gloves were essential for collecting them or you risked leaving the majority of the bounty behind.

The biggest tree on the north edge of our land is a lovely sweet chestnut and it marks the boundary between our plot and Jacques and Isabelle's. Having seen the debris of the chestnuts that had been run over on the road outside the château, we couldn't wait to go and collect our own. Suitably dressed and with wellies on, we set off for a family expedition round the moat to collect our own *marron*, which is the French name that describes the fruit of the chestnut (the *châtaigne*). That first autumn, we were too busy to fully appreciate all the wonderful things growing around us but we were determined not to miss out on everything, so we made sure we would have a bag of chestnuts to roast and nibble on.

Having collected a decent hoard, we pierced them several times to avoid them exploding while they cooked, soaked them in water for half an hour then popped them in the oven for twenty minutes. They were so tasty and smelt wonderful. They were so enticing that you ended up burning your fingers in the haste to peel them. It was a little sad that there were so many chestnuts around our land but we only had time to collect a few, but the beauty of moving to a new life in France was we knew they would be there every year for the foreseeable future and whatever we didn't eat was food for the abundant wildlife.

Hunting is very popular in France in the autumn and I was invited by Jacques to join his family and friends for a hunt on their land. All around the château the land is still owned by the Baglion family and Jacques has several hundred acres. From what we could see he did not farm, instead he had planted trees and set it aside. We had spotted deer from our windows but had yet to see the wild boar everyone talked about. That was probably due to our tendency to look inwards during that first year and not outwards, combined with the fact that Arthur and Dorothy were a little too young to join in spotting wildlife. I decided that I would indeed join them but I would not shoot on this first occasion so I could observe the traditions before participating. Having been in the army for over twenty years, I am a reasonable shot, and being a country man at heart I have enjoyed shooting and fishing for most of my life. In France there is a lot more game than we have in the UK so shooting is popular and the land husbandry appears to treat the game as a resource to be looked after.

Before the day of the hunt, I popped to a local hunting shop and bought the regulation fluorescent orange camouflage waistcoat and a *pibole*. We met on Saturday morning. First on the agenda was a drink and a briefing on the day. There were to be a number of drives, with half the hunters beating and driving the game, and the other half taking positions at the end of the drive to shoot what passed them. There were different horn signals for the end of a drive, for deer and for boar.

It was a beautiful day and a truly French experience. There are very few pheasants in our part of France and, from what I could ascertain, the birds that were flushed were woodcock and snipe, both of which are not easy to shoot. So by the end of the morning there were only a couple of birds bagged despite some enthusiastic shooting.

After the morning drives and flushing, lunch was very welcome and we were treated to Isabelle's game terrine and a lovely vegetable soup. The main course was like a hotpot and dessert was an open apple tart glazed with apricot. Wine was served but I think people were a bit reserved as there was still an afternoon's shooting to come and the drives for the larger game. Still, as we congregated after lunch, everyone was feeling rather mellow and the half-mile

---

*   The French hunting horn.

walk to the start of the drive was probably very well planned by Jacques. When large game is driven the size of the shot in the guns is changed and there is significantly less shooting. I never saw a boar that day, which was disappointing, but several deer were taken.

We made our way back to Jacques and Isabelle's where there were drinks waiting for us. I joined Isabelle and helped with the skinning and butchery and everyone who participated was offered a joint of venison. As I had not shot, I declined that time.

* * *

After months of waiting for the *étude** and then the challenge of finding a contractor to install our septic tank and filter beds, the day had finally arrived. Jean Betram and his team were going to install our new septic system. Inside the château, the pace was picking up as the very real deadline of our wedding was galloping closer. It didn't matter how many hours we worked, there was always lots more to do and, even though progress had been made on lots of rooms, nothing was quite finished.

The installation of the septic tank cost more than £10,000 as we had opted for a system with lower annual costs and a slightly greater outlay. We had confirmed with Jean Bertram and his nephew, Jean Betram (no chance of confusion there!), that the price was a fixed and they reckoned it would only take a couple of days. When the plant turned up on Monday morning before 9am, it was all looking very promising. We confirmed the plan on the *étude* and they were all very chilled about the fact that the waste post-settling-tank (where the filter beds would be) was going across the moat so we were relaxed and looked forward to being spectators rather than workers.

I made time to watch the first hole being dug as it was for the septic tank and near the château itself, and I was a little worried about the proximity to the walls and their foundations. We know our château

---

*   Survey.

is on the site of an earlier château but we didn't know anything about the foundations and whether they were original or new in the nineteenth century. The digging started and some really huge boulders were excavated. It was possible to see the massive rocks that were below the walls and that was reassuring. More interesting was the surprise that the French team had when the hole began to fill with water as they dug down. To place the tank at the correct level they needed the base to be down below the water level. After a cup of coffee and a little head scratching, a call was made by the elder Jean Bertram. Excavation continued, a pump was brought in, and sand and cement was emptied into the puddle at the bottom of the hole. Filling the tank with some water allowed it to settle on the floor of the hole.

Day one had been fun but it was on day two that I was happy I had a fixed-price contract. The trench for the pipe that carried the post-settling-liquid to the filter beds had to be laid across and under the moat but instead it floated . . . I was in the wonderful position of watching not doing, so I enjoyed my view. Obviously the water seeped back into the trench as the sludge was removed. It was like digging a hole on the beach down by the water's edge – the more you dig, the more the hole will fill in from the sides. Some progress was made but it was never going to be a 'trench'.

Then Jean Bertram the younger came up with the idea of damming off one end of the moat. Water levels were down so the hope was it might be possible to slow the ingress of water sufficiently to place the buoyant piping into the bed of the moat. Jean Bertram the older had to be away for several hours and left the rest of the team to wrestle with a *barque*[*], sheets of corrugated iron and tarpaulins. It was great spectator sport, but with lots going on, I was only able to pop in and out, and to be honest I don't think spectators were very helpful as the team tried to manoeuvre

---

[*] A small, unsinkable plastic boat.

on the sludge. All credit where it is due, with the digger shovelling the sludge, the boat moving the barriers and the pump working overtime, they managed to build a dam of sorts and pumped lots of water out of the end of the moat. Next thing I knew, there was no pipe visible and everyone was congratulating each other. Just then, as if by magic, Jean Bertram the older, and obviously wiser, turned up. While the automatic pump in the *fosse septique** and the pipes in the filter bed were connected, we had a snap inspection from the SPANC lady to see all was well. It was her job to ensure regulations had been met and to sign off our sewage system. Our conditions of sale had given us eighteen months to do it. We were quite pleased that only nine months in and we were just about there.

I'm not sure what the young lady said but my joking answer about it being lovely getting a visit from the SPANC must have caused some offence because she muttered something, turned round, got in her car and left. Both the JBs were perplexed. They always got their jobs signed off and this was obviously my fault. About three-quarters of an hour later she turned up again and the JBs practically ran to intercept her so she didn't have to speak to me. To everyone's surprise, especially mine, she was a bit tongue-tied as she asked me to sign the French edition of my *Practical Self Sufficiency* book. I wrote a dedication in English thanking her for her help. She had a quick look around, smiled lots, signed off the work and then drove away. What a result.

With our forever sewage system in and functioning, a major milestone had been met and now we could stop worrying about what happened to our poopage, though two months later we were to find out more in the rather horrible episode of the poop volcano . . .

* * *

*   Septic tank.

Finding the right lights for the château was a challenge that I loved . . . to a fashion. I did not have total freedom as Dick needed to check that it was possible to make them all work and to ensure that they were, well . . . lights and not hanging ornaments! Even with our shortened to-do list and pared-back fittings, there were still lots of lights to get. Before the wedding I needed:

- *A chandelier in the entrance hall – this was important. I bought an antique pineapple light from eBay in America for US$400.*
- *A chandelier in the salon – also important. I found a lovely chandelier on Leboncoin for €320.*
- *A chandelier in the* salle-à-manger *– important again (in fact, I suppose most of them were important!). This was bought for €55 from the slow-moving lady at the brocante.*
- *Two wall lights for the back hallway. These came from the Emmaus for €5 each.*
- *Two lights for the main staircase. For this, I chose two very Hollywood-looking steam engine lights, again from the slow-moving lady at the* brocante. *These were €230 for the pair.*
- *A hanging light for the main kitchen. We went for a classic double billiard table light, which was €20 at the Emmaus.*
- *Wall lights for the bathroom in the honeymoon suite. We chose a pair of Hollywood-style showtime lights from Ikea.*
- *A selection of lights for the vestibule, bedroom and turret in the honeymoon suite. We went for Art Deco wall lights in the honeymoon suite. These were all purchased from the Emmaus at different times and cost between €5–20 each.*

- *Lights in all the other rooms (so people could see!). These all came from the Emmaus and were the cheapest I could find!*
- *Hand-held battery lights for the orangery.*

Even compiling the list took a lot of time and I spent many evenings in our 'horizontal office' looking. In fact, every night I was searching for something. Lights were important, but I was also after a kitchen table, sofas, sideboards, mirrors, rugs and anything else quirky. We had brought a lot of stuff with us but the château is big and it took a lot to fill it!

I have a simple rule for Angela: she can have anything but she can't have everything. That's pretty reasonable and clear. It only becomes tricky if she doesn't quite understand the pain her choices put me through. I get the fact that a pineapple is a sign of welcome (in Hawaii!) and that a light with the original patina is desirable but bringing back to life a light in which the fittings didn't work and the wires were only insulated with paper was a slight inconvenience.

After a trip to the electrical section of Bricomarché*, I took up residence in the back kitchen. I knew it was going to be a long one and the kitchen has the best light in the house, so I brought down an audiobook on my phone and a bottle of water and set to work.

Once the children were in bed, I generally never went far, but I knew Dick would be getting himself worked up with my pineapple light so I slipped downstairs to check. In that moment, my heart melted. He had a foldable table in front of him, his glasses at the end of his nose, looking adorable, and there were old and new cables everywhere. I knew he was not happy, so I just smiled,

---

* A French chain of stores that sell DIY products.

kissed him gently and then ran off fast before I could hear the chunters.

In a château no one can hear you scream. I cursed and I fiddled, trying to thread new wire into the arms of the light. It must have had the wires installed before it was put together because I really struggled trying to get them through the very narrow tubes. Finally I managed to enlarge the entrance holes and get fishing line through by pushing copper wire in first and then pulling the line after it (god bless clove hitches). Then I used the fishing line to pull the cable through. It took a couple of goes before I discovered the 30lb sea fishing line was the best but I had to keep it under tension or the clove hitch would slacken. Six hours later and I had the wire in place so I could think about connecting and attaching the low-energy 'candle' fittings and bulbs. The eight fittings and bulbs actually cost nearly as much as the light but it would have been churlish to mention that to Angela.

As a wedding present, Jacques and Isabelle had offered to cut our grass. It was such an act of kindness that we will never forget it. I can't lie: I actually liked the meadow that had grown with the grasses that had been scorched by the sun, but I knew having it cut was the right thing. There was no way we could say no to their kind offer. Jacques' plan was to cut it twice: once in October and then again just before our wedding. It was not a small task as there were a couple of acres to cut. But he had the equipment to do it and gladly helped.

Jacques obviously loved the fact that his family home was full of activity and coming back to life. In addition to cutting the grass, he and his son Louie made themselves available to help distribute the gravel. Jacques drove the tractor, roughly spreading the gravel, and then Louie raked the ground. Louie is a charming young man – he was eighteen at the time and we loved that he never had a

mobile phone; if we needed to get in contact with him we had to text Isabelle. It was a massive help and, in a day, with their tractor and all the attachments, Jacques and Louie achieved what would have taken us absolutely ages. We did have tractor envy but that would have to wait.

At the end of that day you don't just say thank you and goodbye; we had toiled together so refreshments were in order. The least we could do was have drinks with the family on our new gravel. A little bit of bustling later and trays of drinks and nibbles were out. Soft drinks were the syrups you become used too very quickly in France, diluted with sparkling water. When we first arrived, we used wonder where the squash was, but now, of course, we had grenadine . . . On a warm summer's evening we would have pastis or Suze served with ice or ice-cold water, but this was autumn, so I looked at Jacques and said, 'A whiskey?'

He smiled and responded, *'Bien sûr'**, so crystal glasses, some Black Bush and a small jug of tepid water was produced. A healthy measure and a little splash of water to let the flavour out and then there was lots of toasting and general merriment.

I have to say it was very pleasant but definitely unusual for us to be drinking whiskey as an aperitif on an empty stomach. And, as a bird can't fly on one wing, we had a second healthy measure too. It was a lovely relaxing time and there was lots of smiling, chatting and gesticulating . . .

* * *

We had been busy across a very wide front. Though it may seem logical to do one room from start to finish then move onto the next,

---

* 'Of course.'

that did not reflect the scale of our challenge. With so many rooms you would require the electrician to visit twenty times – a couple of times per room. Or the plumbing would need to be done ten times in ten different rooms. We had just about reached the point when some rooms could actually be finished. Lee and Kyle had been on holiday for most of the seven months since we last saw them but, bless them, they were prepared to come back and get some closure on the heating system.

There are three legs of utilities in the château. The first one provides water, waste, electricity and heating to the family kitchen, the boot room, the dining room and the service kitchen and plumbing to the temporary suite above ours. The second, middle leg provides heating to the temporary suite and would eventually service the *boudoir* (though that was not yet even a glint in our eyes) and the honeymoon suite and toilet. The final leg has heating, plumbing and electricity for the eastern side of the château.

Lee and Kyle came in and had a wander around to see what we'd been up to and then, without any further ado, they set about connecting and commissioning anything that needed to be brought to life. After a couple of very long days, we had all our radiators connected on the first three floors. The honeymoon suite's bathroom was fully functional, which meant, together with our suite and the temporary suite on the floor above us, we had three working bathrooms – plus the temporary loo in the tower room off the dining room. Four loos is a luxury but far from enough for two hundred guests at a wedding – but that was yet to be addressed . . . As they left, Lee did his very famous head shaking, which translates to, 'You are barking, but good luck.' Next time we would see them was going to be at the wedding and we had told them in no uncertain terms that they were not allowed to bring coveralls or any tools.

I have had the privilege of going on a many brides' journeys with them. I often get an early peek of their wedding dresses as we plan every detail together. I have always stood by the sentiment that a huge part of the celebration is in the planning. Dick and I knew we had taken on a mammoth task. Though trying to organise a three-day wedding in a new country, alongside all the renovations and looking after two young children was actually quite amusing. Writing it down now makes me laugh. I'm strong and do not like violins and have few moments in which I cry out of frustration. But the wedding dress was one.

I had spent many evenings and 'children sleeping in the car moments' looking at what sort of dress I would like and I came to realise that I'm just not a wedding dress sort of girl. I never ever found anything that I liked for me and my shape or even anything I could picture myself in. I suppose there was always something more pressing or important and I did not want to think about me. Dorothy was only just one and I moved about wearing maternity bras. I had no idea about my body any more. I guess this often happens after children. I'd spent most of the last nine months in a denim boiler suit but I decided that was not a good look for the big day. Being in another country, I did not know where to even look. Not being in control of this made me sad. So I had a good cry and then immersed myself into the task of finding a wedding outfit.

I took myself up to the old servants' quarters. Next to my workroom was a room with lots of cupboards full of our posh clothes we no longer wore. I decide the first thing I would do was explore what fitted my new post-children body and then I would see if I had anything in my wardrobe that still excited me.

The room was small but the light was beautiful and dappled and it had beautiful wooden floors. I often thought it was lovely conditions for a servants' area. I started taking clothes out of the wardrobe, many items still with covers on. There were capes, dresses from the 1940s, '50s and '60s, kimonos, outfits that I used to wear when hosting, fur stoles, dresses I had made, dresses that did not fit and some that surprisingly did. It was a lovely walk down memory lane. Lots of the items had been purchased for specific occasions and all those moments came flooding back to me.

When I pulled out the 1940s wiggle dress that I was wearing when I met Dick for the first time, I got goosebumps. I loved this dress. I'd nearly worn it to its death. It had a slash neck, which was very forgiving, and little darts that cinched in at the waist. At the front there was a v-shaped panel of fabric which ruched into the waist – this was clever as it took the eye away from the belly. The fabric had a slight stretch to it and was a beautiful lilac floral. The length was also good, just below the knee (like a lady should). I loved this dress and always felt like a million dollars when I wore it – it certainly did the trick on that night, 14 November 2010 . . . So my idea was to have this dress remade in white silk. It was perfect. I felt the weight falling off my shoulders.

It was time to get real about what we could get done in time for our wedding. There were a couple of limitations: our funds and our bodies. At this point, we were functioning on less than five hours sleep a night and the other nineteen hours a day were spent working, so we were getting a bit knackered. We had budgeted pretty well but there was no way we could pay for more horsepower above what we had committed to.

Now in October, Angela was getting frustrated that we had not started to do all the decorative touches she had dreamt of. We were not being idle. It was just a lot of work that took a lot of organising, a lot of sourcing materials and a lot of doing. Deep down she understood that – though unfortunately it was fairly deep down! When we started to take things off our list that would have to wait until phase two, I could see her bottom lip quivering. But it was sensible to make this call as soon as we could to ensure we didn't waste time or effort.

As the windows had mostly had new glass put in and the rotten wood had been filled to make them safe and sealable, we decided a lick of paint over the ugly patches would be enough to see us through another winter. Our suite was going to have to remain untouched. We were comfortable and the children weren't suffering. At best it could be described as looking jaded – more accurately it could be said to be a bit squalid. It wasn't really a place to entertain but actually we loved it and were very happy there.

Apart from the honeymoon suite, the guest rooms would remain very basic as well. Our temporary bathroom on the fourth level was working and four of the rooms could be described as bedrooms, so we agreed no more effort was to go into the guest accommodation.

With the meadow cut and the gravel spread, the outside was also considered done. It would have been great to spend some time on the outside of the orangery but actually the problem would be where to start or stop so it was best to just accept it as it was. For the interior we would have to make do with the mismatched chairs, as the time and budget to cover them just wasn't there. Likewise, we didn't have the chance to go searching for a couple of hundred soup spoons (the one bit of cutlery that hadn't been in the Vintage Patisserie equipment boxes).

It actually came as a relief that we had made some decisions and taken massive chunks off the list. You have to know when to draw the line and we had come so far. I'm sure I knew that at the time as well. Or maybe I'm writing this with the benefit of hindsight. We still had to finish the kitchen, the entrance, the stairways, the salon, the *salle-à-manger*, the playroom and the honeymoon suite and make them as beautiful as possible for our guests. Even a quick tidy, clean-up and some flowers would have taken a good amount

of time. But thank goodness the 'grubby' work was coming to an end. I could not wait to get stuck in without mess being made.

During our search for extra help, Julian mentioned his friend Tina. She lived less than an hour away, was a quick learner and was game to have a go at anything. Tina's brilliant attitude along with her kind and caring nature meant she quickly became part of the team. Our limited funds were the only reason we didn't have her working eighteen-hour days with us – she was a huge help and was really getting stuck into all the woodwork painting. I also found out in later years that she is a great machinist and upholsterer. I quiz her all the time for her knowledge. In time, we also watched Tina and Julian fall in love. They didn't tell me, but I could see how they looked at each other. Tina still works a couple of days a week for us but she now spends most of time with Julian. Happy ever after I say . . .

But with so much painting we needed another set of hands. I felt like if we found someone who could start that very moment and paint 24/7 until the first guests arrived, we may possibly have got all the newly-plastered walls finished. (It had taken Nadine three days to paint the playroom.) I was saying goodbye to Steve the plasterer around this time and I asked him if he knew anyone that could paint. 'My wife Denise is brilliant,' he said. 'She's brilliant because I taught her.' You've got to love a bit of modesty. The very next day Denise flew in with her cape (or actually her brushes).

I'm pretty sure that when Denise arrived she said she was a better painter than Steve. I just had to laugh at having another competitive couple at the château. I explained that we didn't really have time to prime the walls and then do two coats of paint, so I had an idea (an idea that any good decorator would gasp at). If we added a 20 per cent ratio of water to a tin maybe it would water the paint down enough to allow it to go straight on and not clump on the

plaster. 'Let's give it a go,' Denise said, and to everyone's surprise it went on like velvet. It also meant that we got the grand staircase walls done in just a few days.

Even with the new sewage system in, we had insufficient toilets for the wedding guests. Obviously we looked at hiring more nice loos but the price of four toilets for the weekend was €1,800 – ridiculous! We needed to come up with another answer. After a bit of head scratching and research we bought three sheds for less than €100 each, two very cheap flush loos and a chemical cassette toilet. The two sheds were erected outside the château beside the septic tank. A little fiddling with some hoses to connect them to a tap in the workshop and then some creativity with some 100mm waste piping and cutting holes in the sheds gave us two flushing toilets. Now it was just a matter of connecting them directly into the septic tank.

The chemical loo we put in a shed beside the orangery. So that was three more to add to the one in the tower off the dining room, the two in the honeymoon suite, the one in our room and the one on the fourth floor – not terrible, even if some were tucked away. But to relieve the pressure on them we decided that we also needed some *pissoires*, so we stood a urinal we had inherited in the woods beside the orangery, with the pipe disappearing into a rapidly dug and loosely backfilled hole. A few pretty candles and it would actually be very atmospheric. As well as one functioning toilet inside, when we first moved in our château also had a couple of outside toilets at the rear. They were quite special, as both were double seaters. Well 'seats' is a bit of an exaggeration but there was a large plank in each with two holes cut into it so two people could take up residence at the same time, very sociable. They had obviously been neglected, but removing the seats showed that each of the small rooms were actually just floors suspended above large holes that disappeared down below the water level. We had to assume there was some sort of pipe that connected the holes to the moat to allow 'things' to swim in and eat the 'waste'. We decided to take a tired old bath that Angela would never refurbish and put it in one of these outside toilets, over the hole with a 'Pee here' sign above it. All very makeshift and low tech, but cheap.

It had probably been decades since anyone had used the loos so before installing the new urinal I thought it was worth a quick explore to see if there was any treasure in the bottom of the hole. It sort of sounds disgusting in hindsight, but it made sense at the time. Some welly boots and gloves, a spotlight, a bucket and a ladder, and I was off. I'd given myself twenty minutes so there was no messing around.

There was a fair amount of wood from where the box had disintegrated but that was soon out of the way and I started raking around in what felt like rubble. Some lovely bits of crockery appeared – the colours were vibrant despite so much time in the ooze. There were also a couple of small bottles and bits of glass. There was absolutely no treasure but I did discover a tunnel about one inch high that joined the pit to the moat. It was lined with very nice cut stone and looked impressive for a loo output. With my time up it was just a matter of attaching the bath so that no one could fall down into the pit.

In total, our make-do toilet facilities were the best part of €1,400 cheaper than hiring portable potties, and some of them even flushed.

As October drew to an end, our stress levels rose. There are several things in life that are known to be stressful and we appeared to be doing most of them at the same time. We were getting married in two weeks, all our family and friends were coming to see us in our new home and we were entertaining a couple of hundred people in a château that hadn't had running water or electricity eight months earlier. We still knew we would do it; we just didn't know if we would ever sleep again. We also had the niggling feeling that there was so much more we should be doing. It was ridiculous but we felt there were things we were missing. For example, quince cheese. A year earlier, when we had seen the château for the first time, we had taken quince back to Southend and made our own jars. We still had a few left but surely we couldn't miss out on making more in our first year living in France?

··

QUINCE CHEESE

Ingredients

1.5kg quince
1 vanilla pod
Caster sugar

Method

Peel and core the quince, cut it into pieces then put it in a large pan. Cover with water and add the vanilla pod. Bring to the boil and simmer for about forty minutes.

Remove the soft quince from the pan with a slotted spoon and put in a bowl. Discard the liquor.

Weigh the quince, then put back in the pan with an equal weight of sugar.

Slowly stirring regularly, bring up the heat and continue heating and stirring until it transforms into a rich coral-pink paste.

Transfer into sterilised jars and seal.

··

October was a big month. First we got our *étude*, swiftly followed by our sewage system and then we were well and truly plumbed in. Decoration was in full swing and day by day the château was becoming more and more beautiful. The honeymoon suite was looking very special and our wedding was only days away.

CHAPTER ELEVEN

NOVEMBER
(A MONTH OF TWO HALVES)

This was it. Our wedding was two weeks, thirteen days or 312 hours away. Although November is not renowned for good weather, there were blue skies every day in our first year. With an autumn bite in the air, it was the best. Autumn really takes hold in November and, as you look out of the windows of the château, you are greeted with bare branches. On our island we have two rows of lime trees that have been pollarded for over a century, but probably not for 15 years now, so their canopy of leaves was enormous and looked a little out of place on the majestic trunks. The leaves were beautiful and had turned yellow and rusty orange. It was a wonderful sight and we hoped they would hold on a couple more weeks until our big day. Then they could fall off and become part of the château's grounds.

We both knew November was going to be a month of two halves. Up to and immediately after the wedding was going to be high-octane and we would be working on adrenaline. Then there would be the calmness and reflection as everyone thinned out afterwards; we would be by ourselves, without any pressing deadlines, for probably the first time since we arrived in France. We could not wait for either.

Normally in the middle of Autumn we love wrapping up and going for windy, wet walks. As the nights draw in during October, the evenings are a time for comforting, warm stews that cook throughout the day and make the house smell wonderful. We took to putting on the slow cooker and enjoying a warming meal in the evening. The smell of oxtail, onions, red wine, tomato, carrot and seasoning cooking all day is enough to send any hungry carnivore round the bend. To our surprise, Arthur became an oxtail-eating monster. A visit to the local supermarket butchery department in France is a lot less sterile than a supermarket back in the UK. The *abats** section contains those parts of an animal no longer available anywhere other than traditional butchers in UK. Our British visitors stare in morbid fascination at the heads, brains, tongues, ears, tails, hearts, lungs and gizzards that are on sale. As well as eating oxtail, Arthur is a sucker for gizzards, and they are widely available in France, so we decided we would serve them at our wedding, comfited and tossed in a rose jelly we make with an apple or quince base.

We pride ourselves on trying new food at least once and we really wanted to share our passion with our wedding guests. That's what weddings should be all about, in my opinion. Some of the textures can be a bit off-putting, I'll give you that, but over the previous eleven months of experimenting we had tried many things that

---

* Offal.

were definitely not frightfully British. Some were amazing explosions of tastes and others were utterly repulsive, but at least now we know. Dick always orders anything he has not tried before and sometimes when he is eating it I cannot concentrate on my own meal because of the morbid fascination. Andouille and chips sound innocuous enough, especially when it is described as a garlicky sausage. There is even an andouille stall in Borough Market, so it must be trendy. But I'd say be very wary of anyone offering you a chitterlings sausage. The smell makes me gag and the fact that the intestines that have been cut into rings and put into a sausage casing that appears to smell even more 'intestiney' means it's just not for me. The village of Andouille is only a twenty-minute drive from us, so it's a local delicacy, and Dick loves it. We even considered including it on our wedding breakfast menu but, alas, I wanted to enjoy our wedding – not have my head stuck down one of the fancy new toilets.

*Tête de veau** is also a 'thing' in our area. Dick's ordered it a number of times, but has confessed to never having had a good one. I think it's the hairy, spiky bits that throw him. We once took my parents to a posh restaurant (with white table linen, that's how I define posh!) and a bowl of slightly creamy stew turned up with very recognisable bits of a calf's head in it. Dick got the giggles and my mum could not take her eyes off it. For the avoidance of doubt, when I say recognisable, I mean eyelids complete with eyelashes, ears and what could have been lips. I don't know how you'd ever make that look appealing. The sauce was very subtle and the meat had been cooked long and slow, but it was definitely hardcore for a British palette, and again not one for the wedding breakfast menu. But I am still proud that I tried it, before saying no f***ing way.

---

*   Calf's head.

* * *

With every day taking us closer to the big one, we were truly putting lots of jobs to bed. After making the very valid observation that what I considered done was a different done to him, Dick gave me the job of ticking off rooms. So I dug out a clipboard and got to work. It felt good to be able to officially close rooms off but with only just over a week to go I still had nearly ALL the exciting bits to finish – the nuances and little details that would showcase all the hard work gone into the fabric of the château, which Dick refers to as the 'dog work'. With the ratio of our build being 90 per cent dog work to 10 per cent beauty. It's embarrassing but lovely that's everyone oohs and ahhs at the final 10 per cent. But it's teamwork and I will never take credit for what goes into the often unseen.

In the entrance hall, the faux-taxidermy unicorns were placed symmetrically on either side of the entrance. Their faux white fur and faux white manes sat perfectly on the light *gris* walls. As you walked through the double doors the pineapple light hung perfectly in the centre (I hoped that Dick would soon forget the pain of that one!). At the back of the entrance, the original woodwork sat perfectly alongside the red and green stained glass, which was in perfect condition. Above was all the original stonework with the Baglion crest proudly declaring in Latin: 'Any land is home to the brave man.' It was a great reminder of the history of our beautiful home.

Facing each other on either side of the walls were two sideboards I'd managed to find at Emmaus. Each was three metres long and gave us lots of practical surface and storage space. I'd taken apart a Victorian taxidermy case and inside we drew a map of the château, so guests would know where to have a pee-pee. And last but not least, my favourite part of the room; the floor. A wooden flower took centre stage. This was surrounded by hexagonal pieces of chestnut and oak, which gave a stunning two-tone effect. The Bagliones had clearly wanted to ensure impressions counted. It looked very stylish.

As you head into the back entrance, the architecture of the grand double staircase was enough to take your breath away. We had scrubbed the stairs but the original burgundy lino remained for the moment. It felt like it was protecting the stairs and, although faded, you could still see the original gold trim; its faded glory was beautiful and a reminder of those who had walked before us. The lion-head stair spindles were a detail that I fell in love with the very first time I laid eyes on them. Above were my 3D butterflies in rich, deep tones: purples, yellows, reds, blacks – every colour and combination you could think of, launching from the back grand staircase and fluttering forward over the high walls of the château. I was so pleased with how they enhanced the château's original features and brought a sense of our personality.

As you looked back to the front door, off to the right, the walls of the *salle-à-manger* were painted a very light mint green. I had managed to save half of the room's original wallpaper, which had a lovely embossed floral print on. We painted over the wallpaper where it couldn't be saved and the new walls that had been plastered in the same green to bring it together. I loved the contrast between mint green on the walls and the dark wooden panelling that filled the entire bottom metre of the room. It had lost some of its colour and looked a little tired but a stain and varnish later it had bounced back and felt very 'gentleman's room' like. I approved. This room had a large double entrance, a door that led to the turret and two other symmetrical doors, one of which led to a cupboard that housed the Bagliones' original drinks bar. We didn't know this yet but Jenny Strawbridge and Dick's sisters had been busy collecting Irish Tyrone Crystal to fill this space. The faux-taxidermy giraffe and zebra took their residency in this room, as well as a piece of old mahogany which was once a coat rack in the back of the main hallway. In the *salle-à-manger* it had been given a new life as a shelf and was host to twenty-five of my favourite teapots that I had collected over the same number of years.

The paint was still drying in the salon and in the honeymoon suite but Denise had been flying through the rooms and Tina had taken control of all the woodwork and windows. I knew it was just a matter of time now until these rooms would come together as well. Everyone was going for it and we all spent a lot of time scrubbing floors as well. We giggled at the idea we were Cinderellas, all determined to go to the ball . . . If we survived, that is!

By this time we were sleeping less and less, sometimes just two or three hours a night. And then Dick's mum called: the Strawbridges were coming to help, a week earlier than planned. I cried my eyes out . . . we would be able to get back on track.

Next on my list was the grand staircase. The paint I mixed for the walls was light grey and perfectly complemented the original Alpaca *gris* paint that was on the woodwork. It was bigger than my flat in London and a lot more difficult logistically, as you couldn't reach anything. In the centre of the double staircase, was a large six-metre-high window. On either side of the window were two cupboards, each one and a half by two metres, and then there were more windows. We had decided that we would put the steam engine lights in the cupboards, shining onto the walls like a Hollywood film set. The space was huge and without any carpet the sound reverberated.

Over the years, I had collected many vintage Union Jack flags that had flown over official government buildings. They were truly massive. The one that I wanted to mount over the full width of grand staircase was my favourite and had cost me a month's wage many years ago when I didn't have any money to spare.

You can imagine my reaction when Angela had the idea of putting a six-metre-long flag up as a sort of a pelmet above the central window on the main stairs. It was ridiculously high and the only way to get up there was to build our scaffold tower on wheels to its maximum height and then put the platform on top without safety rails. The phrase 'don't try this at home' springs to mind.

The tower was wobbly at the best of times and to get onto the top platform you have to climb through a trapdoor on the platform, as if you tried climbing up the outside it would tip over, so you have to keep you centre of gravity in the middle. I understood all this but it still wobbled enough to make my bum twitch. Somehow I managed to get brackets securely fixed on the left and right of the main window. I then lifted the six-metre length of four-by-two with a large flag artistically draped on it over my head. I had to turn round, place it into location and secure it. It was a very silly idea. To lift the plank with the flag on it I had to face down the stairs and, as I started to lift the bloody heavy flag above my head, everything started wobbling. It was as if I had disco knees, which any rock climber will tell you is pretty shit when you're that high up. Ensuring I was in the middle so it didn't drop to one side or the other was more good luck than good judgement and I was dripping with sweat before I finally got one side, then the other, onto the bracket.

If only we had known we wanted the flag up there when I still had my island in the air for plastering! I have decreed the flag stays there until it disintegrates, as I'm never going up there again. I'm just not built for it.

The Union Jack hung proudly like the château pelmet, drawing your eye to the window below that waited for something special to arrive. Dick knew me well enough to know that I was up to something, but he was in for a big surprise. Not long after this, Broken

Hare, aka Katherine and Jon, turned up with a special delivery. I snuck my head in the back of their van and the box that held wolf literally occupied the whole space.

I had planned to give it to Dick the day before our wedding but, even with a very large château, I had nowhere safe to hide something this big – and no one really wanted to be carrying something like this all the way upstairs just to bring it down again. So that precise moment was perfect! Dick and I were both in work overalls but I pulled him off what he was doing for the special moment. He giggled like crazy when he worked out what it was. He had had exactly the same thought – and nearly got me a taxidermy version. I was so happy I had executed the idea first. And with that, the grand staircase was ticked off as well.

Weddings tend to be a wonderful mix of old and young, so there are lots of ways of calculating how much drink is required for a party. Rules like 'half a bottle of wine per person' allegedly take into account that some won't drink and others will party, but Angela has a fear of running out of literally anything, so she made sure there was half a bottle of each wine per person in addition to the bar. That meant everyone was to get half a bottle of red, half a bottle of white, half a bottle of rosé, half a bottle of white sparkling (in the case of our wedding, this was half a magnum) and half a bottle of red sparkling. Her reasoning was simple: you just do not know what will be popular. Funnily enough, we have never run out of anything, at any function, ever.

By the first week in November, it all began to arrive. First was the magnums of sparkling white. They looked ridiculously stylish with their deep orange and gold labels. There is something so celebratory about a magnum – we had purchased a hundred. We also had an abundance of the red *Chinon*, the white *Touraine* and the rosé *d'Anjou* with the very pretty watercolour label. There were enough spirits to stock a nightclub. The best part was getting to fill our wine cellar for the first time. The *cave* was lined with the most robust and authentic racks. Back in Southend, we had owned a wine rack that we absolutely loved. It had been quite expensive and was actually similar to those we found in our *cave*, except it held about forty bottles of wine. The racking in our cellar had space for about ten thousand. It would take some filling. There were also hundreds of empty bottles in the cellar, which would have been disappointing but for the fact that they were each hand blown and no two bottles were the same. They were history and both looked and felt fragile. Each and every one is unique. We love owning them and, what's more, we've got aspirations to fill them all one day.

Dick had done it; he'd got us over the line. There was still oodles to do from my side but now Dick had to take the reins of the kitchen. With everything happening, the 200 guests we had arriving in under a week had not been our priority.

When the Strawbridge girls drove up to the château our wedding had started. Every pressure felt different. It dawned on me we could have the wedding today as long as our friends and family were there. It was happening. Arthur was jumping with excitement and big tight hugs were exchanged by everyone. Linda, Deanna and Bunny, Dick's sisters, all stood back and looked up. Then Dick's mum put her hands on her hips and smiled. Dick and I watched them and then, for the first time in months, we properly looked up too. We were seeing the château through fresh eyes.

We all went inside for a cup of tea and a look around. One thing the Strawbridges do really well is all speak at the same time and also listen to everyone in parallel. I've got better with practice but it's a skill better learnt when young. My mum has the same skill. I think it's a large family thing.

Before I knew it, Dick and Deanna were sitting down writing a store-cupboard shopping list, amongst a number of other bits and pieces. Two cases of butter, twenty-five rabbits, ten kilos of mushrooms, five kilos of duck gizzards, 30 kilos of white onions, enough potatoes for a small army . . . It went on. I didn't get too involved but I thought to myself, *This must be four or five trips to the shops.* And it was!

Jenny and the girls wanted to 'be useful', as they would say . . . and they were. We were just glad they loved French supermarkets as much as we do.

Mum and the girls coming early was like receiving reinforcements when you thought you were alone. The Strawbridge ladies fill a room. OK, none of us are small, but I don't mean physically. I have grown up surrounded by powerful ladies and Mum, Linda, Bunny and Deanna are truly capable. I love them to bits. As they are family, they get treated slightly differently. That does not mean they were taken for granted, far from it, but we could ask them to do anything we would have a go at ourselves. They had insisted that they stay away from the château so as not to be a drain on us and had hired the gîtes we had stayed in when we first moved to France. The area had been declared Northern Irish and all my family were staying there and at the even larger gîte next door.

I can't actually remember showing them all around. We had good intentions but soon they were playing with the children, saying hello to anyone they met, usually taking the mickey in some way, making us a cup of tea and getting out notebooks to make lists. Families are special and we are blessed.

Next to arrive was Dick's younger (and, as my sister-in-law says, better-looking) brother Bobby, his wife Andrea and their three children, Erin, George and Ru. They flew from Canada, so it was a big deal, and as soon as they landed they wanted to help too.

With the arrival of the Canadian contingent, we had even more horsepower. Bobby is my little but bigger brother. His heart is huge and his family are lovely. I always give Bobby a hard time about his DIY skills, even though he has done lots of amazing work on his house in Canada. It stems from when we were all still serving in the army and we competed in a couple of series of *Scrapheap Challenge* together with my other younger brother, David. We were the 'Brothers in Arms'. I seem to remember phoning up Mummy at one point to tell him off on camera . . .

Everyone had tasks. Angela had always wanted to have a games room where people could chill out and play traditional fête games. There was to be a dressing-up corner with top hats and feather boas as well as a coconut shy, hoopla and a simple but frustrating game where you swing a small metal hoop hanging from string attached to the ceiling so it goes onto a peg on the wall, guiding balls up the walls with strings. It all sounded relatively simple but all we had so far was some coconuts. Jon from Broken Hare had not managed to escape yet and, as he knew where the tools were, he showed Bobby and hung around to help. They did an amazing job and bit by bit we had games. It's a known fact that playing hoopla without any hoops is a tad challenging but we also had no idea where you would buy a hoop, so Bobby made them and they are still around today (a 'round' – did you get that? That is a Steve, Angela's dad, joke).

At thirteen, my nephew Ru was our youngest worker and had not yet earned his spurs as a DIY god, so we had him putting up 'safety fencing' so no one would fall in the moat. What could possibly go wrong?

Jimmy and David came next. Jimmy has known me since the day I was born. We were neighbours and our parents are very close friends. Julie, Jimmy's mum, is American and used to have a huge

garden party every fourth of July with homemade baked beans, barbecued corn, sausages and lots of fireworks that used to scare the life out of me. Jimmy moved to America when I was very young but we are still the best of friends. He was to be my man of honour.

Jimmy's husband David is obsessed with cleaning, which I was secretly very excited about. I flew to Portland some years ago for David's fortieth birthday and we spent the day cleaning. It's his relaxation. I just wish we could have got him out earlier. They were staying in the back room on the fourth floor. It was small but the light in there was always beautiful and I made sure it was cleaner than clean. Jimmy is the vice president of a travel company and David manages serious holiday complexes in special locations like Yosemite. The château was small fry to them. I could immediately see David was getting twitchy looking at the leaves on the ground, so a cup of tea later and they were both out hoovering leaves. The cleaning of the outside world – novel but very effective, and hugely appreciated.

When my brother David arrived with his girls the trio of Strawbridge men was complete. But then it struck us – we were no longer a trio. With the arrival of my eldest son, James, and his family, and Charlotte, my daughter, all of a sudden, we had a proper army of manpower. The complement of Strawbridge men had changed. When we were growing up it had always been Dad and the three of us. Now there were eight of us: me, David, Bobby, James, George, Ru, Indy and Arthur. It had been nearly twenty years since Dad had died but we knew he'd be looking down, watching and laughing with us. He would have loved the fact that we were all together and we missed him.

Jobs were dished out and my daughter Charlotte, also our official photographer, set about capturing what was happening and working out how to photograph the weekend. James headed off to the kitchen with a good supporting team – however, when he discovered the Bison Grass vodka in the freezer he seemed to lose the ability to do sums.

James and his wife Holly and their family live in Cornwall and James was running Posh Pasty, a company that makes the most amazing pasties – some traditional and others more inspired combinations. We had decided that Saturday night was to be 'little plates' – tasty and informal but enough so everyone was well fed. Each wave of food had to have some rationale and, as I'd been living in Cornwall when I met Angela there was an obvious link. Small 'two bite'-sized pasties were obviously going to be needed. After several hours, during which shots were enjoyed by all, they had made enough pastry for all the inhabitants of Laval to come and try a pasty or two each. In fact, we had to send Deanna down to the *fromagerie* for another carton of butter.

As if there wasn't enough support, friends were also arriving thick and fast. If we'd had help like this in March, we could have been ready for a spring wedding!

John and Miguel were friends from London. John and I used to be in a collective together and shared a retail outlet in my London days. The pair of them are the most outrageous, loving and stylish couple I know. They live in east London and Miguel has a high-heel shoe collection that is out of control. They had never been out to the château before so came a couple of days earlier to be useful . . . After a cup of tea I gave them each a paintbrush.

Next my beautiful bridesmaid Taj arrived. She was so inspired by France that she and her partner decided to look for a property there and then. Luckily we got her back in time for the big day and I loved having her by my side.

Then it was Sam and Sophie. I had met Sam through Taj many years earlier. He is an artist but to me he was a friend that I had got to know though many evenings partying in London. His girl-friend Sophie was a darling, an incredible soul who also paints. While they were here in France, we agreed to keep the wine coming if they fancied painting. Thanks to their youthful imagination and obvious skills, plus rather a lot of wine, before long they had painted two barn doors with images of the château and fair-ground monkeys, which gave the perfect finish to the games room, the Château-de-la-Motte Husson sign for the entrance to the driveway, and embellished the walls and helter-skelter in Arthur and Dorothy's playroom. It was the loveliest wedding gift we could have asked for.

Then, a couple of days before the big day, my brother Paul brought my nan over. The two of them flew and I was so happy that my nan could make it. I had hosted her ninetieth birthday in my east London events space before we left for France. My nan managed the four flights of stairs to her party fine on her birthday, but I did wonder how she would cope at the château . . . It turned out there was no stopping her. As soon as she came through the front door, she made all the right noises and as we went around every room in the house she would ask, 'Do you own this too?' It was so sweet. My brother took control of looking after my nan and it was heart-melting. Sadly, my grandma could not come. We are all so close but she knew the travel was too much for her. But she still wanted to know every detail . . . and my mum's six brothers and sisters loved telling her. She received at least seven different versions of our wedding celebrations.

Our dream of a life together in France had started curled up in front of a log fire watching *A Good Year* with Russell Crowe. One scene had stayed with us: the couple were dining al fresco watching a silent movie across a small lake. The movie was accompanied by someone singing and playing a grand piano. It turned to mayhem when it started to rain but the idea of a cinema across a lake had stayed with us and, since we were now living our French dream, why shouldn't we have one too?

My plan was to recreate this for Angela. I knew she loved this scene; she referred to it often. But as it was November, I situated our screen near the château so people could watch it out of the window if it was too chilly or it did actually rain. A team of volunteers built a frame on the other side of the moat and then sheets of plywood were painted with white emulsion and screwed to the frame. We hadn't really thought about it but the positioning of the 'screen' also hid the muddy patch where our new sewage filter bed had been placed. It was meant to be. With power laid to the box that would house the projector we were ready to go. To finish off the 'magical image' I knew Angela was after, festoon lights were hung in the lime trees. The overall effect was exactly the magic we had hoped for. Anyone who had not seen or heard us talk about *A Good Year* would have no idea why there was a silent movie playing on a makeshift screen but we knew and for us it was very special.

* * *

Catering for the gathering was lots of fun. There is an old saying that you can choose your friends but you can't choose your family. We are both very lucky because even if you could choose them, we would both have picked the ones we've got. We knew everyone was going to muck in. In addition to keeping everyone that had arrived sustained, we were getting prepared for two days of festivity. That's a lot of food.

Our friend and chef Alan had not been back since the days of living in the gîtes and his reaction to our progress was lovely. As a wedding present, he was to take charge of the kitchen for our wedding breakfast. We'd discussed the menu at length and had hired in some help for the main event, so his preparation days were to be in the company of the Strawbridge Ladies Kitchen Assistance Squad. He never stood a chance. Kitchens are not a place for democracy and the head chef is not used to getting any abuse, poor Alan. As they say in Ireland, the craic was good and, in his defence, he probably didn't understand half of what was said … But it worked, the team was really efficient and, as well as preparing for the wedding, everyone seemed to get fed.

It was the eve of our wedding. The house was looking lovely, buzzing with family and friends. Alan and the Strawbridges were having a ball in the kitchen and my stylish and beautiful ladies arrived to host, my old Vintage Patisserie team. I was so happy to see everyone and my heart ached at how stylish they all were. I felt I had become rather feral over the months, so for the first time in forever I had had my legs waxed and my nails done. I felt normal.

Tradition says that the bride and groom should not see each other the night before their wedding. We had two small kids, so I guess we had already broken with tradition. But I was really looking forward to having a morning to myself and not rushing. I had been rushing for ten months. That morning, I had a bath and breathed. I felt excited. That may sound crazy, but when you're busy your mind is always two, three steps ahead of what needs to be done. Whereas today I was in that exact moment.

My friend Amanda was there with her daughter. We had met on the vintage scene. Amanda's company is called Lipstick & Curls and she is the only person that I would trust to do my hair on such a momentous occasion. For months I had been wearing berets and headscarves (my five-second hairdo I say). But today I was having my hair down. Something no one had seen in years.

The night before had been hectic. After the Vintage Patisserie girls left, I had been flower arranging until midnight and then I dyed my hair and got Dick, Arthur and Dorothy's outfits packed.

The rest of the night was spent not sleeping and answering texts from everyone that had arrived and was excited to be here. I was tired but the adrenaline was keeping me going.

The morning of our big day had arrived and we couldn't quite believe it. I have to admit for once I didn't think about what state the château was in, what we had achieved or what we hadn't managed to do. The last couple of days had been about sorting out the parties and tasking people to ensure we were as ready as possible. It no longer mattered. We'd finished the evening before in time to get up ... After the briefest of kisses, Arthur, Dorothy and I headed off to join the groom's party four miles away in the gîtes complex.

I knew what time I had to be at the *mairie* and I knew there was no need to rush. It was so relaxing I felt guilty. Arthur and Dorothy were delighted to be there with their big cousins and their nieces and nephew (my grandchildren). Everything was super organised. We had been allocated a room to get changed in, breakfast was available, coffee was on tap and I didn't have anything to do. I could pretend that I was responsible for looking after the children but to be honest I didn't get a look in. I chatted with everyone, and breathed, and paused for photos when Charlotte told me to. It was a very agreeable way to spend a couple of hours. I just wished Angela was there to enjoy it with me.

We all got dressed in our glad rags and travelled the couple of miles to the village in good time. It was amazing. The wedding and wedding breakfast was to be for family and our closest friends as the orangery could only fit eighty guests. But we filled the town square and the villagers were also out in force to wish us well. Everyone was smiling, there were so many people to say hello to and it felt like the whole village were cheering us on. The *mairie* was dressed in his ceremonial sash and was smiling as all our party said '*Bonjour*' the way only the British can. My mum had prepared something to say to him as she had been on the journey to provide information as a *témoin**. It must have made sense as he smiled and immediately responded in the rapid-fire French that is saved for those that are obviously fluent. That'll teach her!

I looked out of the window and the Citroen 2CV was waiting outside the château. My dad knocked on my door and told me how beautiful I looked. It sounds textbook but I could see the total love and pride in his face. There were no cameras, no photographers there. Just the two of us. We linked arms and he walked me down the grand staircase. That staircase was meant for this moment and I felt like I was in a fairy tale. My heart was racing and I felt like I had no idea what was going to happen ... It was exciting and terrifying in equal measures.

I was carrying Dorothy and saying hello to everyone, when a blue Citroen 2CV came tooting through the crowd. Angela got out and smiled and I have to say 'beautiful' is inadequate to describe how she looked that day. I think I was a bit surprised when I saw her as I couldn't remember ever seeing her hair down. I'd fallen in love with her smile the first time I'd met her. It's no exaggeration to say she lit up the whole place. I knew just how lucky I was.

As we drove up to the *mairie* everyone was there. You could feel our mums' happiness radiating over everyone. Family, friends that had been part of the château journey, friends that had yet to see the château, all smiling and proud. This was not just our wedding, it was our celebration of us creating a new life for our family and it felt like everyone was there to wish us well. Within a couple

---

* A witness.

of seconds, I had locked eyes with everyone. Some were already crying. Then Arthur came running out to give me a hug. There was no aisle to walk down but Dick was waiting at the front with unconditional love in his eyes and a soft smile. It was the moment we had been working towards yet had not had enough time to think about. He looked so handsome. It was perfect and, as my dad handed me over to Dick, I felt like the luckiest lady alive. That is how every bride should feel and I knew then without a shadow of a doubt that we had created the right path for us.

The ceremony was better than I had envisioned. I had not expected it to be as full of emotion as it was. Dick's eyes said everything I needed to know and the *mairie* who married us did us proud. With Arthur and Dorothy holding on to us, and our family and friends behind us, there was nothing else we needed. When we were handed a book to officially welcome us as part of the village I was in tears. It was a real feeling of belonging and tradition and I wondered in that moment if our grandchildren would end up being more French than English.

There was nowhere near enough seating for our party but we all got into the room with the *mairie*. It was so lovely that he had learnt some English for the vows, and we had decided to make our vows in French as well to ensure it was legally binding in France. The ceremony felt as perfect as anyone could hope for. Our parents witnessed our formal joining and I have to say I couldn't imagine a better way for us to start married life. The ceremony ended with lots of cheering and congratulations and we savoured several minutes of love-infused chaos before we got into our wedding limousine 2CV for the journey back to the château. The quiet of us being alone in the back of the car was a bit surreal as it was the first time we had been together with nothing for us to actually do. Everything was under control. So I did what any sensible man would do: I kissed my very beautiful wife.

Back at the château the smiling continued and the service was conducted by the Vintage Patisserie girls, who looked stunning and oozed elegance. Glasses were kept topped up and the chatter grew more and more lively. Then we headed over to the orangery.

After lots of trial and error we had found that the only way to seat eighty people in the orangery was to have five tables, each of sixteen, equally spaced. There was just enough room for service and everyone had sufficient space to be comfortable. Each table was overflowing with vintage 'stuff' and flowers. I had used all my favourite props that had been with me ever since I started the Vintage Patisserie. All the tables had vintage games and memorabilia that dated back to before the Second World War and each place setting had vintage china, cutlery and a vintage French napkin. To me, it looked wonderful.

We were the last to enter and were met by a sea of smiling faces, all standing, cheering and waving their vintage napkins above their heads; it's something we will never forget. The napkin waving is something the French do and was orchestrated by Jacques. Neither of us had ever seen it before and it was so moving that no wedding has taken place at the château since without it happening. The orangery was packed – eighty really is capacity for the room – and the next five hours were spent eating and drinking. We had written up the menu but everyone was just happy to sit and see what was put in front of them.

We had grown to take gizzards for granted and even Dorothy at the ripe old age of eighteen months would try them, though that could have been the rose jelly. Even the faint-hearted gave them a go and there were many converts who got excited to find out that they would be served again the following night for those who missed out on day one.

We had thought long and hard about what soup to serve and had decided on a 'white soup'. It is a favourite of mine and is a variation on onion soup. It is an aromatic creamy soup of slowly cooked onions and garlic that we serve with an egg yolk, or a softly poached egg, and *herbes de Provence* croutons. The aromatic element comes from a handful of bay leaves that are whipped out just before the soup is blended. Even served without soup spoons it was wonderful. And the budget had been well spent as the wine teacups were never empty.

After a pause we followed with the fish course: salmon three ways. I had been curing and preserving seriously for years, and we both love the vibrant colour and earthy taste of the cured beetroot. It went extremely well with the sharpness and sweetness of a honey mustard dressing, served with a salmon tartare made with fresh lime juice and zest, dill and finely diced cucumber. Salt and white pepper seasoned it to ensure it stood alone as well as part of the trio. The final element was a salmon fusion fishcake. We often cooked them as a lunch with salad, but the delicate fish cakes that were coated in crunchy panko breadcrumbs added texture as well as the surprising mix of spring onions, olives, coriander, chilli and lime. We didn't see anything left, so our party of food-loving friends seemed to be enjoying themselves.

Serving food in waves allows for a very social wedding. I loved spending time with every group of family and friends, having real time in that moment with them . . . and as the wedding breakfast continued and the drinks flowed everyone got louder and more in love!

After the fish came a palate-cleansing sorbet of blackberries that had been picked by the children and grandmothers. As I watched them harvesting from our abundant brambles, I couldn't help remembering all those years that I had collected blackberries with my mum. Now she was out here laughing and joking with her youngest and oldest grandchildren. The sorbet was not too sweet and another precious gift from the château.

It is far from usual to serve rabbit at a wedding celebration but, on what was a beautiful November day, our tried and tested rabbit stew was an absolute success. With so many courses we were all mobile throughout the afternoon. People were swapping seats and moving around to try to chat with everyone. There were many friends and family we had not spent time with and hugs and catching up filled all the time we were not eating.

Next we served a salad of orange and very thinly sliced fennel with sesame and soy sauce. It was to help digestion as well as setting us up for the cheeses, all of which were local, some of which we had smoked ourselves. It was controversial but we served the cheese before the pudding with our château quince. Even though we are living in France both of us love grazing on the cheese course at the end of a meal. However, with so much to eat, we made our wedding the exception.

We had tried not to make the service too difficult when we had devised the menu. After all, the orangery is a couple of hundred metres from the main kitchen, but Alan, those in the kitchen and the Vintage Patisserie girls could probably have handled anything. They were true professionals and lovely to have around us.

It has been proven, in lots of scientific tests, that no matter how full you are there is an empty pudding-hole to be filled. Poached apples, French mess (a bit Eton-like, but with blackberries as we had lots of them) and a small glass of dessert wine brought the meal to an end, and, boy, did we all do it justice. It was hard to move but we did manage to get back to château for coffee, whiskey and digestifs. A lovely day came to an end with everyone leaving by about 7pm. We think our château guests retired quite early too but to be honest we didn't know as on our honeymoon night we crashed out with the children who had been spoiled with attention and so well behaved.

We both agreed that the day could not have been more perfect.

On Saturday morning we were up bright and early. It was party day with 200 guests due to arrive at 3pm. There was lots to do. The orangery had been cleared and cleaned after the wedding breakfast and was being set up for high tea. That involved setting the scene with all the props that had been in constant use in the days of the Vintage Tea parties in London. There were to be 120 new guests arriving who had not yet been to the château and so first impressions had to be right. The honeymoon suite was transformed into vintage hair salon for any of the girls who wanted their hair or make-up done.

Angela was in her element rearranging the château and the orangery. Meanwhile, the kitchen and utility/cold room at the back of the basement were a hive of activity. I found it amusing that, despite having been on *Masterchef* and run restaurants, I was making the sandwiches and scones for high tea exactly the way Angela had shown me the first time I'd helped her in London nearly five years earlier. Who could have foreseen where we were now? But as my folks would say, 'The harder you work, the luckier you get.'

With the party starting at 3pm, we'd decided food had better start early and keep going in waves all day and evening. There was a cheese table with cold meats in the dining room that was kept topped up and refreshed at all times, but a number of small plates or bowls would also keep coming at intervals to ensure no one got hungry

The first wave was at 3.30pm and consisted of a couple of starters. There was a glazed confit chicken liver salad and a 'light' mushroom and red wine stew. Most people were taken by surprise, even though the menu for the day and the timetable of what would happen when had been put up in several places. These first options were distributed by the Vintage Patisserie girls and everyone was encouraged to try something. Even while the first dishes were being savoured, the tea party started in the orangery for a couple of hours with alcoholic tea cocktails, refined sandwiches, cakes, scones and jam and clotted cream and lots of games to play. People were moving around and enjoying a wonderful day and we couldn't have been luckier with the weather.

As it got a bit darker and people moved back towards the château, the outside games room and the children's playroom was heaving. Food and drink kept coming and, in the early evening, waves of smoked-fish pasties and stew and dumplings were hearty enough to satisfy anyone who still had a hunger. As the evening wore on, we felt the world was ready to try some of the spicy fish soup, made with Val's secret chilli sauce. Turkey burgers appeared to help soak up any excess alcohol. The soup was about a ten on the spicy scale, but that seemed to encourage people to try it even more, so we ordered half a dozen loo rolls to be put in the freezer.

You can tell a party is going well when it is self-sustaining. Just before Emilio got on stage, we decided to do a little thank-you. We knew it was the last time we would have everyone's attention. Standing on the stairs seeing our friends and family all looking up and drunk was the moment! And when the music started it moved to another level. The Vintage Patisserie girls were no longer on duty, they had proven their skills and did us proud and handed over to a team of locals to continue service. My old team were now part of our wedding celebration. There were nearly three times as many of the smartly dressed waiters and waitresses who all got into the spirit of keeping everyone topped up!

The band had set up on the landing of the staircase and our first dance was announced. There was some confusion as the promised number didn't materialise but it just didn't matter. Instead of

Dick and I having a romantic dance, our family danced together, Dick with Dorothy and me with Arthur, then all of us together. It was perfect. After a couple of moments, the wider family joined us, then friends, and soon everyone was in and around the entrance hall dancing, singing and laughing.

Our first dance was lovely and I could tell Angela was as happy as I was. However, it wasn't long before the beat of the music stepped up and we had masses, and I mean masses, of people dancing and bouncing on the entrance hall's ornate floor. I looked around but I was the only one who was shitting himself. It didn't even occur to them that they might end up in the basement. There was a definite movement in the ornate planks but it wasn't that terrible. *What's the worst thing that could happen?* I asked myself. I'd seen the beams that supported the joists and I concluded that, at the most, we'd probably have a catastrophic sag. No one should end up falling too far. A cone and bit of hazard tape and we'd be able to continue.

We were testing the château and it was performing exactly as we had hoped. The waiting staff were tidying and mopping up behind us all and the singing, dancing and eating continued. Eventually our wonderful band gave way to a playlist that had everyone dancing again. In no time at all it was past midnight. Some of the children were sleeping in beds around the château and some of the more sensible guests, as well as some of the less coherent ones, started thinking about their beauty sleep.

Our evening ended at late o'clock but we were mellow and so very happy. We had said our goodbyes to lots of special people who had literally come for the day and those staying a little longer would all be turning up for coffee, orange juice, croissants and jam sometime the next day. We made our way back to our suite after making sure everything was off and safe, full of the feeling of a job well done.

It is so rare that families and friends get together and spend quality time. We had had a very silly, busy year and it was only on the morning after our wedding party that we could actually breathe for the first time. The house was full of people, special people, but there was no urgency and no need to rush. We were saying hello to some, goodbye to others, and there was food and drink on the go all the time. But it just happened; there was nothing to worry about.

Everyone was so helpful that the château seemed to tidy itself, though we did keep finding areas and little packages that needed to be tidied away for weeks to come. Our newly decorated rooms were showing the signs of a good party, but that was only surface issues. The house had well and truly come back to life. It was so sad saying goodbye to everyone. Luckily my mum and sisters were going to stay for a couple of extra days so we had the opportunity to go out for a meal and show them our new home properly. Farewells are sad but it was also wonderful that a couple of days later there were just the four of us, with Jenny and Steve in their gîte at Jacques and Isabelle's next door. We were all but broke but we lived in a beautiful château that made us smile every day. We were happy, we were married, and we were in love.

CHAPTER TWELVE

DECEMBER

The weather had been so kind to us. In fact, everything had been perfect. The build-up to our wedding, the day itself and the wind-down afterwards. Even the humps had all been part of our journey. It had been physically tiring for the weeks building up to our wedding and we had learnt just how little sleep we actually could survive on. But we had been driven by our desire to give each other everything we could possibly want in our celebration and, because of our bloody-mindedness, neither of us would accept anything but success.

It is probably an understatement to say we were rather tired. The short days and colder weather of early December meant we nested, lit log fires and focused our energy on little tasks rather than big projects.

Going out to our chickens on a crisp morning to open their door and give them access to the walled garden was a pleasure. The weeds had died back for the winter and the garden's potential was apparent. Looking to the future, we began to think maybe we would start work in the gardens in the spring.

In December, we took stock of the château, produced lists and prioritised the work. There was a fair bit of touching up and minor repairs as a result of our celebrations, so firstly we started to recover and then to go forward.

I was completely surprised by Angela's list of tasks for the honeymoon suite. I thought it was done but was told, in no uncertain terms, that it was not yet at the standard we needed for our flagship suite and the list grew. Painting, pictures, decorations, skirting boards, boxed-in pipes, better bathroom lighting . . . It was a decent-sized list and I'd never in a million years have spotted that we needed open parasols hanging up over the archway between the rooms but apparently we did! All these tasks would have to be done slowly as we had spent just about every penny we had budgeted for the year.

Shortly after the wedding, Jenny and Steve headed back to see family and were to return, with Nan and Paul, for Christmas. But our first Christmas would have to be quiet and frugal. That was OK as Arthur and Dorothy were just a little too young to understand the excitement of Christmas. Having said that, we did still get into the spirit and took them to several Christmas fêtes in villages around us. Each was different but in them all the feeling of community shone through. In addition to the stalls of crafts and seasonal goodies, there was always a bar serving *vin chaud* [*], cider and beer, and an abundance of sausage and chips. We browsed and chatted and got into the Christmas spirit.

---

[*]   Mulled wine.

Arthur and Dorothy were introduced to a number of *Père Noëls** and in those meetings their characters immediately shone through. Dorothy was having none of it; she saw no reason to talk to a stranger in a red suit, no matter if she was being bribed with a pressie. Arthur, on the other hand, met smiles with smiles and won over all the elves in the queues while we waited to meet the main man.

It was so refreshing, and a surprise, that Christmas didn't really appear in the shops until the beginning of December, but then it was full-on. The range and quantity of lovely food and drink on offer at the supermarkets was mouth-watering and we are so rubbish at resisting temptation. We had to be strong. It appeared that *foie gras* was compulsory and, partly because the French turkeys appeared to be so small and partly because we'd never cooked it before, we decided that capon was to appear on our menu and it has remained there ever since. When we discovered the French did not know what Christmas pudding was, we steadfastly refused to have Christmas lunch without it and arranged for Paul and Nan to bring us one (or two) as we were out of time to make our own.

From the very first moment we had walked into Château-de-la-Motte Husson and seen the beautiful entrance hall, I had been debating with myself where to put the Christmas tree. Indeed, I do believe that thinking about it may have kept me sane in the months when the whole château was a building site, or maybe that's just me being fanciful. I hadn't reached a conclusion when we were doing the renovations, so we had strategically placed sockets to allow us to put our Christmas tree in the hall or in the salon. Since this year was to be a quiet and more intimate gathering, we decided we would go all out decorating the salon. I wanted everything to be

---

* Father Christmases.

perfect. It was nice to hear from Jacques that he remembered the Christmas tree in many locations.

It is only when you look up and remember that your ceilings are nearly five metres high that you realise a six-foot-tall tree just won't cut it. The reality of the high-status rooms had their first disadvantage: we needed to find a tree that was three metres plus but didn't shed any needles and it needed to be at a reasonable price. I sent Dick out to find the one – no pressure.

The choice of tall Christmas trees was limited. So first I methodically went around the garden centres and then the supermarkets. It was still only early December so there were more coming in daily. Tape measure in hand, I held up every likely contender. In the third garden centre there was a lovely Nordmann fir but at €120 it was not quite what I wanted. Eventually, outside a large Carrefour supermarket, I found our first château Christmas tree. It was in the 2.5–3m section but I measured it at 3.2m and at €45 it was great value compared to anything else I'd found. Having checked it a couple of times – it was balanced, the top looked elegant, it was not too thin at the bottom – I guarded it with the tenacity of a terrier until the gentleman came over to serve me.

Over the years, we have collected Christmas tree ornaments together from lots of different places and each has its own story. Some of them don't look great but because of the memories they are our favourites. With so much tree to cover, we decided we needed lots more so we took apart a rather ugly crystal chandelier to provide dozens of glistening teardrop-shaped ornaments. That, another set of lights from the internet, and a couple more really rather ugly ornaments from the local fêtes, and the two of us had a wonderfully romantic night decorating our tree and drinking port in front of our log fire with Bing Crosby and Perry Como singing carols.

We loved the build-up to our first Christmas at the château; this was wonderful family time. It felt like Christmas had arrived and our lives revolved around the children and each other. Naptimes were for the four of us; we went shopping together, went for walks and we smiled an awful lot.

Although, it has to be said, we could not turn off completely. That is not in our nature and we were still making plans for our fledgling business – we started work on the branding, logos, websites and planning our first 'Food Lovers' weekends. Not to forget the dream of our vintage wedding business.

As there would be eight of us for Christmas, we moved the dining-room table into the salon and converted the dining room for Nan so she didn't have to worry about stairs. The salon was big enough for us to have one end full of a sofa and chairs and a log fire, and then the dining table and our Christmas tree at the other.

Christmas started in earnest when the Newmans (Grandma Jenny, Papi Steve, Angela's brother Paul and her nan Jenette) all arrived back at the château. Nan still marvelled at the fact that we owned the whole building and we settled into a routine of playing with the children, cooking, eating, drinking and watching television, with Angela and I slipping away to do the odd little job if we started to twitch.

Just before Christmas, the weather was glorious, so we all went for a walk in our favourite park in Laval. As with all major expeditions, getting everyone out of the door is a bit like herding cats before it all settles down. We parked up and, as it was a hilly park, we put Nan in her wheelchair and Dorothy in her buggy. The sun was shining and we ambled, chatting and enjoying life.

At the entrance to the park, we were met with a mountainous village nativity scene that had obviously been used for decades and dated back to a time before technology. The dozens of houses were about twelve inches high with little characters, some with

Christmas decorations, others scenes from a bygone era. There were artisan shops, *boulangeries*, butchers, cobblers, millers, blacksmiths. The detail was incredible and the children (and the rest of us!) loved looking and pointing them out as we spotted them. We were the only people there and it was very special. We go back there every year at Christmas time and it is still wonderful and special, even though the children are now five years older. After that we walked around the rest of the park, allowed the children to play in the playground, and saw the ducks and geese, plus some rather smelly goats that seemed to poo on demand.

The first Christmas at the château was incredibly special to us. The kids were a year off really understanding that *Père Noël* would be coming down the chimney, but we both love tradition and thought why not start as we intend to carry on . . .? So even though Arthur was only two and Dorothy was one, we gathered together hay and carrots for the deer, made mince pies for Father Christmas and poured a large glass of port. We finished off the traditions for our first Christmas Eve in the family kitchen with four generations of the family getting involved. It was amazing. I think we may have even got my nan a bit pickled, which was good, because we would have hated Father Christmas waking her up when he came down the chimney. All the goodies were left in the salon by the mantelpiece and, as we all said goodnight, I was not sure who was more excited.

Christmas started in our suite with stockings found at the end of the children's beds and all four of us sitting together on our family bed. In one respect, it was a Christmas like no other because both Arthur and Dorothy opened up one toy at a time and played with each in turn . . . When we headed downstairs we trooped into the salon to see if Father Christmas had been. Everyone gathered to see Arthur and Dorothy's faces and I think the kids were just as excited by our faces watching them as they were by the gifts that had appeared under the tree. Whatever created the happy factor, it was there, in abundance.

Our Christmas breakfast was simple: fresh orange juice and a slice of glazed baked ham on toast with homemade chutney or English mustard. Just enough to give us the energy to get through the morning. Then we all sat together in the salon and opened our presents. Dick and I had given each other a budget of £50 to spend and, being competitive as we are, we had both tried to be clever. I bought Dick a second-hand tongue press – the postage took me slightly over the £50, but that had not been specified in the rules. Dick got me lots of bits: real socks to keep my feet warm, handy stationery to keep me organised, a lovely locally made lavender candle and my favourite Mon Cheri chocolates. To be honest, we needed nothing. We both had everything we wanted. But we do both love a challenge . . .

Christmas lunch was celebrated in style with the most amazing roast capon and a very fine bottle of claret we had saved for such an occasion.

We don't believe in stressing over Christmas lunch, so the kitchen is my domain. We always want it to be special but when it's ready, it's ready and, provided everyone's favourite is on the table somewhere, we are happy. Our Christmas lunch will always include our bird, with a lot of sausage meat stuffing to keep it moist (chopped onions, lemon juice and zest and parsley are a must), too much gravy (made from the meat juices and red wine), bread sauce (made with milk infused with bay leaves and an onion studded with cloves and a big knob of butter), roast potatoes and roast parsnips, boiled potatoes to absorb the lovely gravy, al dente Brussels sprouts tossed in lardons, fried cloves of garlic and sweet chestnuts, carrots (cooked in butter and honey) and peas, mashed buttery swede with lashings of white pepper and boiled savoy cabbage. Anything else is just an optional extra.

We didn't even think of pudding until several hours afterwards and it was startling that Nan cleared her impressively stacked plate and was the first to ask about it. Being traditionalists, it was a flambéed Christmas pudding, served with a sweet white sauce, or cream or ice cream for those who wanted.

We ended the year happy, content and broke. We knew there were lots of challenges ahead but we had gone from strength to strength and we could not wait for all that was to come. We seldom got the chance to stop and think about what we had done in that first year so it has been a pleasure to relive it all again in this book.

At the end of 2015, we were uncertain of what our future held. We didn't know when *Escape to the Château* was to be shown on television, or indeed if it would ever be shown. So, as the next year began, we started to live our dream. We worked on getting business in, we had our first wedding and a number of our 'Food Lovers' weekends booked before anyone really even knew we were in France . . .

We still smile every time we turn into our driveway and we still have trouble believing we live in this wonderful place. If the truth be known, we fear that someday someone will find out that we are just a normal family.

Afterword

This year, 2020, has been hard on so many people. It's something that unites us all. In taking the time to write this book we have used the opportunity to reflect on what we have done and our choices in life. But we really do believe that anyone can do something similar to us. We're not silly and don't think its sensible for everyone to buy a château and go through what we have been through but changing your destiny by living your dreams is doable and we'd encourage everyone to 'dare to do it'. It's too easy to talk yourself out of a particular path but, be honest, are your arguments excuses or actual *bona fide* reasons?

We know we are lucky and we pinch ourselves regularly. You just cannot make up the story of how a chap born in Burma in the 1950s met a beautiful girl born in Essex in the 1970s, fell in love, had two amazing children and bought a castle together to live in happily ever after . . .

Acknowledgements

Where do we start?! We could probably write an entire book of acknowledgements and thanks.

For those we have not met – you may have sent a letter, a gift or e-mails of kindness and support. Thank you. You should know that we read and reply to every single one and keep them as part of our history. One day, when Arthur and Dorothy understand, we will show them everything. Thank you for your love of our family. It has meant that Escape to the Château is now in its 7th series; we raise a glass to you and thank you for being here with us!

Our mums – the two Jennys – are the reason we are who we are. They are completely biased, loving and have lived every step with us. Thank you.

Dad (Papi Steve) – for being the biggest kid, and best granddad . . . never grow up.

Siblings, friends and family – you cheered us on from the start. We partied hard at our wedding and for many of you (mentioned in the book of course) you worked for your 'dinner'! Your support keeps us going and we love you to bits.

New friendships:

Our journey has opened many doors (you just need to pick the right ones!). It's a pleasure doing business with you; you have become our Château family!

www.TheChateau.tv – Paul & Emma, Simon, Ella, Matt, Ed and the team. For making the ideas and dreams we had right back at the start of our journey come true on the www. Thank you for being honest, lots of fun, generous, kind and hard working.

Lizi and Alan and our Two Rivers/Château TV co-production team. Lizi, without you no-one would have known that we 'Escaped to the Château'. We are so thankful to finally be in your arms!

The people that look after us:

The Soho Agency: Sophie – our TV mum and the reason we are together . . . What a year! We don't need to say much more – 2020 will not be forgotten!

Cliff – it may not be legal to write what we would like to write . . . Thank you for everything.

Julian – thank you for being by our side through this process. You have been amazing.

Orion Books – Vicky and your amazing team. It's been such a pleasure. You get us, thank you.

Bells & Whistles – Bella thank you for being with us from the start and caring!

Sam Steer – the friend and artist who has brought so many visions to life . . . Our work and friendship goes from strength to strength. Sophie and Lyra – thank you for sharing!

Ian Wallace – for all the beautiful photography over the years!

Ben Turner – thank you for capturing the château in the early days.

Team Château – Chloe, Tina, Steve and Denise, Sacha, Quentin, Meredith, Jane, Amanda, Sandrine and Chermaine, Lydia and Craig . . . We have grown the perfect team. Thank you.

About Us

DICK STRAWBRIDGE is an engineer and an environmentalist. He began his TV career many years ago as a team leader on *Scrapheap Challenge*.

ANGEL STRAWBRIDGE is an entrepreneur who made her name in London with her hospitality business, The Vintage Patisserie. She first appeared on TV in 2010 as she sought investment on *Dragon's Den*.

Later that year Dick and Angel met and fell in love. They now have two children together, Arthur and Dorothy. In 2015, after years of searching for a new home, they invited Channel 4 to follow them on their journey as they bought a derelict château in the Pays de la Loire, so was born the hugely popular series *Escape to the Château*. After extensive renovations on a shoestring budget, the couple married at their family home in November 2015.

They are still living life to the full, and continue to restore, renovate and maintain their château.